LEGAL ACADEMICS

This detailed study of the lived experience of legal academics explores not only the culture of legal academia and the professional identities of law teachers, but addresses some of the most pressing issues currently facing the discipline of law. Given the diverse nature of contemporary legal scholarship, where does the future lie? With traditional doctrinalism, socio-legal studies or critical scholarship? What does academic law have to offer its students, the legal profession and the wider society? How do legal academics 'embody' themselves as law teachers, and how does this affect the nature of the law they teach and study? In the context of the RAE, the QAA and all the other pressures facing universities, legal academics discuss the realities of contemporary legal academia in the UK.

Legal Academics
Culture and Identities

FIONA COWNIE
The University of Hull

·HART·
PUBLISHING

OXFORD AND PORTLAND, OREGON
2004

Hart Publishing
Oxford and Portland, Oregon

Published in North America (US and Canada) by
Hart Publishing c/o
International Specialized Book Services
5804 NE Hassalo Street
Portland, Oregon
97213-3644
USA

© Fiona Cownie 2004

The editors and authors have asserted their right under the Copyright, Designs and Patents Act 1988, to be identified as the authors of this work

Hart Publishing is a specialist legal publisher based in Oxford, England. To order further copies of this book or to request a list of other publications please write to:

Hart Publishing, Salter's Boatyard, Folly Bridge,
Abingdon Road, Oxford OX1 4LB
Telephone: +44 (0)1865 245533 or Fax: +44 (0)1865 794882
e-mail: mail@hartpub.co.uk
WEBSITE: http//www.hartpub.co.uk

British Library Cataloguing in Publication Data
Data Available
ISBN 1–84113–061–3 (hardback)

Typeset by Hope Services (Abingdon) Ltd.
Printed and bound in Great Britain on acid-free paper by
Biddles Ltd, www.biddles.co.uk

For Tony

Contents

Preface	xi
1 Studying Legal Academics	1
Why Study Legal Academics?	1
'Culture' and 'Identity'	4
'Culture'	5
'Identity'	10
Method	14
Conclusion	26
2 Legal Education and the Lived Experience of Legal Academics	27
Legal Education	27
Legal Education: Pedagogy	28
Legal Education: Policy	30
Legal Education: Approaches to Law	35
Inaugural Lectures and Other Occasional Writing	38
Historical Perspectives	39
Empirical Surveys of the Legal Academy	41
The 'Private Life' of Legal Academia	42
Conclusion	47
3 Inhabiting the Discipline of Law	49
Approaches to Law	49
A Discipline in Transition: From Doctrine to Socio-Legal Studies	54
The Impact of Feminism	60
The Future of the Discipline	63
Possible Difficulties Ahead	65
Anti-Intellectualism of Law	69
Conclusion	72
4 The Legal Academic Career	73
Careers and the Culture of Academic Law	73
Reading Law	73
The Legal Academic Career: Vocational or Academic?	75
Academia as Second Best	79
The Qualities/Skills of a 'Good' Academic Lawyer	81
Getting On	86

Success	92
Conclusion	95

5 The Experience of Being a Legal Academic

Introduction	97
Proud to be a Legal Academic?	97
Job Satisfaction	101
Autonomy	104
Variety	105
The Worst of Times	107
Working at Home	111
Work-Life Balance	113
Conclusion	118

6 Teaching and Research in the Legal Academy

Teaching	121
Lecturing as Performing	124
Teaching as Part of Professional Identity	129
The Institutional Attitude to Teaching	130
Research in the Legal Academy	133
The RAE effect	135
Evaluation of the RAE	138
Conclusion	141

7 Inside and Outside the Academic World

Introduction	143
Administration	143
Outside Concerns	151
Networking	153
The Changing World	159
Conclusion	165

8 Identity Matters

Introduction	167
Gender	168
Class	175
Race, Ethnicity and Legal Academics	181
Sexual Orientation	183
Dressed for the Part	186
Conclusion	196

9 Conclusion	197
Introduction	197
Law as a Discipline	197
The Changing Culture of Academic Law	199
Different Perspectives on the Culture of Law: Old and New Universities	200
Key Aspects of Professional Identity	201
Other Identity Matters	203
'Culture', 'Identities' and the Discipline of Law	204
Bibliography	207
Index	223

Preface

Exploring the lived experience of legal academics has been a very enjoyable experience. Like many such experiences, it would not have been possible without the assistance of other people. I would, of course, particularly like to thank all the legal academics who so willingly gave up their time to talk with me, and who were so generous in answering my questions so fully.

This book would not have appeared without the support—emotional, intellectual and of every conceivable kind, which I receive on a daily basis from Tony Bradney. My debt to him is impossible to repay. The experience of living with that particular legal academic is profoundly satisfying.

I am also very grateful to Mandy Burton, who patiently read and commented on a number of draft chapters. Bela Chatterjee, Jeff Murray and Alex Mackenzie have offered enthusiastic support, and their interest in the project has been heartwarming. Bill Felstiner gave me the courage to 'take as long as it takes', thus ensuring that I worried more about the quality of my ideas than the RAE!

Mark Bell, Andy Boon, Ray Cocks, Pascal Lorber and Trevor Buck have all patiently answered my queries and supplied me with additional material. Sue Smith, specialist in Government Publications at the University of Leicester, has willingly unearthed obscure data and Jo Goacher used her administrative skills to excellent effect in the early stages of the project. I would like to thank all of those people.

I would also like to thank the Society of Legal Scholars for the grant which allowed me to go and visit, often on several occasions, the research sites which I chose. Some of the research for this book was carried out during a semester's study leave from the University of Leicester.

Finally, I would like to thank Richard Hart, for believing in a somewhat unusual 'legal' project.

Fiona Cownie
Leicester, June 2003

1
Studying Legal Academics

WHY STUDY LEGAL ACADEMICS?

THE PURPOSE OF this book is to provide an extended analysis of the 'lived experience' of legal academics teaching and researching law in English universities. By 'lived experience' I mean that I want to examine the everyday professional lives of legal academics, in order to uncover the culture of academic law as it is found in university law schools, as well as the professional identities of those who research and teach it. My investigation encompasses the attitudes of legal academics, situated in a wide range of institutions, to teaching and researching law, their perceptions of themselves as members of the academy, the extent to which the study of law permeates their lives, how they 'embody' themselves as law teachers, and how their social background, as well as their gender, affects the construction of their professional identities. It also involves exploring their views about the discipline of law itself, whether the nature of academic law is changing, and what it might look like in the future. Finally, I want to acknowledge that this 'lived experience' takes place in a particular context, that of the organisation variously called a law department, a law school, or law faculty, and within the larger organisational context of the university, which itself is affected by policies emanating from government and other national and supranational bodies.

The purpose of exploring the culture of legal academia is twofold. Firstly, it is a contribution to our knowledge of the academic profession. Clark argues that there are many reasons why '. . . the academic profession ought to arouse our curiosity and elicit serious study':

> Academics train the members of an increasing number of leading fields outside the academy; its ideas speak to economy and politics, to social order and culture; and its leading scientists produce knowledge and technique in such world-transforming fields as atomic energy, biotechnology and computerization. In so many ways, and more than before, it touches the lives of the general public. Yet, in the face of such importance, how much do we know about the development of this profession, other than in simple numerical terms?
> (Clark, 1987: 2)

Investigating academic lawyers is, then, a step towards increasing our knowledge of a profession which has hitherto been subject to remarkably little scrutiny by its members, even though they are arguably best equipped to carry out the kind of serious investigation which is called for:

2 *Studying Legal Academics*

> Observers have long noted that academicians study everything but themselves, a remarkable failing in an estate composed of scholars and researchers devoted to the task of assisting others to understand the natural and social phenomena that make a difference in shaping the modern world. Of this we can be sure: the academic profession makes a difference. We can hardly know too much about it.
> (Clark, 1987: 2)

Or, as Geertz has put it:

> We know very little about what it is like, these days, to live a life centred around, or realized through, a particular sort of scholarly, or pedagogical, or creative activity. And until we know a great deal more, any attempt to pose, much less answer, large questions about the role of this or that sort of study in contemporary society—and contemporary education—is bound to break down into passionate generalities inherited from a past just about as unexamined in this regard as the present.
> (Geertz, 1983: 163)

In finding out more about academic lawyers, my second objective is to discover more about the discipline of law itself. In doing so, I am making a contribution to what Becher (1989), following Geertz (1976), has called 'an ethnography of the disciplines'. This enterprise calls for detailed qualitative studies of all academic disciplines, in order to contribute to our knowledge of the higher education system and the way it functions. The discipline, says Clark, is the 'primary going concern' of higher education (1983: 76); it is also the 'dominant force' in the working lives of academics (1983: 30). In order to better understand higher education, he argues, we need to better understand the disciplines:

> It is around the formidable array of specific subjects, and their self-generating and autonomous tendencies that higher education becomes something unique, to be first understood in its own terms . . . Field by field, the academic search for progress leads to alternative interpretations of the world . . . Knowledge will remain a divided and imperfect substance. In its fissions and fusions we come closest to a root cause of the many odd ways of the higher education system.
> (Clark, 1983: 276)

By examining the everyday lives of legal academics, their attitudes towards, and beliefs about, teaching, research and administration, their contacts with colleagues in other institutions and (occasional) conference attendance, I want to question what this tells us about academic law. Do we teach in a certain way? What are we trying to do when we are teaching our students? What are the criteria we use when deciding what to research? What are the qualities of a 'good' academic lawyer? What do the answers to these questions tell us about our beliefs about the nature of law itself?

It was Trow who pointed out that:

> By far the greatest part of what is said in print about higher education is directed towards its public life, and toward decisions that involve agencies outside the colleges and universities—decisions about the size of the system, its costs, governance, and the

like. The private life of education is what actually happens in the classrooms, the
libraries, the laboratories, at the desks and in the offices—the moment-by-moment-,
day-to-day activities of teachers and students engaged in teaching and learning.
(Trow, 1975: 113)

When research into the private life of the university is focused on one particular discipline, it can tell us much about the ways in which academics construct that discipline, their perceptions of its intellectual and political strengths and weaknesses, what qualities are valued in those who are recognized as experts, or achieve high status. By exploring the perceptions, views and attitudes of legal academics, I aim to contribute to debates about the nature of academic law, its place in the academy, its epistemology and its future development. One can also form views about the nature of law schools, the kinds of values they are transmitting, and their potential for producing cultivated human beings and/or potentially desirable employees. On a more pragmatic level, knowledge about specific disciplines can also inform policy-making, making it more responsive and effective, enabling policy-makers to understand the complexities of the higher education system, and undermine '. . . the crudely naïve assumptions . . .' which they may otherwise make (Becher, 1991: 130).

Agreeing with Bourdieu (1988) that the academy is a site of power, I would also argue that the ways in which legal academic careers are made, defended and destroyed have far-reaching consequences, in terms, for example, of the research which is carried out, that which is valued and that which is given little attention, that which attracts large numbers of younger scholars, and that which is left to the 'maverick'. Thus, academic careers have profound effects upon what makes up 'the academic discipline of law'. In addition, although some have argued that the characteristics imported into the academic profession by individual members from their personal background and prior experiences are unimportant (Clark, 1987: 107), I would accept Huber's argument that academic disciplines cannot be understood without taking into account social factors, since '. . . there are traits associated with disciplinary cultures which cannot plausibly be connected only with the epistemological characteristics of knowledge domains' (1990: 243). Social factors, such as class and gender, also play important roles in shaping the careers of legal academics, while the ways in which law teachers 'embody' themselves, to students and to others, both inside and outside the academy, provides further evidence of their attitudes and values, and the ways in which they construct their professional identities. In terms of teaching, the choices which law teachers make about the subjects which are offered on the law syllabus and the ways in which they are taught will influence generations of law students, while law teachers' relationships with others in the academy, as well as with the legal profession and others outside the academy, are also likely to contribute to the shape of legal studies in the future.

I would therefore agree with Valimaa (1998: 126) that 'it is both theoretically and empirically controversial to use disciplinary cultures as the sole explanatory factor of academic behaviour.' Thus, I would argue that in studying the culture of a specific discipline it is important to acknowledge the influence of the 'micro' level of personal identity, of class and gender, of location in a particular type of institution, and a particular type of department, upon the professional lives of individual legal academics, as well as the 'macro' level of national policies, emanating both from government and elsewhere (Knorr-Cetina and Cicourel, 1981). I have therefore used the concepts of 'culture' and 'identity' to indicate that I aim to provide an understanding of the whole range of what Sally Falk-Moore (1978), in another context, called the 'semi-autonomous legal fields' which go to make up the picture as a whole—in this case, the range of different influences upon the lives of individual legal academics which overlap and interact with each other in the complex mesh which makes up their professional identity of 'legal academic' as it is lived out in the university law school, and what this means for the academic discipline of law.

'CULTURE' AND 'IDENTITY'

In taking account of both the 'macro' and the 'micro' influences on legal academics, I am thus exploring the culture of legal academia as it is constructed and experienced by academic lawyers. Influences external to individuals—the department, the institution, and the society in which they are situated—will clearly influence, to varying extents, that culture. Yet the individual professional identities which are forged by and within that culture are also of considerable interest when trying to understand how legal academia works out. Henkel argues that,

> . . . the concept of identity itself has been of central symbolic and instrumental significance both in the lives of individual academics and in the workings of the academic profession . . . Traditional academic reward systems reflect the cultivation of an institutionalised individual within a community of peers.
> (Henkel, 2000: 13)

Key to understanding legal academia, therefore, is the interplay between the culture of the discipline as a whole, and the individual academic identities forged within that culture.

These two concepts, 'culture' and 'identity,' are thus central to my analysis, and I agree with Alvesson that when using such concepts, '. . . a well-elaborated framework and a vocabulary in which core concepts . . . are sorted out, is necessary for understanding . . .' (2002:1). In the sections which follow, therefore, I set out the theoretical basis of my study, indicating the ways in which these fundamental concepts will be used to explore the 'private life' of legal academia.

'CULTURE'

Raymond Williams, one of the founding fathers of cultural studies, famously describes culture as 'one of the two or three most complicated words in the English language' (1983: 87). The concept of culture is one that has proved useful to researchers from a wide range of disciplines across the arts and social sciences. However, the very flexibility of the notion of culture, wherein lies its broad appeal, can also prove its undoing. As Alvesson notes: 'Many people referring to culture seem to do so in a very vague way and it is important to use the concept without losing focus, direction and interpretative depth' (2002: 3).

In *The Idea of Culture* (2000) Terry Eagleton argues that:

> It is hard to resist the conclusion that the word 'culture' is both too broad and too narrow to be greatly useful. Its anthropological meaning covers everything from hairstyles and drinking habits to how to address your husband's second cousin, while the aesthetic sense of the word covers Igor Stravinsky but not science fiction. Science fiction belongs to 'mass' or popular culture, which floats ambiguously between the anthropological and the aesthetic. Conversely, one can see the aesthetic meaning as too nebulous and the anthropological one as too cramping. The Arnoldian sense of culture as perfection, sweetness and light, the best that has been thought and said, seeing the object as it really is and so on, is embarrassingly imprecise, whereas if culture just signifies the way of life of Turkish physiotherapists then it seems uncomfortably specific.
> (Eagleton, 2000: 32)

'Culture' then, is not an easy concept to deal with, but, as Bauman argues, it is the very ambiguity of the concept which makes it '. . . such a fruitful and enduring tool of perception and thought' (Bauman, 1999: xiv).

In saying that I wish to explore the 'culture' of university law schools, I am drawing on ideas of culture developed in a number of different disciplines, but primarily in cultural anthropology and organisation studies. 'Culture' is a slippery concept, even for anthropologists; Geertz (1975: 4) notes that in the first twenty-seven pages of a chapter on the concept of culture, Kluckhohn defined culture in eleven different ways, including 'the social legacy the individual acquires from his group,' 'the total way of life of a people,' 'learned behaviour,' 'a way of thinking, feeling and believing,' and 'a storehouse of pooled learning'. In his own anthropological research Geertz himself espoused a concept of culture which he described as essentially a semiotic one:

> Believing, with Max Weber, that man is an animal suspended in webs of significance he himself has spun, I take culture to be those webs, and the analysis of it to be therefore not an experimental science in search of law but an interpretative one in search of meaning. It is explanation I am after, construing social expressions on their surface enigmatical.
> (Geertz, 1975: 5)

6 Studying Legal Academics

One of Geertz's main contributions, in his theoretical analysis of the idea of culture (the concept around which the whole discipline of anthropology arose) is his emphasis upon Gilbert Ryle's idea of 'thick description' (1975: 6). Seeing a boy rapidly contracting the eyelid of his right eye, to engage in 'thick description' is to be able to interpret that gesture not just as a wink, but as 'a boy practising a burlesque of a friend faking a wink to deceive an innocent into thinking a conspiracy is in motion'. Analysis involves 'sorting out the structures of signification . . . and determining their social ground and import' (1975: 10):

> What the ethnographer is in fact faced with . . . is a multiplicity of complex conceptual structures, many of them superimposed upon or knotted into one another, which are at once strange, irregular and inexplicit, and which he must strive first to grasp and then to render. (Geertz, 1975: 10)

In terms of a qualitative study of legal academics, this approach does indeed involve 'making the familiar strange' (Delamont 1996: 147), having sufficient sensitivity to professional practices, common assumptions and taken-for-granted behaviour firstly to notice, and then to interpret, what is talked about and done. Culture, viewed in this way, is not a structure, but a continual process of 'becoming' (Billington et al, 1991: 29).

In taking this approach in the particular context of universities, which are, in some senses, organisations, I am also drawing on work carried out in organisation studies, and in particular by Mats Alvesson, who has written extensively about the culture of organisations (1993, 2002; Alvesson and Billing, 1997). Alvesson writes that culture can be understood '. . . as a theoretical tool for developing sensitivity for differentiation, inconsistency, confusion, conflict and contradiction' (1993: 120). He argues that in order to take as many dimensions of organisational culture as possible it is necessary to incorporate multiple perspectives into research:

> The perspective I am proposing can be called a multiple cultural configuration view. It assumes that organisations can be understood as shaping local versions of broader societal and locally developed cultural manifestations in a multitude of ways. Organisational cultures are then understandable not as unitary wholes or stable sets of subcultures, but as mixtures of cultural manifestations of different levels and kinds. People are connected to different degrees with organisations, subcultural units, profession, gender, class, ethnic group, nation, etc; cultures overlap in an organisational setting and are rarely manifested in pure form. It is especially important to keep in mind the existence of cultural traffic—that organisations are not cultural islands, but are affected by the societal culture.
> (Alvesson, 1993: 118)

As Sackmann et al (1997) have noted, this interpretative approach falls within a naturalistic paradigm, which assumes not only that reality is socially constructed, but that it is multiple (1997: 25). Along with researchers working on organisational culture, I find the definition of culture put forward by Sackmann et al, while not ideal, useful in encapsulating my approach:

The core of culture is composed of explicit and tacit assumptions or understandings commonly held by a group of people; a particular configuration of assumptions and understandings is distinctive to the group; these assumptions and understandings serve as guides to acceptable and unacceptable perceptions, thoughts, feelings and behaviours; they are learned and passed on to new members of the group through social interaction; and culture is dynamic—it changes over time, although the tacit assumptions that are the core of culture are most resistant to change.
(Sackmann et al, 1997: 25)

Culture, then, is about beliefs, values and customs (Billington et al, 1991: 4). In terms of studying legal academics it involves paying attention to the way people live their lives in law schools, focusing on the norms and values which they share *because* they are legal academics.

The Cultural Approach to Researching Higher Education

My interest in culture is not, for present purposes, a general one. I am interested in the culture of academic law, in uncovering the assumptions and understandings of academic lawyers about their professional expertise, and in their attitudes and behaviours. Examination of the academy has long been the concern of researchers in the field of higher education studies, and there is now a body of literature about various aspects of the professional lives of academics, much of which can be found in specialist academic journals such as *Studies in Higher Education, Higher Education Review, Higher Education in Europe* and so on. Tight (2002) has identified seventeen specialist higher education academic journals published in the English language outside America, many of which contain material relevant to the current study, which is referred to in later chapters. In addition, there are substantial numbers of monographs, ranging from those which are concerned with the nature of the academic profession as a whole (such as Halsey's *Decline of Donnish Dominion*, 1992) to those whose concern is with a particular aspect of academic life, whether it is teaching (Andre and Frost, *Researchers Hooked on Teaching*, 1997) or the place of women in the academy (Brooks, *Academic Women*, 1997). Again, these are referred to throughout this book, when it is relevant to do so. However, the vast majority of this literature is general in nature, in the sense that it is concerned with exploring aspects of academic life as it is lived by all members of the academy. To date, no extended study of academic lawyers has been published (Becher and Trowler, 2001: 53).

In the field of higher education studies, the idea of an 'academic culture' as a tool of analysis, as it has been developed by European researchers, is rooted in CP Snow's discussion of the two academic cultures of arts and sciences, antithetical and unable to communicate with each other (1959). Snow's discussion has been described as '. . . a landmark in the development of the cultural understanding of higher education, because it promoted an interest in higher education consisting of cultural entities' (Valimaa, 1998: 123). Among those who have adopted what Valimaa has called 'the cultural approach' to the study of higher education, the work of Tony Becher stands out as seminal. Indeed, the inspiration for this book came originally from my reading of his work, in particular *Academic Tribes and Territories* (1989). This study, which has been described as having '. . . many of the attributes that enable a study to become a classic in its field' (Williams, 1990: 352) has made an outstanding contribution to the qualitative examination of higher education. Becher's thesis was that '. . . the ways in which particular groups of academics organize their professional lives are intimately related to the intellectual tasks in which they are engaged' (1989: 1). In other words, his interest lay in exploring the academic culture of different disciplines, to see whether the discipline to which academics belonged affected their attitudes, behaviour and way of thinking.

Between 1980 and 1987, Becher gathered data from interviews with academics in twelve different disciplines (including law) (1989: 175). In each case, he started by exploring the characteristics of the discipline itself, its specialisms, its nearest intellectual neighbours. Next he moved on to epistemological matters, including the role of theory, the importance of specialised techniques and so on. His third area of interest was career patterns, including questions about how new members were inducted into the discipline and how specialisms were chosen. This was followed by questions about reputations and rewards, such as the criteria for professional recognition, terms of praise and blame, and prizes and other marks of distinction. Becher also looked at professional activity: forms and rates of publication, the structure of personal networks, the extent of teamwork. Finally, he explored his respondents' value-systems, the extent of their involvement in their work, the aspects of their jobs which they considered particularly rewarding or unrewarding and their stereotypes of fellow practitioners and of those in other disciplines (1989: 2). From Becher's work emerges a comprehensive overview of a range of disciplines situated in contemporary universities. His book, now in its second edition (Becher and Trowler, 2001) is a rich source of information about how academics belonging to different disciplines think, how they organise their research and their careers, their publication practices and their views of themselves and of other inhabitants of the 'academic territory'.

However, although Becher has explored many different aspects of contemporary academia, one of the necessary limitations of his work was that in dealing with twelve different academic disciplines, there was clearly a limit to the extent of his analysis in relation to any one of his chosen subjects. Becher himself suggested that,

> much more remains to be done in the way of a systematic study of the nature of knowledge fields and the cultural aspects of the communities engaged in their exploration . . . The understanding of each of the 12 disciplines could also be given greater dimensionality and depth by pursuing the type of close observation suggested by Geertz (1976) in his prospectus for 'an ethnography of the disciplines' and adopted by Evans (1988) in his study of modern linguists.
> (Becher 1989: 179)

The project to create 'an ethnography of the disciplines' is one which has been notably ignored by the majority of higher education researchers, a fact which Becher himself comments on in later work which looks at unexploited opportunities for research on higher education (1991). Becher speculates that the reason for this may be (a) because this area lacks the 'authoritative sweep' of policy-centred research (which is a strong field within higher education studies) and (b) because it calls for particularly demanding and time-consuming fieldwork (1991: 123). However, he goes on to make a strong case for the value of what he terms 'meso-qualitative' research, emphasising not only that it can contribute to our knowledge of the higher education system and our understanding of the way in which it functions, but also the more utilitarian contribution such research can make to the development of higher education policy (1991: 130, 131). A central aim of my research, then, is to build on Becher's work, and thus contribute to the creation of 'an ethnography of the disciplines'. The study reported here aims to uncover the complexity of the discipline of law as it is taught and researched in contemporary universities, not just in an effort to communicate with policy-makers, but as an attempt to reveal aspects of the nature of the academic study of law which do not lend themselves to examination by other more traditional methods of enquiry.

Using the Cultural Approach to Study Academic Law

In exploring the nature of academic law, my perspective is, however, slightly different from Becher's in that I am less concerned with the disciplinary epistemology which fascinated him so much, and more with the nature of the professional identities of academic lawyers. Becher's main interest lay with the disciplines themselves, and the interplay between people and ideas, though in the second edition of *Academic Tribes and Territories*, more attention is paid to changes in the higher education system, to the effects of increasing regulation and managerialism and to the variety of institutions encompassed within the higher education system (Becher and Trowler, 2001: ch 1). It is noticeable, however, that even in the later edition, Becher and Trowler do not give equal amounts of attention to all aspects of disciplinary culture, preferring instead to '... give sustained attention to one among a number of structural factors which have differential, and fluctuating, degrees of cultural influence' (2001: 25). It was also, as the authors' comment 'a self-imposed limitation' of the original empirical research upon which Becher based his study, that it did not enquire into the lives of respondents as private individuals (2001: 147), and although in the second edition of the book there is discussion of the effects of gender and ethnicity on academic careers, the exploration of more personal matters, and their relationship to the formation of professional identities, is far from extensive.

Among those who have taken up the challenge to create an ethnography of the disciplines, the work of Colin Evans is particularly important. He has written two extended studies in this genre: *Language People* (1988) and *English People* (1993). These are qualitative studies, concerned with the disciplines of modern languages and English respectively. Evans' approach differs from Becher's, in that he characterises his primary aim as being to explore 'the lived experience of a group of people' (1988:1). He is thus much more concerned than Becher with aspects of his respondents' identities—the fact that many staff in modern language departments had entered into cross-cultural marriages, for example (1988: 83), or the effect of gender on academic careers (1988: 150–56; 1993: 115–26). My approach is in some ways closer to that of Evans, though unlike his work on 'language people' I am not at this stage concerned with exploring the student experience of involvement with a discipline.

The work of Becher and Evans, therefore, has been influential in providing a stimulus, and to some extent, a model, for my work. In general, however, contributions to this genre of research are hard to find, so that, as Delamont says, '. . . there is today no solid body of data on the ethnography of higher education and few attempts to study the occupational cultures of those who work in higher education . . .'(1996:146). Becher and Trowler (2001: 52) refer to a small number of studies of particular disciplines, noting that physics has been the most popular area for study, while other scientific disciplines remain relatively unexplored. The social sciences and humanities, and particularly the discipline of law, are in terms of disciplinary ethnography, they note, relatively uncharted waters. The culture of academic law is therefore an area which is likely to repay extended investigation.

Toma argues that the work of legal academics takes place in at least four cultures concurrently; they are: the academic profession, the academy as an organisation, the discipline and the institution type. To these he would add the paradigm (ie the perspective—doctrinal, socio-legal, critical legal, feminist and so on). 'Like other components of faculty culture, paradigms represent deeply incorporated assumptions and values that guide behaviour among faculty' (1997: 682). In examining the lived experience of academic lawyers, I have engaged with all of these. In addition, I agree with Valimaa that in order to fully understand a culture, it is important to consider the professional identities of the academics who inhabit it (1998: 131). I have therefore considered not only legal academic culture, but legal academic identities. This approach also enables me to take seriously Alvesson's idea of 'multiple cultural configuration' (1993: 118).

'IDENTITY'

'Identity' refers to the ways in which individuals and collectivities are distinguished in their social relations with other individuals and collectivities. It is the systematic establishment and signification of similarity and difference between those entities. In relation to individuals, identity is our understanding of who we are are and who other people are, as well as other people's understanding of themselves and others (Jenkins, 1996: 4–5). If we accept the interactionist premise that our sense of self is socially constructed, then the linking of culture and identity becomes clear—our culture is an important influence upon the way in which we think of ourselves. Our identities are constructed in '... specific historic and institutional sites, within specific discursive formations and practices, by specific enunciative strategies' (Hall, 1996: 4).

Just as 'culture' is a complex and contentious concept, so is 'identity'. As Stuart Hall says: 'There has been a veritable discursive explosion in recent years around the concept of identity ...' (1996: 1). For Giddens, for example, identity is a distinctively modern project within which individuals can reflexively construct a personal narrative which allows them to understand themselves as in control of their lives and futures (1991). The postmodern contribution to the debate on identity emphasises its fluidity, and the way in which individuals are fragmented into a number of selves, so that different 'selves' may emerge in different contexts. Much of the postmodern critique of identity has centred on dissatisfaction with the notion of an integral, unified identity. Anti-essentialist critiques of ethnic, racial, class and national identity are of considerable importance here, as well as postmodern analyses of the endlessly performative self (Butler, 1999). Acknowledging the strength of these critiques, Hall nevertheless argues that the concept of identity should not be abandoned, but it should be reconceptualised as a question of 'identification':

> In common sense language, identification is constructed on the back of a recognition of some common origin or shared characteristics with another person or group, or with an ideal, and with the natural closure of solidarity and allegiance established on this foundation. In contrast with the 'naturalism' of this definition, the discursive approach sees identification as a construction, a process never completed—always 'in process' ... Though not without its determinate conditions of existence, including the material and symbolic resources required to sustain it, identification is in the end conditional, lodged in contingency.
> (Hall, 1996: 2)

One of Hall's key points, then, is that identities are never unified, but always fragmented and multiple. Since individuals have multiple identities, they may differ in their relative significance in different situations. This is as true of their professional identity as 'academic lawyer' as it is of other aspects of their identity. Although many academic lawyers would no doubt conceive of their professional identities as relatively stable entities, reflecting clearly defined values, attitudes and so on, this perception is deceptive. Writers such as Hall would argue that professional identity depends very much on the context in which the individual is embedded.

In conceptualising the task of exploring the professional identity of academic lawyers, in addition to the theoretical insights just discussed, the work of Erving Goffman has also proved useful, especially the dramaturgical approach he first put forward in *The Presentation of Self in Everyday Life* (1990). Goffman's great achievement was to make us think again about everyday behaviour within a framework of the analysis of social interaction. He 'possessed an extraordinary ability to appreciate the subtle importance of apparently insignificant layers of everyday conduct' (Manning, 1992: 3). Goffman talks of the 'performance' which an individual puts on in his or her interactions with others. An individual uses a range of expressive equipment to achieve a performance; this includes the setting (furniture, décor, etc) and the 'personal front,' made up of appearance, such as clothing, gender, age, racial characteristics, speech patterns, posture, facial expressions and manner, which may be meek, haughty, aggressive, conciliatory, etc. An individual can give a range of performances on the basis of this personal front. Performances tend to be 'idealised,' that is to say they may be modified to fit in with the expectations of the society in which they are presented, which may involve concealing action which is inconsistent with those expectations. Fronts add dramatic realization to performances; they help performers convey everything they wish to convey in any given interaction (Goffman, 1990: ch 1). As a comprehensive account of everyday life, Goffman's dramaturgical perspective is inadequate; but it is a very useful metaphor, which clearly points to the types of factors to take into account when examining professional identity (Manning, 1992: 54). Goffman's work can clearly be related to Giddens' conception of the 'reflexive project' of the self in modernity, and the way in which he conceptualises individuals as continuously engaged in 'a practised art of self-observation' (1991: 75–76). It is also possible, without doing undue violence to the original concepts, to relate Goffman's work to postmodern ideas of the fragmentation of the self.

Professional Identity

In relation to identity, just as with culture, it is important to keep in mind the 'macro,' as well as the 'micro'. As Giddens has pointed out, modernity must be understood at a 'macro,' institutional level, but 'the transmutations introduced by modern institutions interlace in a direct way with individual life and therefore with the self' (1991: 1). In this context, the work of Bourdieu is especially useful. Bourdieu was concerned with what individuals do in their daily lives, but was emphatic that social practice cannot be understood either solely in terms of individual decision-making, or solely in terms of social structures. He used the notion of 'habitus' to bridge these two ideas. 'Habitus' in the sense of a habitual or typical condition, only exists in and because of the practices of actors and their interaction with each other and with the rest of their environment; it consists of sets of dispositions (attitudes, 'taste,' linguistic and bodily traits—ways of talking, moving, making things, and so on). Habitus, embodied as 'hexis,' combines the individual (the personal) with the systematic (the social). It is the mediating link between individuals' subjective worlds and the cultural worlds which they share with others. (Bourdieu, 1977; Jenkins, 1996: 74–84). Bourdieu's notion of habitus has been criticised for being too deterministic, giving precedence to social structure over subjectivity, and failing to acknowledge the role of the sort of deliberate, knowing, decision-making that Goffman, for example, would emphasise (Jenkins, 1996: 97). However, even his critics acknowledge that Bourdieu offers useful insights into examination of socially competent behaviour, of 'accepted ways of doing things' (Jenkins, 1996: 98). In the specific context of work on academia, I would argue that Bourdieu's work yields a dynamic theory, which allows one to move between 'culture' and 'identity,' and examine the relationship between the two (McNay, 1999). In doing so, it serves to remind us of the necessity of taking account of structure and agency—the 'micro' and 'macro' which Knorr-Cetina and Cicourel (1981) argue for so powerfully. As Jenkins notes:

> Individual identity—embodied in self-hood—is not meaningful in isolation from the social world of other people. Individuals are unique and variable, but selfhood is thoroughly socially constructed; in the processes of primary and subsequent socialisation, and in the ongoing processes of social interaction within which individuals define and redefine themselves and others throughout their lives.
> (Jenkins, 1996: 20)

In this view, social identity is never unilateral—it is not enough to assert an identity. That identity must also be validated (or not) by those with whom we come into contact. It is this social aspect of identity which underlines the importance of Goffman's work. His ideas of 'impression management strategies' draw attention to the performative aspects of the construction of identity, and to the fact that identity is embedded in social practice.

Identity as a Device for Analysing the Culture of Academic Law

From the disciplines, says Clark '. . . come self-identities that may be more powerful than those of mate, lover, and family protector, or those that come from community, political party, church and fraternal order' (1983: 80). Exploring the culture of legal academia, on this view, inevitably involves coming up against identity. Henkel, on the other hand, argues that it is not just the discipline, but also the institution to which academics belong, that is important. She argues that the discipline and the institution are the main communities within which academics construct their identities, their values, their modes of working and their self-esteem (2000: 22). Developing these ideas further, Valimaa sees identity as a process based on dialogue with *significant others*. The crucial question for researchers is therefore to identify these significant others. Valimaa argues that, drawing from the research of Clark (1987) and Tierney and Rhoads (1993), attention should be paid to the discipline, profession, institution and nation (Valimaa, 1998: 132). Identity describes the interactive processes between an individual and structures, or institutions.

Identity has thus been singled out as a key concept by higher education researchers. Henkel's work, in particular, is valuable for its insights into the interplay between higher education policy and the professional identities of individual academics. She stresses the duality of academic identity, which, she says 'embodies the argument that individuation is the primary goal of individual academics, but is at the same time the product of the embeddedness of those individuals in communities' (2000: 148). In adopting this approach, Henkel's work clearly has resonances for the present study. However, it does not attempt to throw much light on the ethnography of particular disciplines, and law was not one of the disciplines from which data was collected (2000: 23). In focusing on law I want to draw on some of the general observations, both at the macro-level of policy, and the micro-level of professional identity, which flow from work such as Henkel's, but to particularise them within the specific context of the law school, thus allowing some exploration of what all this means for the professional identities of individual legal academics, as well as for the discipline of law as a whole.

By using *both* the concept of culture, *and* that of identity, I hope to avoid the main problems which Eagleton identified in his analysis of the concept of culture, so that I will neither reveal merely the minute details of the professional lives of a few English legal academics nor simply add to our knowledge of the epistemology and ontology of law without putting those theoretical considerations in the context of the academic lives within which they are framed.

METHOD

In focusing on the discipline within which I myself work as an academic, I am taking up Bourdieu's challenge to 'exoticize the domestic' (1984). Delamont has criticised existing work on the sociology/anthropology of higher education for failing to challenge the familiar, encapsulating instead, she argues, '... an essentially taken-for granted view of the sector' (1996: 146). In carrying out the research for this book, then, one of my objectives has been to 'make the familiar strange' (Delamont, 1996: 147).

The present study is what Becher called 'meso-qualitative' (1991; 130, 131). Broadly speaking, it is based on a philosophical position which is concerned with how the social world is experienced by legal academics. It is based on semi-structured interviews with fifty-four legal academics working in university law schools in England, carried out during the eighteen months between June 2001 and December 2002, this being a method of data generation which is sufficiently sensitive to the social context involved to produce meaningful results.

Access

The negotiation of access proved unproblematic. I wrote to the heads of department of each of the departments I had selected, asking whether they would mind if I interviewed their staff, and if not, whether I could tell the staff that there was no institutional objection, making clear that whether individuals talked to me or not was entirely a matter for them. I adopted this method because my previous experience of interviewing in academia (Addison and Cownie, 1992; Cownie and Addison, 1996) had shown that, in new universities particularly, people tended to agree to be interviewed more readily if their head of department had given the project some sort of official sanction. Having obtained 'permission' from heads of department (most of whom emphasised they were not in a position to give permission, but were nevertheless happy for me to convey their support of the project), I then telephoned individual academics, explaining the project, its sanction by their head of department, and the scope of the interviews. This approach resulted in all the departments and all the individuals I approached agreeing to participate in the project; in only two cases did my first choice of interviewee say 'I will be interviewed if you can't find anyone else—but I'm really busy just now' and in both those cases it was easy to find another participant. My experience was thus significantly different from that of other researchers trying to gain access to large white-collar bureaucracies (Crompton and Jones, 1988). One explanation for this may have been that as an 'insider,' I was already known by those involved, even if I was not personally acquainted with them. Several of the respondents volunteered the fact that their familiarity with my previous work on legal education was a significant factor in causing them to agree to be interviewed. Given that I was asking people to talk about their everyday working lives, and that I already had an established reputation in the field of legal education, both as a researcher and as an activist through my involvement in various professional organisations, I appeared to have been able to satisfy the respondents' need both to understand the purpose of the interview and to feel that I was trustworthy (Buchanan et al, 1988: 59).

Interviewing

The interviewees were all guaranteed anonymity. I was conscious that the same factors which appeared to strengthen the likelihood of respondents agreeing to talk to me (namely, their knowledge of me as an 'insider') might prove disadvantageous if they did not believe that the contents of their interviews would remain confidential. I therefore stressed the confidentiality of the interviews, explaining that no individual would be identified. To increase confidence I also explained that I would not identify the institutions involved either. (Of course, academia being a small and gossipy world, I could not prevent interviewees themselves from disclosing that they had been interviewed, nor from asking other people whether they had).

In the event, interviewees provided many hours of richly detailed responses to my questions; occasionally, if making a potentially controversial disclosure, they would check to see that 'This is all anonymous, isn't it?' but, in general, confidentiality did not seem to be a big issue. This was probably because of the nature of the subject matter; the majority of topics discussed were not of a sensitive nature; it was unlikely that respondents would have been embarrassed, even if their responses had been attributed, except in relation to one or two questions. The extensive data I obtained appears to confirm that respondents were willing to share their detailed views with an interested insider; this view is supported by the frequent comments made by respondents about how much they had enjoyed the opportunity to think and talk about the issues raised in the interviews, and their inevitable invitation to 'Get in touch if there's anything else you want to know'.

Establishing a rapport with interviewees is a vital part of the research process. Curiosity about issues relating to the professional identity of individual legal academics is not enough. A close relationship with respondents has to be established quickly, if good quality data is to be elicited. While skills such as the order in which questions are posed, the manner of the interviewer and the ability to listen sensitively are all vital (Sudman et al, 1983), none of these are effective if merely deployed mechanically (Buchanan et al, 1988: 60). Previous experience of conducting similar interviews (Cownie and Addison, 1996; Bradney and Cownie, 2000) has allowed me to develop my own style, which, while attempting to capitalise on the advantages of my intimate knowledge of the situation I am investigating, also attempts to guarantee the requisite amount of objectivity needed to interrogate it (Muetzelfeldt, 1989).

Each interview lasted between one and two hours. Interviewees were free to choose the venue for their interview, provided that it was quiet. Most interviews took place in respondents' offices, but on occasion they took place in respondents' homes or elsewhere. The interviews thus took place in a space where interviewees felt at ease, and were more likely to express truthful views.

Interrogating the Data

All the interviews were tape-recorded, and I then transcribed them, producing written transcripts. The production of transcripts, though very time-consuming, proved an important part of the research process, through which I was able to begin the process of 'immersion,' which enabled me to interpret the data. Having experimented with transcription done by others, I would agree with Buchanan et al (1988) that transcription by the researcher is preferable, since it provides a much greater degree of accuracy than is generally possible otherwise, and also enables the researcher to begin the process of identifying the themes and topics which will eventually form the basis of the analysis. The process of analysing the data is a long drawn-out one, which involves reading and re-reading the transcripts, identifying, modifying and re-working the themes which emerge (Burgess, 1982: 235). This is an iterative process, which helps define the categories that ultimately become the main focus of the analysis (Gerson and Horowitz, 2002: 217). Interpretation of data is, as Denzin has argued, '. . . an art; it is not formulaic or mechanical' (2000: 317). Despite that, it is still a process which has to be carried out rigorously; the aim is to create a mechanism for moving back and forth between data, research questions and the 'intellectual puzzle' which lies at the heart of the study (Mason, 1996: 120).

Sampling

As with most qualitative studies, I do not make any claims that my sample of respondents is statistically representative of my subject as a whole. Indeed, that is not the point of the research. Like Evans, my interest is not with the question 'How representative is this?' but with the question 'What does this represent?' (Evans, 1993: x). Nevertheless, I hope to have explored some general issues which go beyond the concerns of individual legal academics, and the sampling strategy I employed was designed to enable some general conclusions to be drawn, without overstating the case. The methodology I have used is a kind of theoretical sampling, directed at validity of findings, rather than representativeness of study population. 'Theoretical sampling' is a term usually associated with Glaser and Strauss' treatise on grounded theory (1967), but its logic and practice has become part of a tradition of qualitative research. Finch and Mason emphasise that for some degree of generalisation to be possible it is essential for the sampling processes to be *systematically* carried through (1990: 28, emphasis in original). With this in mind, I chose research sites and respondents which reflected variations in institution, status, experience and gender.

There are sixty-seven university law schools in England which offer 'qualifying law degrees' (ie degrees which are accepted by the legal profession as the 'academic stage' of legal training) (Bar Council, 2002). Just over half of these are located in old universities. The universities containing the seven law departments in which my respondents worked comprised four 'old' universities and three 'new' universities. The institutions were selected so that they included an elite law school in the 'golden triangle' of Oxford, Cambridge and London, an old-established civic, a new civic, and three former polytechnics, all located in cities of varying sizes. Their varying attributes were chosen in order to increase the validity of the data obtained. A number of researchers have stressed the importance of taking account of institutional diversity when researching the higher education sector. As Scott notes, British higher education is very fragmented. 'Its keynote is not homogeneity, as is commonly alleged, but institutional diversity' (1995: 49). Other writers, such as Clark (1987; 1995), Henkel (2000) and Shattock

(2001) have also noted the importance of institutional diversity when considering the culture of academia. My choice of departments therefore attempted to reflect a variety of different institutional settings. I also took into account the need to include departments displaying a range of 'research orientation' (i.e. attitudes towards the importance of research), since the research culture of a department in which academics work is an important variable. It has often been noted that, although theoretically there are three aspects to the academic job (teaching, research, administration), in practice, it is research which is valued within the academic community as a whole (Halsey, 1992: 185; Becher and Kogan, 1992: 112). Given the differences which may be experienced by academics situated in departments with varying attitudes to research, it was important to include data which reflected this. As Becher and Trowler comment, '. . . generalizations from data derived from elite academics in elite institutions have become increasingly tenuous' (2001: 27). The departments chosen covered the whole range of results achieved in the 1996 Research Assessment Exercise (the last one which took place before I started interviewing) and included one law school which did not enter its staff for assessment at all.

In deciding to pay particular attention to gathering data from academics situated in a range of institutions, my approach differs substantially from that of Becher's original study. In relation to law, Becher's empirical data was gathered from interviews carried out between 1980 and 1987 (1989: 175). He interviewed twenty-four academic lawyers, who worked in university law departments at Kent, LSE, Southampton and in California (Berkeley) (1989: 178). He selected these law schools on the basis that they were regarded by colleagues in the law department at his own university (Sussex) as 'reasonably prestigious within their disciplinary communities,' because those departments 'most clearly delineate and embody the central values of the discipline' (1989: 3). However, in the second edition of his book, co-authored with Paul Trowler, Becher does not focus solely on elite institutions, but draws on two further empirical studies: an ethnographic study of a new university in England (Trowler, 1998), and a study of twenty-four newly-appointed academics in five disciplines in a range of ten Canadian and English universities (Knight and Trowler, 1999; Trowler and Knight, 1999) (Becher and Trowler, 2001: 26). Becher and Trowler say that they have now broadened the scope of their enquiry to take into account changes in the nature of higher education, acknowledging increasing institutional diversification (2001: 27). However, it remains the case that the bulk of their data appears to emanate from elite institutions.

The academics I interviewed were all legal academics working full-time in university law departments, thirty-three in old universities and twenty-one in new universities. They were all located in academic (as opposed to vocational) departments, though two of them taught, for a minority of the time, on the Common Professional Examination course (a one-year course which teaches law to graduates of other disciplines). Only a small minority of university law schools in England offer the professional training courses for intending barristers or solicitors (www.legaleducation.org.uk; www.lawcabs.ac.uk). More importantly, academics teaching the Bar Vocational Course or the Legal Practice Course (the training courses for would-be barristers and solicitors), are involved in the 'vocational stage' of legal education, which is exclusively directed towards enabling students to enter the legal professions. The professional experiences and concerns of these legal academics are frequently very different, therefore, from legal academics engaged in the 'academic stage' of legal education, which may or may not be a precursor to legal practice, and offers an education in law in much the same way as a degree in history offers an education in history. Consequently, I did not interview any legal academics who were employed solely to teach on vocational courses. The academics I interviewed were all, therefore, engaged to varying degrees in the traditional academic tasks of teaching, research and administration.

Individual academics were selected so as to include varying levels of status and experience. Status is a relevant factor, because there is (unsurprising) evidence that the status of an academic affects their view of their job (Thorsen, 1996: 474). Length of experience as a legal academic was relevant, because one of the aspects of culture which I wanted to explore was the respondents' views on any changes in academia which they had experienced. In each law school I interviewed roughly equal groups of lecturers, senior lecturers (principal lecturers in new universities) and readers/professors. They formed roughly one quarter of the full-time academic staff of each law school in the study. In terms of experience, I evolved three broad categories: 'early career' (up to 10 years' experience), 'mid-career' (10–20 years' experience) and 'experienced' (more than 20 years' experience), and selected respondents with a range of experience at each level of seniority. My respondents comprised eighteen experienced academics, fifteen mid-career and twenty-one early career academics, giving a broad range. I interviewed twenty-six professors/senior staff and nineteen lecturers, thus broadly reflecting McGlynn's 1997 findings about the spread of senior/lecturer positions in relation to legal academia as a whole (1998: 41).

I also wanted to interview both men and women. Gender has long been a contentious issue in academia as a whole, and there is a burgeoning literature on the place of women academics (see Brooks, 1997; Morley and Walsh, 1996; Brooks and Mackinnon, 2001, all of which contain extensive bibliographies on this subject). As I indicated above, writers on the legal academy have also recently begun to address issues relating to gender in relation specifically to legal academics (Collier, 1991, 1998, 1998a, 2002; Cownie, 1998, 2000b; McGlynn, 1998; Wells, 2000, 2001, 2001a, 2002). Their work has shown not only that women find it hard to gain recognition and promotion in the legal academy, but that masculinity, as it is worked out in law schools, plays a complex part in that process. These were issues that I wanted to explore further. The group of legal academics I interviewed included thirt-five men and nineteen women. This gives roughly the same gender balance as that found by McGlynn in her 1997 survey of legal academia (1998: 41). Women were slightly over-represented in the early career group, as compared with McGlynn's figures, but this reflected the distribution of men and women in the law schools I visited.

Another factor I was interested in was what Toma calls 'paradigm' ie, academic lawyers' approach to the study of law (doctrinal, socio-legal, critical legal and so on). Toma argues that scholars working in different paradigms view the purposes of their work differently, apply different evaluative standards, rely upon different methods and frameworks, and accept different values (1997: 679). Shared paradigms define scholars in the same manner as disciplines, but this is a factor which is often ignored, despite the fact that paradigm is as important as the discipline if we are going to understand the settings within which enquiry takes place (Toma, 1997: 681). However, I decided not to use this as a criterion of selection, because my pilot study revealed that there is wild variation in which the terms describing different paradigms are used, and trying to identify, in advance, academics working in different paradigms would have endangered the integrity of the study as a whole. For instance, in the course of the interviews which I carried out for this study, legal academics describing themselves as 'black-letter' then went on, without any apparent sense of contradiction, to talk about how they regarded knowledge of policy, feminism and other arguably socio-legal perspectives as vital to their work, both as researchers and teachers. When questioned, they were surprised to find that anyone might regard them as in any way socio-legal, because they did not do empirical work, and they regarded themselves as very focused on the law, whereas their perception of socio-legal studies was that (a) it was exclusively empirical and (b) it rather ignored legal rules. Having discovered these anomalies at an early stage, I explored them with my respondents in more detail during the interviews, having decided that this was the best way of understanding the significance of 'paradigm' to academic lawyers.

In taking into account these particular variables when selecting law schools and respondents, and in relating them to relevant structural factors, I am reasonably confident that I have gathered together data which reflects legal academia as a whole, thus satisfying Woods' injunction to 'make the case' of validity (1986). However, my basic position remains firm; this is a qualitative study, and the sample of people I interviewed is not intended to be statistically representative. As Evans says:

> When the aim is to describe and understand a complex, shifting reality in some depth, when one is working with the sheer messiness of human reality, it has to be recognised that the apparently 'unrepresentative' individual is expressing something vital ... (Evans, 1988: 5)

'Conversations with a Purpose' and the Location of the Self

Following in the tradition of Becher and Evans, and influenced by Geertz's ideas of 'thick description,' qualitative interviews appeared the most appropriate method to gather information from my respondents. As Sackmann et al comment in the context of organisation studies, deciphering the specific meaning of a given cultural group in context requires in-depth probing to gain an insider's view rather than imposing an outsider's perspective (1997: 35). My interviews thus drew on Burgess' idea of a 'conversation with a purpose' (Burgess, 1984: 102). Burgess describes 'a series of friendly exchanges in order to find out about peoples' lives,' and notes the way in which, when he was carrying out his own research in Bishop McGregor school, teachers and pupils often asked him for information (1984: 105). Since I was interviewing a group of people with whom I share a profession, and sometimes membership of the same professional organisation or subject specialism, I adopted Burgess' attitude, that to refuse to engage in conversation if it was initiated by my respondents would damage the relationship which I had established, and thus damage the quality of my data (1984: 105). While I did not initiate conversations about matters apparently unrelated to the project, I participated in them if they were initiated by the respondents, and inevitably some of these conversations proved highly relevant to the subject of my research.

Discussion of interviews as 'conversations' inevitably brings one to a consideration of the location of the self in research such as this. Feminist writing on methodology has for some time stressed the importance of reflexivity (Stanley and Wise, 1983, 1993; Gelsthorpe, 1992; Adkins, 2002; Skeggs, 2002):

> Based on an epistemology that considers all knowledge to be socially constructed, it begins with the acknowledgement that the identity of the researcher matters. She is unavoidably present in the research process, and her work is shaped by her social location and personal experiences.
> (Roseneil, 1993: 180).

Feminist methodologists have stressed that the presence of the researcher as an ordinary human being cannot be avoided,

> ... it isn't possible to do research (or life) in such a way that we can separate ourselves from experiencing what we experience as people (and researchers) involved in a situation. There is no way we can avoid deriving theoretical constructs from experience, because we necessarily attempt to understand what is going on as we experience it. The research experience itself, like all other experiences, is necessarily subject to ongoing 'theorizing,' on-going attempts to understand, explain, re-explain, what is going on.
> (Stanley and Wise, 1983: 161)

Adopting this perspective involves a rejection of positivist notions of the possibility of objectivity, and embracing a hermeneutic/interpretative epistemology, which assumes that all human action has to be understood within the context of social practices, research as much as any other social practice. It is therefore crucial to be aware of one's own assumptions, pre-suppositions and so on (Scott and Usher, 1996: 20). This kind of personal reflexivity draws attention to the fact that the self that researches has an autobiography, marked by the signification of gender, sexuality, ethnicity, class, etc—socio-cultural products that are part of the practice of writing, and which have effects on the form and outcomes of research (Scott and Usher, 1996: 38).

My own location within this research is inevitably a very particular one. This is a piece of research carried out in university law schools among academic lawyers. It is of relevance to know that I too am an academic lawyer, who currently works in a law school located in an 'old' university. It is also relevant to know that through my published work (e.g. Bradney and Cownie, 1998), and through the position which I held for six years as Vice Chair of the Socio-Legal Studies Association, I am identified with the socio-legal paradigm within legal scholarship. I am also known as someone with a specialism in matters of legal education, not only in terms of research, but because I am currently Chair of the Legal Education Committee of the Society of Legal Scholars, a position which involves, among other things, interaction with the two professional bodies in law, the Bar Council and the Law Society, and includes some responsibility for negotiating the 'Joint Statement' which governs the content of law degrees for those wishing to enter the legal profession. Many of my respondents would also be likely to identify me with a feminist approach to law. Since much of my recent work (Cownie, 1999, 1999a, 2000, 2000a, 2000b; Bradney and Cownie, 2000) has been about various aspects of the university law school, anyone who was interested could have located me within a particular genre of research, and a particular view on the nature of the university law school as offering a liberal education in law. Many academic lawyers would also be aware that I am married to another legal academic, Professor Tony Bradney, with whom I regularly carry out joint research (e.g. Bradney and Cownie 1998, 1999, 2000). Some of them would know that I am a Quaker, and that I spent five of the last ten years carrying out 'insider research,' doing participant observation in a Quaker Meeting, which was subsequently published as *Living Without Law* (Bradney and Cownie, 2000).

The boundaries between ethnography and autobiography are contested; they are fragile and blurred. How much (more) is it relevant to reveal? When does reflexivity become self-indulgence? In discussing where I myself am located in relation to the research which has formed the basis for this project, I have attempted to contextualise the data and its analysis in sufficient detail to allow the reader to see where I am 'coming from'. Some of the effects of my identity upon the research process become immediately apparent, in the context of the discussion of 'insider research' which follows; others will become more relevant as the text progresses.

'Insider Research'

The issue of reflexivity, which I have discussed in the context of feminist methodologists, is one which is also being debated by ethnographers, and the debate here is of particular relevance to a piece of research such as this which is carried out in a familiar setting. 'Insider research' does not appear at all in Gold's classic categorisation of field roles (Gold, 1958), and is frequently not discussed in textbooks on methodology. Nevertheless, some writers argue that the best qualitative researchers are those who are already familiar with the setting and the phenomena which they are studying. Riemer, for example, points out that insider researchers benefit from a number of advantages, including shared language and a set of experiences, which enable them to avoid irrelevant questions (1977). Coffey, who locates her work within current debates within feminism, post-modernism and post-structuralism, notes that some aspects of ethnographic research are still relatively neglected, notably the multiple relationships which exist between the researcher self, the field and the people of the field. She argues that it is important to take account of the fact that fieldwork 'helps to shape, challenge, reproduce, maintain, reconstruct and represent our selves and the selves of others' (1999: 8). She is critical of the conventional wisdom of ethnography, which is based on a duality of observer and observed, with the ethnographer being encouraged to adopt the role of an ignorant outsider. Over-familiarity, on this view, is problematic, and is a particular issue for those carrying out fieldwork in familiar settings; methods texts emphasise the need to maintain a sense of strangeness (Hammersley and Atkinson, 1995; Delamont, 1992). Estrangement or alienation has thus been seen as a positive analytical tool, and the denial of self as an epistemological necessity (Coffey, 1999: 21). Coffey characterises the dichotomy between involvement and immersion, rapport and over-rapport, as unhelpful and crude:

> The issue is not necessarily one of conversion, immersion or not, but a recognition that the ethnographic self is the outcome of complex negotiations. Moreover, the definition and location of the self is implicitly a part of, rather than tangential to, the ethnographic research endeavour
> (Coffey, 1999: 36)

There is, of course, considerable debate among sociologists and anthropologists about the advantages and disadvantages of 'insider research'. Conventionally, one is cautioned that familiarity may be a problem; it is important not to take anything for granted, or overlook things because they are so familiar (Burgess, 1984: 24). For an insider 'there is a danger of missing the sense of wonderment and discovery' (Douglass, 1992: 129). Roseneil has described the potential difficulty of being too close 'to see the sociological significance of that which appears to be completely normal, or to form criticisms' (1992: 192).

Of course, there are also advantages to insider research. One of the more obvious problems a researcher can face is the difficulty of learning a new 'language,' whether literally, in the case of some anthropological studies, or metaphorically, in terms of technical language or jargon. As Barley has noted, a reading of some seminal anthropological studies would suggest that, once in the field '. . . the anthropologist transforms himself into a linguistic wonder-worker'

(1986: 44). In the case of legal academia, understanding jargon and technical language was not a problem for me. That left me free to be 'a thoughtful and analytic listener, or observer, who appraises the meaning of emerging data . . . and uses the resulting insights to phrase questions that will further develop the implications of these data' (Dean et al, 1967, quoted in Burgess, 1982). Being what Adler and Adler characterise as a 'complete-member-researcher' also has a number of advantages in allowing the researcher the deepest possible access to the community studied. As an insider, one is more likely than 'outsiders' to avoid asking meaningless questions and to be able to probe sensitive areas with greater ease (Adler and Adler, 1987: 67–84). In addition, being an insider can act as a form of triangulation, since one is able to take a knowledgeable view of misinformation (whether deliberate or inadvertent) (Roseneil, 1993: 189).

In my case, my previous experience of doing insider research on another topic over an extended period (five years) had given me experience of subjecting that with which I was familiar to an academic critique (Bradney and Cownie, 2000). In relation to the issue of detachment, I would agree with Coffey that the conventional problematising of over-familiarity in fieldwork should be treated cautiously, since all ethnography involves a mixture of familiarity and detachment:

> The ethnographic self actually engages in complex and delicate processes of investigation, exploration and negotiation. These are not merely professional tasks. They are also personal and social occupations, which may be lost if we revert to an oversimplified model of fieldworker as ethnographic stranger . . . The image of the heroic ethnographer confronting an alien culture is now untenable, and fails to reflect much of what ethnographers do, if indeed it ever did reflect the lived reality of fieldwork (Coffey, 1999: 22)

The process of fieldwork can best be understood as a series of real and virtual conversations and interactions with informants and significant others; all of these dialogues help us to navigate pathways and understandings through the research. It is critical reflection which is key; not only as regards the relationship of researcher and researched, but as an aspect of the authorship of the final text. Authorship needs to be a self-conscious activity. This does not mean that all ethnography will be autobiographical, but, like Coffey 'What I am advocating is an awareness of the fact that we are responsible for the reconstruction and telling of the field'. The text is an important mechanism 'through which we express, construct and represent ourselves. This is so, whether or not we explicitly choose to write about ourselves as part of the public process of documenting the ethnography' (Coffey, 1999: 160). Adler and Adler are clear in regarding insider research as fruitful:

> We believe that the native experience does not destroy but, rather, enhances the data-gathering process. Data gathering does not occur only through the detached observational role, but through the subjectively immersed role as well.
> (Adler and Adler, 1987: 84)

Overall, as someone who wished to explore the 'private life' of legal academia in detail, the advantages of being an insider outweighed the disadvantages, since, as Adler and Adler comment, while some detachment may be sacrificed, the depth of the data gathered is a valuable compensation (1987: 81). It is important to remember, in this context, that 'academic rigour' and 'insider research' are not mutually exclusive. As Bourdieu showed in his study of French academia, *Homo Academicus* (1984), an authoritative account can best be produced by a *reflexive* encounter with the 'known,' the apparently familiar. It is a process of 'participant objectification,' which seeks to avoid the false choice between the unreal intimacy of a subjectivist position and the equally misleading superiority of objectivism (Jenkins, 1992: 47).

Location

In considering the scope of this research, it should be noted that it is confined to English law schools. There is an extensive legal education literature in the US, as pluralistic in approach as the UK literature discussed above. Similarly, in Canada and Australia, there is much research on this topic. A lot of this work adds to our knowledge of the academic discipline of law as it is lived, researched and taught in those countries. Some of it I will refer to during the course of my argument. However, the experience of being a member of the tribe of academic lawyers in England is, I would argue, a culturally-specific one. Membership of the discipline of law is something that all academic lawyers have in common; indeed, as I have argued above, it is the discipline which is the primary unit in higher education. However, as Burton Clark has shown:

> Around knowledge specialities, each national system develops a division of labor that becomes traditional, strongly institutionalized, and heavily influential on the future ... The meta-institutional nature of the disciplines and professional fields of study is a salient and distinctive part of the character of the higher education system ... But, on the institutional side, national systems have evolved quite different structures ... (Clark, 1983: 6)

While academic lawyers have many things in common, the lived experience of being an academic lawyer differs significantly in different countries; one should not assume that experiences as a legal academic in one jurisdiction can automatically be transferred to another jurisdiction. In taking this view, I would agree with Clark, who has pointed out the danger of limiting research to a single country, then using it '... to assert what the academic life is like everywhere'. The fundamental purpose of Clark's extensive comparative study of higher education was to show how the basic elements of higher education systems '... vary across nations, with fateful effects' (1983: 2). My aim is to uncover the culture of academic law as it is taught in England. It does not mean that the ideas and theories I discuss have no wider interest; I hope they will stimulate others to question the culture of their own law schools, and to think further about a number of specific issues which I raise. But I would not claim that what I say about English law schools will *necessarily* apply to those in Scotland, Wales or Northern Ireland (though some of it may do so), far less Canada, Australia or the United States.

CONCLUSION

I have tried, in this brief introduction, to set out the purpose of my study of legal academics, and to explain what I hope it will contribute to our knowledge of the discipline of law and the academics who research and teach it. I have outlined the theoretical background to the two concepts of culture and identity which I propose to use in order to illuminate the lived experience I am aiming to uncover, and I have tried to show how these concepts will enable me to look at both 'macro' and 'micro' aspects of the subject. In discussing our existing knowledge of higher education, and legal academia in particular, I have acknowledged the work that has already been carried out, but also indicated the gaps which I hope to fill.

In terms of methodology, agreeing with Alvesson and Skoldberg (2000: 288) that 'Good qualitative research is not a technical project, it is an intellectual one,' I have tried to explain the criteria I used for selecting research sites and respondents, and to clarify my theoretical position as interpretative, leading to a concern with reflexivity, and with research as a social process. I have also explored the implications of 'insider research,' drawing from the work of feminist anthropologists to critique the scepticism with which such research has sometimes been regarded.

In the chapters which follow, I first set the scene for this project by situating it within our existing knowledge of the culture of legal academia. I then go on to explore a number of aspects of the lived experience of legal academics, beginning with an examination of the legal academic career, going on to focus on specific matters such as teaching and research, before turning to aspects of professional identity and the 'embodiment' of legal academics.

2

Legal Education and the Lived Experience of Legal Academics

LEGAL EDUCATION

So far, I have been attempting to situate this study in its wider intellectual context within research on higher education and on the sociology of organisations, and within the relevant theoretical debates in the social sciences and humanities. I have also discussed the methodology which underpins the empirical investigation of legal academia in which I have engaged.

I now want to situate this project within the specialism of legal education. There is a wide range of research and writing which throws light on various aspects of the legal academy in the UK and provides a range of different insights for anyone interested in the 'private life' of the law school, although this literature does not always seem to have reached a wide audience outside the legal academy. Becher and Trowler, for instance, who are two very experienced researchers into the tribes which can be discovered in contemporary institutions of higher education, comment in relation to the discipline of law that '. . . with the exception of an interesting discussion by Campbell and Wiles (1976), the attempt at a literature search drew a complete blank' (Becher and Trowler, 2001: 53). Yet there is so much writing on various aspects of legal education that it has been argued that legal education is as much a specialism within the study of law as is land law, criminal law, or any of the other generally-accepted fields of legal study (Bradney, 1997). While the primary purpose of writers on legal education is to contribute to our knowledge of some aspect of the legal academy, and not to provide insights into the culture of the discipline of law, it is nevertheless the case that their writing provides, for those who are interested in such things, a rich source of information about the 'tribe' of academic lawyers and their 'territory', the discipline of law.

In the discussion which follows, I aim to outline some of the main ways in which writing about legal education could help us discover more about the culture and identities of academic lawyers and their discipline. I also identify what it is that the existing studies do not address, thus revealing the gap in our knowledge which my work seeks to fill. To do justice to all the published research on legal education would take a book in itself, so I can do no more than point to some of the main contributions. In adopting that approach, it is inevitable that I will leave out some work which others may feel is more deserving of inclusion than some items which I have included. Hard choices have to be made; and readers should bear in mind that this is not a comprehensive overview, but a survey with a particular objective—merely to act as an illustration of the kind of research which already exists which might throw light upon the legal academy and its inhabitants, the tribe of academic lawyers. Much of the work which I do not specifically mention here is discussed at a later stage in the book.

LEGAL EDUCATION: PEDAGOGY

Writing about legal pedagogy gives us valuable insights into the culture of academic law. It throws light on the variety of ways in which academic law is taught, as well as pointing up debates and controversies, indicating the ways in which different approaches to the discipline are developing, and the extent to which trends apparent elsewhere in the academy have permeated the law school.

When people outside the specialism think about research into legal education, my personal experience is that they invariably do so in terms of writing about teaching. It is certainly true that a perusal of the pages of specialist journals (notably *The Law Teacher* and the legal education section of *The Web Journal of Current Legal Issues*, but also the *International Journal of the Legal Profession* and *Legal Ethics*) as well as general academic legal journals such as the *Modern Law Review*, *Legal Studies*, *Law and Critique* and the *Journal of Law and Society*, not to mention the subject-specific journals such as *The Company Lawyer*, reveals that there is a great deal of discussion about the pedagogical practice of law teaching. Some of these discussions have a long history; for example, legal education has often been the topic of the President's Address to the Society of Public Teachers of Law, which for many years was published annually in *Legal Studies* and its predecessor, *The Journal of the Society of Public Teachers of Law*. As early as 1925, Professor WS Holdsworth considered 'The Vocation of a Public Teacher of Law' (Holdsworth, 1925), while recently, Professor Richard Card's Presidential address explored a similar topic in his consideration of 'The Legal Scholar' (Card, 2002). These are just two of a whole series of addresses on legal education which have been delivered over the years (see also, for example, Stallybrass, 1948, 'Law in the Universities' and Llewellfryn Davies, 1956, 'Problems of Legal Education'). Recent concerns about pedagogy expressed by writers on legal education in other contexts range from lamentations about the lack of theoretical knowledge of education among law teachers (Webb, 1996; Cownie, 1999 and 2000), to debates about the introduction of legal skills and clinical legal education (Grimes, 1996; Brayne, 1996) and the place of legal ethics in the academic legal curriculum (O'Dair, 1997 and 1998).

The activities and publications of the United Kingdom Centre for Legal Education (UKCLE) and its predecessor, the National Centre for Legal

Education (see www.ukcle.ac.uk) which form the law component of the Learning and Teaching Support Network, can also provide a window on pedagogic aspects of the culture of academic law. Publications emanating from these sources range from a series of 'teaching and learning manuals' focused on specific subjects, such as family law or legal system (Burton et al, 1999; Bradney and Cownie, 1999) to guidance notes on teaching legal research (Clinch, 1999) and a series of briefing papers on assessment in law. These materials give an insight into the wide range of approaches, pedagogic activities and assessment vehicles which can be found in the contemporary law school.

There have been a number of edited collections of work on the pedagogy of the legal academy, which give valuable insights into aspects of academic legal culture. In Peter Birks' *Examining the Law Syllabus: The Core* (1992) and *Examining the Law Syllabus: Beyond the Core* (1993) authors address fundamental issues relating to the teaching of their specialist subjects, such as the proper relationship between property law and trusts (Swadling, 1992) or contract and tort (Hepple, 1992). *Teaching Lawyers' Skills* (edited by Webb and Maugham, 1996) focuses on skills-based learning, at both the academic and vocational stage of legal education. Its primary concern is to illustrate the extent to which the debate about legal skills has moved away from the behavioural, outcomes-led models of the 1980s, to an increasingly reflective model (Webb and Maugham, 1996: xxv). It is a fundamental aim of the authors to blend theory with practice, and in choosing to do this, their work illustrates the way in which legal education itself is moving away from an exclusive concern with the inculcation of a narrow range of technical skills towards a more overtly theoretical approach to legal education. A similar concern also underlies the special issue of the *International Journal of the Legal Profession* on 'Theory in Legal Education' edited by Sherr and Sugarman (2000). Authors contributing to this collection are self-consciously addressing the relationship between law, theory, and legal education. In doing so, they draw on a wide range of literature, much of it from outside the discipline of law; the editors note 'the increasing diversity' of legal education; their basic premise is that theory should not be seen (as it has often been in the past) as separate from substantive law and legal education (Sherr and Sugarman, 2000: 167). On the other hand, Brayne, Duncan and Grimes' collection, on clinical legal education, takes a more vocational approach to legal education. Subtitled *Active Learning in Your Law School*, it concentrates on illustrating how learning the law by 'doing the things that lawyers do' can improve the quality of what is learnt (Brayne et al, 1998). The diversity of approaches which can be found within the culture of contemporary legal academia is equally well illustrated by some of the other contributions to this genre, such as the collection of essays which introduce the perspective of critical legal scholars to the debate, edited by Peter Fitzpatrick and Alan Hunt, *Critical Legal Studies* (Fitzpatrick and Hunt, 1987) and that edited by Ian Grigg-Spall and Paddy Ireland, *The Critical Lawyers' Handbook* (1992). A perusal of some of these collections would provide rich pickings for anyone interested in the tribe of 'academic lawyers', since they reveal much about the ways in which legal academics teach, write about and conceptualise their subject.

Further information about the legal academy is provided by a range of empirical evidence relating to the praxis of teaching various legal subjects which has been gathered over the years. Among these are two surveys of the teaching of jurisprudence: Cotterell and Woodliffe (1974) and Barnett and Yach (1985), a survey of legal method/legal system teaching (Lynch et al, 1992) and a survey of company law teaching (Snaith, 1990). There is also a survey of the extent to which clinical legal education is included in the undergraduate law curriculum (Grimes et al, 1996). From these we discover, for example, that at the time these surveys were carried out, jurisprudence teachers were interested in the movement of their subject from a largely compulsory status in the syllabus to a predominantly optional status (Barnett and Yach, 1985: 154) and that law schools have a high rate of consensus about the need for foundational legal instruction which covers not only basic information about the legal system, but instruction in the skills necessary to use legal material effectively (Lynch et al, 1992: 219).

Writing about the pedagogy of the legal academy is of interest to ethnographers of the discipline, then, because it throws light on an important part of academic legal culture. However, it is, for the most part, very much confined to the public life of the academy. What it does not generally do, other than by implication, is reveal the attitudes of individual legal academics to the task of teaching law, their philosophy, values, beliefs about education and so on. It is these aspects of the private life of the law school that my work seeks to uncover.

LEGAL EDUCATION: POLICY

In addition to the extensive literature on legal pedagogy, some of which is outlined above, there is also a range of writing which is focused on the nature of the legal academy itself. Birks' edited collection, *Pressing Problems in the Law: What Are Law Schools For?* (1996) pursues the debate about whether law schools should be 'academic' or 'vocational', with spirited contributions from both sides of the debate, while the similar volume *Reviewing Legal Education* (Birks, 1994) is located firmly in the debate surrounding proposals by the legal professions relating to the academic stage of legal education. Birks expressly points out that these volumes contain 'personal insights into the life and purposes of law schools' (Birks, 1996: vi), thus pointing up the way in which they contribute to our knowledge of the culture of academic law.

The Law School: Global Issues, Local Questions (Cownie,1999a), brings together scholars from a number of common law jurisdictions to address issues ranging from the future of law schools in the context of globalisation, to the policy of higher education in Europe, while *Transformative Visions of Legal Education* (Bradney and Cownie, 1998) addresses new developments in legal education, such as legal ethics, and the use of information technology in the law school, as well as the effects of recent socio-economic policies on the nature of the legal academy, including the increasingly market-driven state pressures on law schools, and the effects of 'new public management', including league tables, increased accountability and so on. These two collections therefore open up a range of policy areas for debate, and in doing so, aim to illustrate '. . . the increasing professionalisation of legal education research' (a comment which throws light on the way in which scholars engaged in legal education research may feel work in this area has been perceived by other members of the legal academy) (Cownie, 1999: vii).

One of the major debates in the UK 'policy' arena has centred on the purpose of the university law school. Should law departments be producing good lawyers or, as Roger Brownsword has put it 'good citizens', ie providing a liberal education in law rather than a narrowly vocational one (1996 and 1999)? The question of the appropriate balance between training law students in the skills they need to be professional lawyers, and providing them with a liberal education which will equip them to be independent critical thinkers, is a topic which has attracted much attention since law became firmly established in the academy in the nineteenth century (Sugarman, 1986). Dicey, one of the most famous nineteenth-century jurists, entitled his inaugural lecture as the Vinerian Professor of Law at Oxford '*Can English Law Be Taught at the Universities?*' (Dicey, 1883). He began by concluding that practitioners would give a resounding 'No' to that question:

> They would reply with unanimity, and without hesitation, that English law must be learned, and cannot be taught, and that the only places where it can be learned are law courts or chambers.
> (Dicey, 1883: 1)

Dicey then sets out to show why the practitioners' answer is wrong. Learning the law by the traditional apprenticeship method leads to an arbitrary, partial legal education, any instruction depending on the goodwill of the (untrained) pupil master. As the unfortunate pupils soon find out, 'Many excellent lawyers have no talent as teachers' (1883: 3). If they try to teach themselves by reading some books, this attempt is doomed to failure, since the available legal literature replicated all the inadequacies of legal training:

> Our best works, such as Smith's Leading Cases, are at bottom a mere accumulation of notes on detached points of curious, rather than useful, learning. They are deficient in all general conceptions, in all grasp of principles, in all idea of method. . . . Turn, for example, to a writer whose book was twenty years ago the student's guide to the law of contract. Mr JW Smith opens his treatise with a chapter on the 'Nature and Classification of Contracts'. Of the nature of a contract he tells his reader nothing. What he does tell them is that agreements consist of contracts of record, contracts under seal and simple contracts. He first substitutes division for definition, and then gives a division which, for absolute uninstructiveness, may be compared to an attempt

to classify animals by diving them into dodos, lions, and all animals which are not dodos or lions.
(Dicey, 1883: 13)

On the other hand, argues Dicey, academic legal education can provide a rational introduction to the subject, based on expert work by law dons who can reduce the morass of legal rules to an orderly set of principles, and teach their students to analyse the law in a rigorous and logical manner (Dicey, 1883: 20). Meanwhile, legal academics will set to and create the high-quality legal literature which is so badly needed. In making his argument, and setting out so clearly the role of the legal academic, Dicey was justifying the existence of law as an academic discipline, speaking, in some senses, more to the academy itself than to the practitioners who appear to be at the forefront of his mind (Sugarman, 1991). He was also setting out, at a very early stage in the history of academic legal education, the debate between practitioners and academics about the nature of legal education which has continued, in some form or other, to the present day.

There are numerous contributors to this debate, which goes right to the heart of the place of law in the academy. Some writers have tried to fuse the gap between academia and practice. In the 1960s, we find Kahn Freund describing the opposition between vocational and academic legal education as a 'false antithesis', arguing that a legal education must include very academic matters, which might not seem to bear much relationship to the needs of the legal profession, but that this does not mean that legal education is irrelevant to practice; on the contrary, people should understand how well such an education fits law graduates for professional life (Kahn Freund, 1966: 123). At around the same time, we find William Twining discussing 'Pericles and the Plumber' (Twining, 1967). Two images of 'the lawyer', he argues, have dominated the literature, when it comes to discussing the purpose of legal education. The first is the lawyer as plumber—essentially, someone who is master of certain specialised knowledge and certain technical skills. 'What he needs is a no-nonsense specialised training, to make him a competent technician'. A liberal education is a waste of time for such a person. Think what effect it would have on our central heating systems if plumbers had to study the history and philosophy of plumbing (Twining, 1967: 397). At the other extreme is the image of the lawyer as Pericles, 'the law-giver, the enlightened policy-maker, the wise judge.' This type of lawyer needs, among other things, a breadth of perspective and a capacity for independent and critical thought (Twining, 1967: 398). Twining then goes on to explore how one might reconcile '. . . the liberal tradition with the demands of the world of affairs . . .' If legal education is to develop successfully, he argues, we must question the general working distinctions, such as 'education' and 'training', 'academic' and 'practical', 'theory' and 'practice', which, while useful in some contexts, have become frozen into rigid dichotomies (Twining, 1967: 421).

Recently, this theme has been taken up by Hepple, in his inaugural lecture at Cambridge '*The Renewal of the Liberal Law Degree*'. Hepple reiterates Kahn Freund's criticism of the 'false antithesis' between liberal and professional legal education (Hepple, 1996: 471), and goes on to endorse the approach found in the *First Report on Legal Education and Training* issued by the (now-disbanded) Lord Chancellor's Advisory Committee on Legal Education and Conduct (ACLEC, 1996) (of which he himself was a member), which proposed that the academic and vocational stages of legal education should be much more closely integrated, with liberal values and transferable professional skills permeating the entire experience. Hepple sees this as a revival of an older vision of law as a liberal discipline, and repeatedly makes the point that students must be able to view legal problems from a broad range of social and political perspectives, informed by theory, for 'Unless the student can make those connections between the particular and the general which theory should provide, he or she will fail to comprehend the wider universe in which the law operates' (Hepple, 1996: 483).

Other writers, taking slightly different perspectives, have also explored the relationship between the academy and legal practice. Birks, for instance, has argued that there should be a close partnership between academic lawyers on the one hand and judges/legislators on the other. He sees the legal academy as discharging a public and constitutional function, contributing not only to the improvement of the law, but to its legitimacy (Birks, 1996a). Savage and Watt, on the other hand, argue for what they describe as 'a more harmonious relationship' between academic lawyers and practitioners, seeing the law school in more utilitarian terms, as a 'House of Intellect' for the profession (Savage and Watt, 1996). Meanwhile, in addition to work already discussed, Twining has made a series of substantial contributions to the policy debate surrounding the nature and purpose of legal education, including a number of articles (eg, Twining 1967, 1982, 1988, 1995, 1996, 1998), his series of Hamlyn Lectures, published as *Blackstone's Tower: The English Law School* (1994) and his collection of essays, *Law in Context: Enlarging A Discipline* (1997). Twining is, as Birks has said 'one of the few leading English jurists to have devoted serious time to the theory and practice of legal education'(Birks, 1994: xi) (Birks himself being another example). Comments like this, made as asides in longer pieces, often prove very revealing, in terms of the culture of academic law; it is a culture, for instance, in which 'leading English jurists' apparently do not generally devote their time to the serious analysis of legal education.

Returning to the 'academic versus vocational' debate, Bradney has been an outspoken critic of the vocational aspects of legal education, arguing strongly that university law schools should offer a liberal education in law, and expressing strong disapproval of legal scholarship which is utilitarian in nature, designed to satisfy the short-term needs of the legal profession for clear explanatory descriptions of the law:

> A history of British scholarship during the twentieth century would probably omit any mention of legal writing. The dominant ethos within law schools has been to do work which was 'saleable' (Wortley, 1965: 258–59). Given the relative sizes of the academic and professional markets, that which was saleable was for the legal professions. The fact that many academics were also practitioners increased the likelihood that such research as was done would be oriented towards the interests of the practitioner. Contact with the professions foreshortened the horizon-limiting research to that which was of immediate use to the practising lawyer.
>
> But if universities are seen as places which deal with 'the theory of things' (Fehl, 1962: 28), rather than looking at things themselves, this kind of pedagogic writing simply fell outside the central function of the university. The research agenda of law schools distanced them from other disciplines within the university.
> (Bradney, 1992: 14)

Bradney is not alone in lamenting the intellectual poverty of academic legal scholarship. In an article on 'English Legal Scholarship', published in 1987, Wilson argued that the academic discipline of law up to that point had been essentially undistinguished, in intellectual terms, largely because its main claim to a place in the university had been that it was desirable that future members of the legal profession should have a university legal education:

> [It may be that Law is] neither sufficiently scholarly to be attractive to scholars, nor sufficiently legal to be attractive to lawyers. If putting 'legal' in front of 'scholarship' was like putting 'plastic' in front of 'cup', than adding 'English' is like adding 'disposable'. The words, though high-sounding, have a similar function to the words 'disposable plastic cup'. Each adjective strengthens the message that one cannot expect much in terms of quality, or long-term utility, from it.
> (Wilson, 1987: 819)

Despite his apparent cynicism, Wilson goes on to argue that there is hope for the discipline of law, if academic lawyers look for new ways of analysing law, and refuse to be bound by the traditional approach of which he is so critical (Wilson, 1987: 853).

Legal academics have also engaged with policy on a wider scale, analysing its effects on legal education as it has emerged from the Quality Assurance Agency (Bell, 1999; Bradney, 1996, 1999, 2001; Brownsword, 1994) and the Research Assessment Exercise (Vick et al, 1998; Campbell et al, 1999), as well as from the legal profession and Government (McAuslan, 1989; Twining, 1982). There has also been discussion about the relationship of the legal academy with industry, and, in particular, of the role of commercial sponsorship in academic law departments (Bradney, 1992; Bright and Sunkin, 1991; Bradney, 1990). Here Bradney has again been an outspoken critic, painting a bleak picture of the way in which law schools, strapped for cash, bowed to pressures to accept money from private firms (usually law firms) rather than maintaining their independence by relying exclusively on (inadequate) state funding. The maximum money available from sponsors, notes Bradney, is small in comparison with the needs of law schools. 'In any event . . . "for what is a man profited, if he shall gain the whole world, and lose his soul?" ' (Bradney, 1990: 146).

The perspectives which are adopted by all these writers, the concerns which they choose to address, and the ways in which they do so, are all clearly informed by their background as academic lawyers. Consequently, perusal of such work enables the reader to gain considerable insights into the attitudes of the legal academy, and into its relationship with other institutions in society. Here again, however, such insights must be gained by interpretation of materials produced for other purposes. Generally, policy work does not record the attitude of legal academics, either collectively or individually, to the relationship of the legal academy with the legal profession, the assessment of their research and teaching, or how they feel about being on the receiving end of the changes which are currently taking place in the academy. These are the sorts of issues which I have been able to explore with contemporary legal academics in a range of different institutions, working within different legal paradigms, at different stages of their academic careers.

LEGAL EDUCATION: APPROACHES TO LAW

Another major area of writing about the legal academy (which is highly significant, in terms of understanding the discipline in an ethnographic sense) is that which explores the approach which should be taken to the researching and teaching of law. Traditionally, law has been analysed and taught from a doctrinal, or 'black-letter' perspective, which concentrates on examining statutory materials and the reports of judicial decisions as the sole means of understanding the law (see Twining, 1994: ch 6). Critics have referred to this approach as 'technocentric'; students are taught to see the law in purely technical terms, as an autonomous system, with discernible boundaries between law and morality, as well as between law and other academic disciplines (Thornton, 1998). There is frequently a close relationship between the adoption of a black-letter perspective, and a belief in the purpose of the law school as producing legal practitioners.

However, since the 1960s, the legal academy has witnessed the emergence of other approaches to teaching and researching law. Foremost among these (numerically, at least) has been the 'law in context' / socio-legal studies approach, which has given rise to a flourishing professional association (the Socio-Legal Studies Association). The socio-legal approach has been analysed quite extensively in the literature. In Thomas' collection (Thomas 1997), aspects of the politics of socio-legal research are explored (the relationship with funders and users of empirical research, for example), alongside analysis of a range of legal specialisms, each author drawing out the distinctive contribution of a socio-legal perspective to the development of scholarship in a particular area of law. Others who have analysed the contribution of socio-legal studies include, for example, Campbell and Wiles (1976); Twining (1997a). The socio-legal approach has the potential for application to all areas of legal study, including those areas often perceived as very 'black letter' in nature, such as company law (Cheffins, 1999), contract (Wheeler and Shaw, 1994) or tort (Cane, 1997).

Law schools, as is the case with other parts of the academy, have also seen the emergence of a critical school (Critical Legal Studies, or CLS). While the growth in influence of CLS has been most noticeable in the United States (a development ably chronicled in Austin, 1998), the Critical Legal Studies movement has also taken root in British university law schools, and has spawned a number of significant contributions to the legal education debate. Legal education has featured in several collections of critical scholarship. In the collection on *Critical Legal Studies* edited by Fitzpatrick and Hunt (1987), we find, alongside considerations of the contribution of CLS to specific legal fields, a discussion of 'Critical Legal Education in Britain' (Thomson, 1987) which identifies as one of the key features of critical legal education the ability to provide,

> . . . an enabling perspective, that is to say a form of understanding which enables students to overcome their experience of powerlessness through recognising the sources of it . . . Seen in this light, critical legal education 'involves bringing to consciousness the taken for granted in and about law so that we can recognise what it means.'
> (Thomson, 1987: 194)

The Critical Lawyers' Handbook (Grigg-Spall and Ireland, 1992) contains a number of essays on critical legal education, exploring the nature of a critical approach to the teaching of a range of legal subjects, as well as a contribution from Duncan Kennedy on 'Legal Education as Training for Hierarchy', in which he argues that traditional legal education involves '. . . ideological training for willing service in the hierarchies of the corporate, welfare state' (Kennedy, 1992: 51). Other contributions to the legal education debate include Peter Goodrich's critique of Twining's *Blackstone's Tower* (Goodrich, 1996), in which he writes of the experience of being a law student as one of 'progressive disappointment':

> Law school stole my hopes of change and robbed me of any surviving sense of the relevance of my inner world, of poetry, desire, or dream, to the life of the institution. My experience of law school was of the denial of the relevance of my experience of law school. The irony of that paradox, of the experience of repression as a form of knowing, of the embodiment of denial as a mode of being, is the secret of the school's success as a rite of reproduction: an institutionally managed trauma gives birth to a conforming or believing soul.
> (Goodrich, 1996: 59).

The student experience of learning law is an important focus of critical examination, addressed also by Peter Rush in his article 'Killing me softly with his words: hunting the law student' (1990):

> Orthodox legal studies continually addresses itself to its students: the tradition of textbook writing could be said to constitute an immense effort on the part of the

orthodoxy to define itself in relation to the student, to construct legal studies as legal education. Such however is not the tale told in critical legal studies. The image of the orthodox constructed within critical legal studies is that the lecturer is all-too-present and the student is all-too-absent; the student is the victim of authority.
(Rush, 1990: 26).

A further indication of the weight given by some critical lawyers to legal education can be found in the fact that the first issue of the CLS journal, *Law and Critique* was a special issue on legal education (Volume 1, Number 1, 1990).

Feminism, too, has made a significant contribution to the development of the discipline of law, with a slow but steady increase in the number of law schools offering courses specifically considering the law from a gender/feminist perspective (McGlynn, 1998: App 2) as well as a similar increase in the integration of gender/feminist perspectives into the substantive legal curriculum (McGlynn, 1998: App 3). Feminists have not only introduced a new set of theoretical ideas with which to analyse the subject, now expounded in an extensive body of literature (recently reviewed in Conaghan, 2002), but have opened up new approaches to teaching, a clear example of which is provided by the article in *Law and Critique* written by participants in the 'Feminist Perspectives on Law' course at the University of Kent, with commentary provided by Susie Gibson (Feminists, 1990). The aim of this course was first to explore a feminist perspective on law, and secondly to explore the possibilities of a feminist teaching method 'that is, we were to emphasise the importance of personal experience, co-operative work with shared responsibility for one another and for the course, and a feminist educational ethic going beyond individual acquisitiveness' (Feminists, 1990: 48). The series of 'feminist perspectives' books published by Cavendish has been particularly influential in bringing feminist work to the attention of the legal academic community. Titles in the series range from examinations of the 'core subjects', such as *Feminist Perspectives on Equity and Trusts* (Scott-Hunt and Lim, 2001) and *Feminist Perspectives on Criminal Law* (Nicolson and Bibbings, 2000) to examinations of *Feminist Perspectives on Employment Law* (Morris and O'Donnell, 1999) or *Feminist Perspectives on Health Care Law* (Sheldon and Thomson, 1998).

Familiarity with these different approaches, and the arguments put forward to support or criticise their adoption, enables anyone interested in finding out about the way in which law is taught in the academy to put together a reasonably comprehensive picture of what goes on in the law school. However, as with the other materials discussed above, writing about these subjects is rarely qualitative; it does not allow you to see beyond the public face of law teaching, to find out how much law teachers enjoy teaching, whether they think they are good at it, to what extent they adopt any of these different approaches, or what they think they are trying to do when they are teaching their students. It is that kind of issue which I have been able to explore with the law teachers who have talked to me.

INAUGURAL LECTURES AND OTHER OCCASIONAL WRITING

Inaugural lectures are another relatively significant source of information about the legal academy, which give a sense of the development of the discipline over time. Legal education has been quite a popular topic on such occasions. Apart from the early example of Dicey, discussed above (1883), there are numerous other examples. One of the most powerful of these is Gower's inaugural lecture, delivered at the LSE in January 1949 (Gower, 1950), in which he attacks the 'complacent apathy' with which people have come to regard legal education, and criticises the paucity of published material on the topic (Gower, 1950: 185). His critical analysis of the state of legal education addresses the failings of both academic and vocational legal education, and laments the lack of co-ordination between the two. He goes on to set out a comprehensive programme of reform, using the experience of the United States and other countries to inform his ideas. Gower's lecture, extending over sixty-eight pages of the *Modern Law Review*, is an early example of a distinguished legal academic (familiar to most academic lawyers as a company lawyer) taking legal education very seriously. His exposition is detailed, scholarly and incisive, and forms a major contribution to the history of legal education.

Examples from later eras abound, including, from my own university, the inaugural lecture of the founding professor of the law department, which ranged widely over a number of issues which have remained central to debates in legal education—the place of the discipline of law in a university, the need to study law in its social context, the merits of joint degrees (with economics, politics or sociology, for example) and the relationship between the academic and vocational stages of legal education, to name but a few (Grodecki, 1967). Recently, Hepple, Leighton and Sherr have all used their inaugural lectures to explore issues in legal education, Hepple arguing for 'The Renewal of the Liberal Law Degree' (Hepple, 1996), Leighton looking at some of the key challenges facing contemporary law teachers (Leighton, 1996) and Sherr exploring the purpose of legal education in the context of profound changes in the legal profession and within the higher education sector as well (Sherr, 1998).

Professors of law have, from time to time, written thoughtful and provocative 'occasional pieces' about the university law school and the discipline of law as it is studied there. These contributions, made by those who would be unlikely to describe themselves as specialists in legal education, but rather as property lawyers, constitutional lawyers and so on, also provide interesting insights into the development of the discipline and its culture over the years. Within this genre is Bridge's discussion of the role of academic lawyer *qua* academic (rather than *qua* lawyer) (Bridge, 1975), and McAuslan's call for positive and well-informed action by academic lawyers in the face of increasing external pressures upon university law schools (McAuslan, 1989). From such writing, we can discover a lot about the opinions of individual academic lawyers about a range of issues relating to the academy, and in particular to legal education.

Members of the judiciary have also, from time to time, contributed to debates about legal education. While they themselves are not members of the academy, in the sense of being full-time academics, the relationship between academia and the judiciary is quite a close one (Duxbury, 2001), and judges' comments on legal education can throw light on the academy as it is seen from the point of view of a close 'outsider'. Within this genre, we find a range of opinions, from judges who believe that the function of the law school is to serve the needs of the legal profession (Lawton, 1980) to those whose views are remarkably similar to some of the law professors discussed above; the Lord Chief Justice, for example, talks of legal education as including '. . . not only the skills of a traditional black-letter lawyer, but also the ability to identify the broad principles which are involved in creating a just society subject to the rule of law (Woolf, 2000: 269).

Under the heading of 'occasional writing' also come pieces of journalism which legal academics occasionally engage in. Recently, some apparently light-hearted (but essentially serious) insights into the culture of legal academia have been provided by the Editor of *The Reporter* (the newsletter of the Society of Legal Scholars), Professor Tony Bradney, whose editorials have catalogued the pressures experienced by law school staff in an era of diminishing resources ('the university has decided that this year we will be able to budget for a book') (Bradney, 2002a), praised the high quality of work which goes on, despite low morale (Bradney, 2002b), and urged law teachers to defend academic freedom before it becomes merely 'the freedom of academics to do what they are told' (Bradney, 2003). That these pieces have been regarded by others as relevant to their research is an indication of their ability to capture something of the flavour of contemporary legal education (see, for example, Collier, 2003).

Nevertheless, while inaugural lectures and other occasional pieces provide interesting insights into the culture of academic law and the professional identities of legal academics, these remain essentially public pieces of work. In carrying out my research, I have been able to move beyond the public arena, to uncover the 'private life' of the law school.

HISTORICAL PERSPECTIVES

The history of legal education is a much-neglected subject, and as yet there is no comprehensive survey of the history of legal education in England. Such an enterprise would be of considerable interest to anyone trying to understand the discipline of academic law and legal academics, but it is a task which lies outside the scope of this book. Suffice to say that any such history would mention, as significant early figures, Blackstone, Austin, and Bentham, and that these figures have already received significant attention, though not necessarily from the point of view of their contribution to legal education; see, for example, the discussion in Twining (1989). David Sugarman's examination of the early history of legal education in England (Sugarman, 1983 and 1986) provides invaluable analysis of the politics of the emerging discipline of law and its relationship with the academy, while overviews can also be found in Cownie (2000a) and Bradney and Cownie (2000).

Literature of a quite different kind, which also gives us insights into the private life of legal academia, is that devoted to recording the history of various law schools. In Lawson's *The Oxford Law School 1850–1965* we can find chapters on 'The Age of the Professor' and 'The Rise of the Tutors', which give us a range of insights into the private life of the law school, as well as much biographical discussion about the lives of various legal academics. On Anson, for instance, we find Lawson writing that:

> Besides occupying the Wardens' Lodgings he kept a flat in London, and rented the great house at Pusey in Buckinghamshire. He knew politics, and later, a great deal of administration, from the inside, and he also took a considerable part in the administration of the University . . . Anson was as a young man a mid-Victorian Liberal. Like his friend Dicey he deserted Gladstone on the issue of Home Rule for Ireland and thereafter became more and more Conservative.
> (Lawson, 1968, pp. 77–78)

In a small booklet recording the first 60 years of the Law Faculty at the University of Birmingham (Bosworth, 1987), we find this description of Charles Smalley-Baker, the first holder of the Barber Chair of Law:

> It is easy for us to criticize and even laugh at Charles Smalley-Baker. He has been described as 'a snob, a name-dropper, a dictator' as a 'lover of flummery' who 'dressed and looked more like a bookmaker than a professor'. Photographs of him show a face which is very smug and self-satisfied, and it is true he did not underestimate his own role when making reports on the progress of the Faculty.
> (Bosworth, 1987: 12)

While clearly not primarily written with the intention of adding to our knowledge of the private life of the law school, such documents can prove invaluable in allowing us to put legal academic life in context, and in prompting us to make comparisons with our contemporary experience of legal academia.

William Twining's essay detailing the history of the discipline of law in the University of London, written as part of the 150th anniversary celebrations of that institution, provides much interesting analysis into the politics of legal education as interpreted by an 'insider' (Twining, 1989). Another glimpse of the 'private life' of the legal academy can be found in Phillip Pettit's article, detailing the history of the Society of Public Teachers of Law (now the Society of Legal Scholars) during its first fifty years (Pettit, 1983). Abel Smith and Stevens' *Lawyers and the Courts* (1967) also contains some interesting insights into the history of legal education.

Legal Education and the Lived Experience of Legal Academics 41

In Twining's essay on the 'Wandering Jurist' (Twining 1997a) we find information about a legal academic legal career which began in the 1950s and is still continuing. This piece acts as an introduction to a collection of essays entitled *Law in Context* (Twining, 1997). Twining writes:

> In order to set these pieces in an appropriate and coherent context it is necessary to say something about my personal odyssey and the locales that were the settings of these essays. What follows is akin to the reminiscences of a foreign correspondent describing situations in which he has found himself doing work that inspired him to write. (Twining, 1997: 2)

'What follows' is a piece of personal history which has rich pickings for those interested in the private life of the law school. There are glimpses of life as a law undergraduate at Oxford in the 1950s, followed, after a period as a 'travelling scholar', by a chair at Belfast in 1966, and the launch of the 'Law in Context' series in the following year. This was the period of the Ormrod Committee on Legal Education, as well as the 'Troubles' in Northern Ireland, and the two are inextricably mixed in this story of legal academia. Professor Twining was appointed to a chair at Warwick in 1972; in this new law school he had the opportunity to contribute to the development of the law in context approach. At Warwick, this general approach was to be implemented in every course, with each academic expected to rethink their field in broader terms than exposition and analysis of doctrine. A move to UCL in 1983 saw the continuation of an interest in international legal education, particularly through the Commonwealth Legal Education Association, and finally there is a consideration of some of the main policy issues facing legal education at the end of the twentieth century. This essay, together with the others that accompany it, gives considerable insights into the politics and everyday life of legal academia, pointing up some of the controversies, the weaknesses and the strengths of academic law as it is practised in English universities from the point of view of a knowledgeable and scholarly 'insider'. The work mentioned here provides just a few examples of the way in which material which is often written primarily with 'history' in mind can inform our exploration of the culture of legal academia as it is found in law schools today.

EMPIRICAL SURVEYS OF THE LEGAL ACADEMY

Quite apart from the empirical evidence about legal pedagogy gathered by the surveys relating to specific legal specialisms discussed above, there have been a number of other surveys which have aimed to uncover a range of data about the legal academy. Foremost among these are the extensive 'Wilson' surveys of law schools, carried out by Professor John Wilson (joined from 1975–81 by Dr Stan Marsh). During the period 1966–93 three surveys and two interim supplements were published (Wilson, 1966; Wilson and Marsh, 1975, 1978, 1981; Wilson, 1993). These surveys gathered a wealth of empirical information about law schools, including data on student numbers, selection of students, the syllabus, methods of teaching and assessment, the qualifications and experience of staff, library facilities, secretarial support and liaison between law departments and outside bodies. This data is particularly valuable because it is much more detailed, in relation to law schools, than that available from the Higher Education Statistics Agency or any of its predecessors. The three original surveys were followed by a similar survey by Harris and Jones, published in 1996, focusing on very much the same issues, but including, for the first time, data collected from both 'old' and 'new' universities (Wilson had surveyed 'old' universities, while a team from the Association of Law Teachers (Harris et al, 1993) had surveyed 'new' universities). The survey by Leighton et al (1995) focused specifically on legal academics, and gathered together not only data on their qualifications, teaching methods, reading habits, consultancy activities and research activities, but also on their attitudes and priorities in relation to the ability to carry out research, good quality administrative support, flexible working opportunities, student numbers and improved pay. These surveys provide researchers and others with a range of empirical data about law schools, legal academics and law students; they also provide some insights (often tantalisingly brief) into the discipline of law itself, but they are almost exclusively quantitative in nature, and, apart from a little material in the 1995 survey by Leighton et al, they are not, therefore, a good source of qualitative information about the issues which are central to my investigation.

THE 'PRIVATE LIFE' OF LEGAL ACADEMIA

I would argue that although we can glean much information, both about the tribe of academic lawyers and their territory, from the work which has just been discussed, it is work which, for the most part, belongs to the 'public life' of academic law. A few writers have, however, ventured into the more private aspects of legal academia, and from their work, we can begin to see the type of insights which can be gained from such an approach.

In *Blackstone's Tower* Twining is explicit in emphasising the insights which could be gained by adopting an anthropological approach to the study of the law school. Chapter 4 is entitled 'Law School Culture: A Visit to Rutland' and in it Twining sets out to examine the culture of English university law schools by taking the reader on '... an impressionistic tour of an imaginary law school', which he names 'Rutland' (Twining, 1994: 66). We begin with a brief historical introduction:

> The University of Rutland is a civic university of the middling sort, founded in 1930 ... During the 1960s it rapidly outgrew its original suburban campus, captured further territory, some neighbouring and some far-flung, where it demolished, converted and erected a motley collection of unmemorable buildings.
> (Twining, 1994: 66)

Next we are taken on a tour of the department, past the notice 'Denning House—Faculty of Laws', which allows for a discursion on the positivist heritage which leads to a Faculty of Laws *(leges)* rather than Law *(ius)*, and into the building itself, where we find the porter, backed up these days by video surveillance. Along the corridor we come to the noticeboards, with their student timetables, notices relating to the sale of student textbooks, recruiting visits by law firms, and Law Society events. It is not long before we arrive at a recent exercise in public relations:

> ... a case exhibiting a sample of recent publications by the Faculty, four slim monographs, about a dozen fat books addressed to the student market (three of which are past their third editions) and a number of offprints with obscure titles, which some might think are self-addressed. No room could be found here for rather more lucrative publications, such as nutshells (or other student aids), contributions to loose-leaf practitioners' services, and occasional journalism. First impressions suggest that this is primarily a teaching institution, which is quite vocationally-oriented, but which is trying to build up its research profile.
> (Twining, 1994: 69)

The final section of the 'case study' is devoted to 'events' and allows the author to look at faculty appointments and open days. All of this material is used to allow the author to make comments about the culture, values and attitudes of the inhabitants of Rutland's law school, relating them to the existing academic literature on higher education and on legal education in particular. Witty and entertaining though it is, Twining's imaginary ethnography has a serious point, which is to point out that, in a context where there are hardly any empirical studies about law students and legal academics, such work could greatly increase our knowledge.

Another contribution to the literature on the private life of legal academia is Goodrich and Mills' discussion of the dynamics of race in the internal culture of law schools (Goodrich and Mills, 2001). In the course of their analysis, Goodrich and Mills express their disquiet at the lack of reaction from the legal academic community to an assertion by a reviewer in the *Cambridge Law Journal* that critical race theory, though containing some writings 'which are clearly important and insightful', mostly consists of 'anti-intellectual ranting by people who are unwilling or unable to construct proper arguments' (Kramer, 1996: 152), together with other similar remarks made in the course of a book review published in the same law journal a few years later (Kramer, 1998), where the same reviewer talks about critical race theory in the following terms:

> Faddish creeds such as Critical Race Theory and postmodernism have yielded little apart from intellectual flabbiness. Possessed of neither talent nor training in philosophy, the followers of such creeds have not hesitated to display their lack of competence to the world by putting forward arguments (or ostensible arguments) that are too lamentably feeble and assernine to deserve any response other than contemptuous amusement.
> (Kramer, 1998: 612, quoted in Goodrich and Mill, 2001: 23).

Goodrich and Mills' view of legal academia is that it has been found wanting:

> That these remarks were published in a law review edited by professional legal academics is surprising. That their publication has to date elicited neither comment nor response is shocking. . . . Whatever the epistemic status of these generalisations, however, their publication in two of the top university law reviews in England must be taking as according at the least a certain credibility and gravamen to the views propounded.
> (Goodrich and Mills, 2001: 23)

The problem, for Goodrich and Mills is that critical race theory has failed to establish itself within the English legal academy, and that these remarks constitute one of the few occasions on which it has been mentioned in leading law journals. They argue that the dismissive tone of these remarks does not invite engagement or dialogue, and that it will contribute to the silence about race which they see as permeating legal academia (2001: 24–25).

Recently, there has been a flurry of publications which have sought to uncover a different range of theoretical / qualitative information about the tribe of academic lawyers. There are still only a handful of scholars working in the area, but in terms of an ethnography of the disciplines, it is a welcome development. The majority of these scholars have, however, to date, focused their work on issues relating to gender and the law school. Richard Collier's interest lies with masculinity and the teaching and studying of law. In 'Masculinism, Law and Law Teaching', he examines the relationship between men and feminism in the legal academy, looking at the sexual politics of law teaching, and arguing that:

> Whilst in sociology there has occurred a certain reflexivity about the masculinism of both sociological method and the epistemological status of the sociological enterprise, within legal scholarship men do not seem to have been keen to address the masculinism of law and legal education. It has been in the development of an explicitly feminist legal theory that the masculinity of law . . . has been a central question.
> (Collier, 1991: 429)

Collier's call for a critical engagement with masculinity and his emphasis on the relationship of the power of law and the power of men is revealing in the light it throws not just on the nature of law, but on the values and practices which, he argues, are part of the everyday life of the law school (Collier, 1991: 446).

In what has become one of the best-known pieces of work on the private life of the law school, ' "Nutty Professors", "Men in Suits" and "New Entrepreneurs": corporeality, subjectivity and change in the law school and legal practice' (1998) Collier goes on to explore the relationship between the social production of heterosexual masculinities and the 'making of men' as practising lawyers and legal academics. He argues that:

> . . . the (sexed) bodies of women and men are constituted at particular moments and settings as having differential access to 'knowledge' resulting from their embodied social locations in a gendered world . . . the constitution of 'professional' masculine

bodies and subjectivities can be seen as important factors in the production and maintenance of the continuing marginalization and discrimination of women.
(Collier, 1998: 45)

As far as the private life of the law school is concerned, Collier uncovers a number of aspects of that life which have hitherto remained hidden. Others have noticed the differences in status of men and women in the legal academy (see McGlynn, Wells and Cownie, below), but it is Collier who has explored in most depth the playing out of the close relationship of law and masculinity in the law school. It is this idea which he develops further in '(Un)Sexy Bodies: The Making of Legal Professional Masculinities' (Collier, 1998a), where he explores insights from recent scholarship on the relationship between identity, subjectivity and corporeality in relation to the 'masculine' cultures of legal education and practice. What interests him is the 'conceptualisation of the *social dynamics* whereby discrimination is reproduced and legitimated on a daily basis in the field of law' (Collier, 1998a: 23, italics in original). Relating this to the growing literature on the gendering of organisations and bureaucracies, Collier points out the complexity of the processes whereby historically practices have been constituted by reference to a masculinist vision of professional work and the implications of this for both legal practice and the law school. Central to his analysis is a critique of the ways in which mens' subjectivities remain predicated on a dualism between 'public' masculinities and 'private' domains. While men in power do not perceive the transformation of mens' relationship with children as a pressing concern, he concludes, little is likely to change.

Most recently, Collier has sought explicitly to contribute to work on the 'private life' of the law school in his article 'The Changing University and the (Legal) Academic Career: rethinking the relationship between women, men, and the private life of the law school' (Collier, 2002). Collier argues that academics, as 'new knowledge workers' within an increasingly corporatised (masculinist) working environment, have experienced a shift in the dominant gender configuration of higher education. This has implications for what a 'successful' academic career entails (Collier, 2002: 20). Work which cannot be measured in terms of 'outputs' (such as counselling students) becomes formally invisible. The more masculinised university values a model of performativity which encourages, as Margaret Thornton has noted (Thornton, 2000) 'the relentless promotion of self at the expense of good citizenship.' Given that the boundaries of academic work are so indeterminate, Collier argues that the effects of increased demands from the university are playing out differently for men and women (Collier, 2002: 22). Even with the increase in scholars working in the socio-legal and critical legal paradigms, Collier has little optimism for the future 'There is no reason to believe, in short, that the dominance of men has shifted simply because a new intellectual terrain has evolved or because lip service is now paid to gender equity' (Collier, 2002: p28). I will return later to many of the issues raised by Collier's body of work. For now, it is sufficient to note that here is one legal academic who takes 'the private life of the law school' very seriously.

Clare McGlynn's work has been particularly useful in providing empirical evidence about the position of women in the contemporary academy. Her book, *The Woman Lawyer: making the difference*, though primarily about women in legal practice, contains two chapters which discuss the legal academy as it is experienced by female students and staff (McGlynn, 1998). Research for the book included gathering data on the relative numbers of male and female academic staff (by grade) in UK university law schools, detailed information about law schools offering courses specifically considering the law from a gender/feminist perspective, as well as courses which though primarily about, for example, tort, criminology, jurisprudence, address gender issues (see McGlynn, 1998, Appendices 2 and 3). Her inclusion of testimonies from some women who have experienced life in university law schools also gives us a rare insight into the private life of the discipline of law through the eyes of four individuals (three of them among the 14 per cent of female law professors then existing in university law schools).

Celia Wells' contribution to this area arises out of a recent series of articles on women in the law school (Wells, 2000, 2001, 2001a, 2002). She writes that her research was prompted by her own experiences as a professor in a leading UK university (Wells, 2001: 120) and her work analyses a number of common explanations for the position of women in UK law schools. Among the insights into the private life of the law school offered by her survey of women law professors, is the fact that, for a significant number of her respondents, entering the academy was seen as preferable to pursuing a career in legal practice, particularly at the Bar, which was perceived as a particularly unfriendly environment for those who were not white, male and 'public school' (2002: 9). Only a small minority of her respondents (20 per cent) thought that gender had had no effect on their careers, or on their relationships with students, colleagues, heads of department or others in the university. The vast majority (the remaining 80 per cent) believed not only that gender had had a significant effect on their careers, but there was an increasing tendency for it to do so with those in positions of authority, such as heads of department (2002a: 11). Promotion to a chair appeared to polarise womens' experience, with some finding that it made things better 'Once I became a professor I found—without any real rationalisation—that all doors opened and suddenly one was credited with a talent hitherto unrecognised!', while for others it made things worse, so that promotion caused greater difficulties, as male colleagues perceived the increased competition as a threat (2002: 29). As a background to her enquiries, Wells notes:

> ... the image of the ideal law professor may be an exaggerated version of images of the ideal professor. Law, like the academy, is associated with values of rationality, objectivity and neutrality. Since there is plenty of evidence that women are perceived as less competent and authoritative than men in many work situations, and that this

becomes more acute for women in professional roles, these (assumed) legal values may contribute to what might be thought a double jeopardy for women law teachers. (Wells, 2001; 119)

I have argued elsewhere that by studying the position of women academics in British law schools one could discover a lot about the discipline of law as a whole (Cownie, 1998). I argued there that since we know even less about the position of female legal academics than male, researching their professional lives might be as good a place to start as any, and that the amount of work which could be undertaken amounted to '. . . a new research agenda'. In later work (Cownie, 2000b) I have argued that the position of women in law schools is a complex one, which involves both the difficulties arising out of gender and sexuality which are clearly indicated by recent work on the legal academy, and some advances for women, who now play significantly greater roles both within their own institutions and in academia as a whole than historically has been the case. In exploring this complexity, it will be necessary to identify the ways in which law, masculinity and the educational setting of the university may combine to suppress what Gilligan (1982) would term 'the feminine voice' in the law school. An important aspect of such work is to reveal more about the relationship between gender and the law school in the academic law, and there is much of importance still to be done. This is work to which I hope to contribute in the future. However, given the paucity of information with which we are currently working, in terms of my primary interest, which is the 'private life' of legal academia as a whole, I have come to realise that it is arguably even *more* important to establish a baseline, to explore the nature of legal academia through the eyes of *all* its inhabitants, both male and female, to get an overall picture, before focusing on the more particular issues surrounding gender.

CONCLUSION

Published work on legal education can provide an interested observer with a wide range of information about the culture of academic law, and the professional identities of the academics who inhabit it. Nevertheless, despite the occasional forays into the private life of the law school such as those which have just been discussed, we still lack any *sustained* qualitative examination of the lived experience of legal academics. Published work about the 'private life' of law schools remains very sparse, and that which there is does not provide us with a comprehensive examination of legal academia as a whole. There is still no extended study of the everyday life of legal academics working in Britain. It is that gap, above all, which I hope to fill with this book.

3
Inhabiting the Discipline of Law

APPROACHES TO LAW

THE APPROACH WHICH legal academics adopt when analysing law and legal phenomena is of considerable importance, in terms of the culture of academic law. Toma argues that 'Scholars working in different paradigms view the purposes of their work differently, apply different evaluative standards, rely upon different methods and frameworks, and accept different types of values' (Toma, 1997: 679). This is certainly true of academic law, where the traditional doctrinal approach to legal analysis, based upon a conception of law as an internally coherent body of rules, analysed using the same techniques of precedent and statutory interpretation that are used by judges in courts, has been subjected, since the 1960s onwards, to a number of different critiques. These alternative paradigms, notably socio-legal studies, feminism and critical legal studies (or CLS), not only use different methods of analysis, drawing in both methods and theoretical insights from other disciplines in the humanities and social sciences, thus inevitably using different evaluative standards, but also address different subjects, not all of which are susceptible to rule-based analysis. The different approaches which are adopted by legal academics when they analyse legal phenomena go right to the heart of the 'webs of significance' which Geertz identified as lying at the heart of a culture (Geertz, 1975: 5). Although for the purposes of analysis I have treated these various approaches to law as if they were clearly distinguishable, it is important to remember that this is not necessarily the case. These classifications are not rigid, as will become apparent from the analysis of my research which follows.

Doctrinal or 'Black-Letter' Law

Becher and Trowler begin their discussion of academic law by giving a brief general account of their view of the subject, which is derived from the data gathered from their respondents:

> In academic law, 'the centre of the subject is a body of rules'. The concern of its proponents is 'mainly with ordering a corpus of knowledge: it is a largely descriptive pursuit'. Law, one respondent observed, 'is the object, not the method, of study—it can only be the method of practice'. There is a constantly changing body of material arising from new legislation—'everything is always in a state of flux'. There is 'a

tradition that law is value-free': it is arguable that 'it is more resistant to ideology than some subjects'. Nevertheless, 'it leaves open the possibility of a critical, ideological function'. The subject allows 'room for shades of opinion', 'an absence of certainty, no clear-cut rules'. However, 'some aspects are uncontentious'; there are 'shared criteria of judgement'; 'a substantial consensus—at least until recently'; and 'validity in some areas within the existing norms'.
(Becher andTrowler, 2001: 31)

The description of academic law as 'concerned with a body of rules', 'a largely descriptive pursuit' and with 'a tradition that law is value-free' is recognisable as a description of a particular approach to the study of law, the positivist or doctrinal approach, which has also been referred to as 'technocentric' (Thornton, 1998: 372). It is commonly acknowledged that legal positivism has been the dominant form of academic legal scholarship since law schools were established in English universities at the end of the nineteenth century, when the concern of the early legal academics in Britain was to establish their area of expertise as 'the science of law', thus justifying their membership of the academy (Sugarman, 1986). A major part of the doctrinal tradition is the conception of law as autonomous, with clear boundaries between law and other subjects. Being taught to 'think like a lawyer' involves learning how to separate 'legal' issues from the other types of issue (moral, political, social, and so on), which may seem to be raised by the material under consideration (Kennedy, 1982: 594). The power of doctrinal (or, as academic lawyers frequently refer to it, 'black-letter') law to insist on casting every situation it looks at in its own terms (Smart, 1989) lies behind the description of legal education as a process which 'steals one's soul'. 'Law school . . . doesn't create selfish, aggressive people—but it does provide the intellectual equipment with which recipients can justify and give force to beliefs and actions most people would wholeheartedly condemn' (Goodrich, 1991, quoted in Thornton, 1998: 377). But it is the narrowness of the doctrinal approach, with its belief in law as a self-contained body of rules, which has attracted most criticism. As Adams and Brownsword comment:

> . . . to say that black-letterism is concerned with describing the operation of the law would be to overstate its scope; for what it purports to describe is the content of the formal legal materials (the content of the relevant statutes and precedents, and so on), not the operation of these rules in practice.
> (Adams and Brownsword, 1999: 30)

Socio-Legal Studies

The more modern critiques to which legal positivism has been subjected, particularly since the early 1970s, do not accept that law is composed of an autonomous body of rules, nor that it is 'neutral' or 'value-free' (Campbell and Wiles, 1976: 547). Of these critiques, arguably the one which has engendered the most widespread interest among legal academics is the socio-legal, or 'law in context' approach (Bradney and Cownie, 2000: 6). Socio-legal studies is difficult to define, because of the diversity of research and teaching carried out under that name; it can, for instance, include feminist work, as well as work which is (almost) indistinguishable from that done by critical legal scholars.

In its review of socio-legal studies, published in 1994, the Economic and Social Research Council ESRC defined it as 'an *approach* to the study of law and legal processes' which 'covers the theoretical and empirical analysis of law as a social phenomenon' (ESRC, 1994: 1, emphasis in original). From its inception, it was regarded as an innovative and exciting departure for the discipline of law (Twining, 1974: 163). Since the establishment of the Socio-Legal Studies Association in 1990 it has developed rapidly, so that by1994, the ESRC noted that socio-legal studies had '. . . achieved a very wide dispersal among UK higher education institutions', with at least sixty-five universities and five independent research institutes conducting socio-legal research (ESRC, 1994: 24 and Appendix 1).

Interest in socio-legal studies has been characterised as '. . . the emergence of a new legal paradigm' (Thomas, 1997: 19) and socio-legal scholarship as '. . . the most important scholarship currently being undertaken in the legal world' (Cotterell, 1995: 314). Socio-legal studies, then, forms an important part of the academic legal scene, and certainly deserves a mention in any analysis of contemporary legal academic culture. Its existence gives an insight into a fundamental division among academic lawyers, since those who adopt this approach do so because they find the traditional doctrinal analysis inadequate as way of explaining the truth about law (Twining, 1974: 163). Criticism of doctrinal analysis of law not only gave rise to socio-legal studies, however; it was also the foundation of Critical Legal Studies or CLS.

Critical Legal Studies

The critical legal studies movement originated in the USA in the late 1970s, and rapidly spread to a number of other countries, including the UK, where the first critical legal conference took place in 1984 (Fitzpatrick and Hunt, 1987: 1). Critical legal studies is self-consciously radical; while there are disparate views about many of the intellectual debates which take place, both among critical scholars themselves, and with scholars outside the movement, it nevertheless still appears accurate to characterise critical legal scholars as '. . . reacting against features of the prevailing orthodoxies in legal scholarship, against the conservatism of law schools and against many features of the role played by law and legal institutions in modern society' (Hunt, 1987: 5). Characterised in this way, CLS shares much with socio-legal studies, and membership of the two movements is not necessarily mutually exclusive, with some legal scholars working within both paradigms (evidenced by publication in both critical legal and socio-legal academic journals, for example). The difficulty of separating critical legal scholarship from other alternative paradigms has been noted by one of leading British critical legal scholars, Peter Goodrich, who wrote of critical legal studies in the UK:

> What substantive literature exists indeed lacks any distinctive programme, seldom adopts a self-consciously critical label, and is scarcely differentiable from extant socio-legal, contextual, or more explicitly political analyses of regulatory forms.
> (Goodrich, 1992: 195)

Even in terms of its concern with theory, which those outside the field might arguably have regarded as one of the distinguishing features of critical scholarship, Goodrich sees critical legal studies as 'fragmentary', and not clearly separable from existing jurisprudential literature and debates (Goodrich, 1992: 196).

Despite its clear links to existing debates, however, it would be inaccurate to regard critical legal studies as 'just another form of socio-legal studies'. Goodrich has argued more recently that what differentiated members of the critical legal studies movement from those focusing on socio-legal studies or a feminist analysis of law was '. . . the absence of any direct relation to legal doctrine or substantive rules of law'. Critical lawyers were thus characterised by their possession of a '. . . fractious hostility to legal rules' (Goodrich, 1999: 345). Some of the other features of critical legal scholarship have included a predominant concern with a range of 'theories', including, in earlier work, Marxism, (reflected in, for example, Cain and Hunt's edited collection of readings, *Marx and Engels on Law*, 1978) and more recently, a particular interest in the possibilities of literary theory and analysis, and a concern with '. . . eros and alterity, of other laws and laws of the other' (Goodrich, 1999: 344). Critical legal studies would also, in the view of some scholars, include feminism, as well as critical race theory. As Naffine has pointed out, the relationship between critical legal studies and other critical interpretations of law is complex; in the case of feminism, she argues,

> . . . we may observe an interesting relationship between critical scholars and feminists. To many critical theorists, it would seem that feminists represent the intellectual vanguard of legal theory. For example, feminist work is now accorded prominence in critical conferences and in the more critical journals. But all is not harmonious. Certain feminists have openly taken issue with the critical theorists, regarding them as masculine in their orientation and concerns . . . Other feminists regard critical scholars as 'fellow travellers' . . .
> (Naffine, 1993: 79)

Here, as with the other approaches to law, the lines are not clear-cut. Other general characteristics of critical legal scholarship, however, would include a concern with critique as a political strategy for social transformation, and an explicit concern with legal education, with '. . . teaching practices which will foster the development of politically active, critical law students . . .' rather than conventional forms of legal education which attempt '. . . to destroy all critical thought so as to produce an alienated and subordinated person . . .' (Grigg-Spall and Ireland, 1992: x). While the extent to which critical legal studies in Britain has succeeded in attaining its radical objectives remains a matter of debate (Goodrich, 1999), it is nevertheless a part of the legal academic culture which was known to all my respondents, and which deserves a place in any analysis of the 'tacit understandings' of academic lawyers (Sackmann et al, 1997: 25).

Feminism and Law

The application of feminist ideas to the analysis of law was stimulated, as in other disciplines, by the second wave of feminism in the 1960s and 1970s. In its early manifestations, feminist work within the legal academy tended to take the form of work on 'women and law', which revealed the exclusion of women and women's issues from the focus of legal study, and concentrated on opening up to academic legal analysis areas of particular relevance to women such as domestic and sexual violence and discrimination on grounds of sex, and also began to point out the ways in which law, though apparently neutral, in fact excluded or disadvantaged a disproportionate number of women. A classic example of such work is Atkins and Hoggett's *Women and the Law* (1984).

New ideas about the social construction of gender were reflected in Katherine O'Donovan's groundbreaking consideration of *Sexual Divisions in Law* (1985) which moved the debate on, focusing as it did on the possibility of law playing an active role in the constitution of gender, providing the basis for feminists and other academic lawyers to elaborate a critique of law's role in the constitution of sexuality. Building on work such as O'Donovan's, and that which sprang from it, feminist legal scholars have gone on to develop a significant body of work on feminist legal theory, which now interacts with other critical movements such as post-modernism, post-structuralism, critical race theory and psychoanalysis. The way in which feminism has gained ground within the legal academy over the past twenty years is well documented by Conaghan, in her recent review of the current state of feminist legal studies (Conaghan, 2002), in which she notes the way feminist scholarship not only engages with the 'core' subjects, such as tort and property law, but with new fields such as healthcare law. Conaghan summarises the contribution of feminism to legal scholarship thus:

> First, feminist legal scholars seek to highlight and explore the gendered content of law, and to probe characterizations positing themselves as neutral and, more specifically, ungendered. Secondly, they are part of a cross-disciplinary feminist effort to challenge traditional understandings of the social, legal, cultural and epistemological order by placing women, their individual and their shared experiences, at the centre of their scholarship. Thirdly, feminist legal scholars seek to track and expose law's implication in women's disadvantage with a view to bringing about social and political change.
> (Conaghan, 2000: 359)

The question which has remained largely unanswered until now (at least in terms of the lived experience of academic lawyers) has been the precise extent to which the traditional doctrinal approach to the study of law has been challenged by the alternative paradigms which can be found in the contemporary legal academy.

A DISCIPLINE IN TRANSITION: FROM DOCTRINE TO SOCIO-LEGAL STUDIES

Doctrinal law has been such a dominant feature of the landscape in English university law schools that, prior to undertaking this research, I had expressed some scepticism (Cownie, 2000b: 72) about the onward march of socio-legal studies as characterised by some commentators, notably Bradney (1998: 73), who described doctrinalism as 'now entering its final death throes.' However, when I asked my respondents how they would describe their approach to teaching and researching law, on a scale from black-letter at one end to critical legal studies at the other, half of all the respondents described themselves, without hesitation, as taking a socio-legal or CLS approach to teaching and researching law.

Looking at the responses as a whole, noone described themselves as taking a purely CLS approach. Overall, about 10 per cent of respondents described themselves as taking a socio-legal/CLS approach, 40 per cent as adopting a socio-legal approach, and the remaining half described their approach as black-letter. Respondents were quite evenly distributed across both genders and the whole range of experience, although those adopting a socio-legal approach tended to be slightly more likely to be situated in an old university:

> I don't believe in the pure doctrinal approach which involves just looking at cases without reference to any other kind of discipline—that's akin to astrology, and I wouldn't dream of trying to inculcate that into students.
> (professor, experienced, male, old university).
>
> ... I've always had a more social scientific view of where law was located, and the other thing is, some of the particular subjects that I'm interested in within legal scholarship, like family law and social welfare law, are inherently socio-legal. I mean, family law was a socio-legal subject before the phrase socio-legal was invented, almost.
> (senior lecturer, mid-career, male, old university)

A range of critiques of doctrinal law thus appear to be firmly established as part of the culture of academic law, though it is socio-legal studies which emerges as the major challenger. CLS has the relatively marginal status among respondents that Goodrich ascribed to it when he commented that 'critical legal studies has not transformed the institution, it has not dramatically changed the law school curriculum, nor has it had any great impact upon the legal profession' (Goodrich, 1999: 359), echoing his earlier comments about '... the marginality, the low status, and limited impact of critical legal studies in England' (Goodrich, 1992: 200).

Scepticism about legal positivism does not mean that legal academics using a socio-legal paradigm regard knowledge of the content and techniques of doctrinal law as unimportant. On the contrary, several of the respondents stressed that in order to be a good socio-legal lawyer, it is imperative to have a good grasp of the law. In saying this, respondents were reflecting an attitude which has been widely held by socio-legal scholars since the early days of the 'law in context' movement (Twining, 1974: 167):

> I mean, it is terribly important to me that people know the law, that they have an accurate knowledge of the black-letter law. What isn't important to me, and what drives me crazy, is the kind of minute doctrinal arguments that you get in law journals sometimes. I mean, I can see how some people might be amused by that, but it leaves me cold. So far as I'm concerned, you must be accurate about the law, but it's completely useless unless you have a critique or a politics around it. I say politics in the widest sense—unless you have a view on it—but equally, it's completely useless to have a view if you don't know the law.
> (principal lecturer, mid-career, female, new university)

> Well, instinctively I'm a critical lawyer, but I honestly don't think you can be a critical lawyer unless you've got a firm grasp of the black-letter; that's crucial . . . There's no point at all in introducing students to what are complex critical frameworks if they have a very poor grasp of black-letter law, because, I mean, what Crits are doing is a criticism of black-letter law and its concepts and its discourse. Now if students don't understand black-letter law, then the critical framework is meaningless.
> (senior lecturer, mid-career, male, new university)

Of the 'black-letter' half of my respondents, the smaller part (just under a fifth of the total) described themselves, *without qualification*, as taking a black-letter approach. The larger part (about a third of the total) described themselves as adopting a black-letter approach, but with an immediate qualification that this did not mean that they concentrated solely on legal rules. They also thought that it was important to introduce contextual issues (social, political, economic and so forth). These respondents came from both types of institution, both genders and all stages of experience:

> [My approach is] Predominantly black-letter, but law can only be understood in the context in which it exists. So, bearing in mind that I teach contract, there are a lot of relevant economic points and a lot of purely policy decisions—and in consumer law quite a lot of important social issues—so I'm quite law in context really—the subjects are ones you can explain that way.
> (professor, experienced, male, new university)

> I'm not right at the black-letter end [of the scale]. In fact, I've become less black-letter than I once was. I'm not sure how much that comes through in what I teach, though it comes through a bit. I try to give more attention to the political context in which rules are being formulated and applied.
> (professor, mid-career, male, old university)

> To me, contract wouldn't come alive without looking at what people in business do, without looking at what consumers' problems are. At a sort of basic level, contextualism

seems to me to be intrinsic to what I am trying to put over. But I'm a rules person, if you know what I mean. I try and look at the rules as variable shifting things within that context, and certainly am not going down the road of saying 'What are the rules anyway?'
(principal lecturer, mid-career, male, new university)

These responses illustrate the extent to which 'black-letter' and 'socio-legal' are terms which need to be treated with caution. Some of those describing themselves as 'black-letter' appeared to be adopting a very similar, not to say identical, approach to others who described themselves as 'socio-legal', so that the line between legal academics adopting a doctrinal perspective and those adopting a socio-legal perspective is not always clear. The fluidity of these two concepts is clearly reflected in some of the comments people made about themselves:

I regard myself as a little island of hard-nosed black-letter commercial law in a sea of legal theory. Having said that, because my subject is competition law, it is uniquely grounded in economics, and because I have an economics degree, there are black-letter competition lawyers out there who complain that my approach is too heavily economics-based and too heavily theory-based. But I think of myself as a black-letter lawyer...
(reader, mid-career, male, new university)

Somewhere probably between black-letter doctrinal analysis with an appreciation of theory. I mean, I try not to just give an exposition of the law, but to see other aspects, what kind of policy objectives it's following, what's the kind of trend behind this. Definitely not socio-legal. I've always had difficulty with that question—you know, people ask you 'What kind of research do you do?' And I always find it quite hard to answer. Because I like to talk about cases and things I just assumed that I must be a doctrinal black-letter lawyer.
(lecturer, early career, female, old university)

Doing something like public law and human rights, I don't think you can be too black-letter, because it involves a number of competing theories, and I wouldn't view that as being necessarily black-letter, but equally there are certain doctrines and rules that you have to put across to them, and you have to convey the information properly.
(lecturer, early career, female, old university)

Comments like these illustrate graphically the extent to which black-letter law has become 'diluted', in that it is frequently combined with an analysis of policy objectives or other social phenomena in a way which would have been an anathema to legal academics at the beginning of the twentieth century, who were determined to establish 'the science of law' (founded exclusively legal rules) as the basis of the academic discipline of law (Sugarman, 1986).

Self-ascription as 'socio-legal' or 'black-letter' may therefore have more to do with a matter of emphasis, or a desire to indicate a political view, as much as with an *actual* difference in approach. Self-ascription as 'black-letter' by some of those who had moved far away from pure doctrinal analysis also appeared to arise out a belief that socio-legal refers exclusively to empirical investigation of the law, using standard quantitative social science methodology. Such a definition of socio-legal studies would be regarded as too narrow by both the ESRC, which (as I showed above) used a very much broader definition of socio-legal studies in its review of the subject in 1994 and by the Socio-Legal Studies Association, whose relevant definition is set out in its Statement of Ethical Practice:

1.2 *Scope*

> 1. Socio-legal studies embraces disciplines and subjects concerned with law as a social institution, with the social effects of law, legal processes, institutions and services, and with the influence of social, political and economic factors in the law and legal institutions.
> 2. Socio-legal research is diverse, covering a range of theoretical perspectives and a wide variety of empirical research and methodologies.
> (SLSA, 2001)

When I raised the matter with some of the respondents whose work seemed to me inherently socio-legal, though they were not describing themselves as such, their reaction was universally one of surprise that I should regard them as anything other than black-letter. In their view, socio-legal had a strong association with empirical work, which they did not carry out themselves; consequently, they did not regard their interest in policy, or other extra-legal matters, as socio-legal. Several other respondents explicitly displayed diffidence in describing themselves as adopting a socio-legal approach for this sort of reason, even though they were also uncomfortable with describing themselves as black-letter lawyers:

> Some people feel more comfortable with saying they're a black-letter lawyer because that's primarily what they are. I think they fear that if you're going to do socio-legal research then you would have to have read certain books, you have to have done certain courses, whereas in fact they might be doing some of those things anyway, it's just that they don't feel qualified to do it. Certainly in my own case I tend to think of myself as a black-letter lawyer, but some of the materials that I use might suggest otherwise. (senior lecturer, experienced, male, old university)

The result of this exclusive association of 'socio-legal' with 'empirical' in the minds of some academic lawyers is that the socio-legal community may be arguably be larger than it appears to be according to my data, or to other measures, such as membership of the Socio-Legal Studies Association.

Another reason for reluctance to describe oneself as 'socio-legal' may be to do with a perception that being socio-legal does not do much for one's image as an academic lawyer, particularly in terms of promotion, in much the same way as some feminists feel (on this, see, for example, McGlynn, 1998: 51). Although there was no evidence from my data that this was the case, this perception may have some basis in reality. If one accepts the argument that socio-legal approaches are more overtly 'academic', they belong to a very different intellectual culture from that of traditional doctrinal law, and members of the

58 Inhabiting the Discipline of Law

traditional culture may not value these new approaches as highly as they do the expository tradition. That was certainly the view of Campbell and Wiles, discussing the emergence of a socio-legal approach in the mid-1970s:

> The new socio-legal approach is regarded as subversive by some law teachers . . . To these critics the proper domain of the law teacher is 'hard law' or 'black-letter law'—the careful analysis and exposition of positive or written law. Their resistance to possible encroachments from socio-legal researchers who wish 'to broaden the study of law from within' or to teach 'contextual law', is reinforced by suspicions that socio-legal work is too much concerned with the policy of the law, and sometimes even with the politics of the law . . .
> (Campbell and Wiles, 1976: 550).

The most interesting implication of the data I have gathered, in terms of the culture of academic law, is the support it gives to the view that a significant shift has taken place in the approach taken by academic lawyers to the analysis of their subject. My data allows me to surmise with some confidence that pure doctrinal law no longer dominates the legal academy in the way that it used to. Only a fifth of my respondents could agree with the professor in a new university who said decidedly that his approach was 'Very much black-letter, there is no doubt about that.' Despite a spirited defence of doctrinal analysis by some (Jones, 1996, esp at 11; Savage and Watt, 1996), it appears that in its pure form it is an approach adopted by only a minority of those working in English law schools. The current approach to black-letter law was summed up by one respondent, who said:

> . . . I think what it means to be black-letter is actually different from what it meant to be black-letter fifteen years ago—or certainly when I started thirty years ago. I think everybody contextualises to a point. That doesn't mean they theorise, or want to be involved in all sorts of broader issues, but I think that they do approach it more broadly—in that sense I think context is always there now . . .
> (reader, experienced, male, old university)

Looking at the culture of the discipline as a whole, it becomes clear that, whatever they call themselves, the majority of academic lawyers occupy the middle ground between the two extremes of pure doctrinal analysis and a highly theoretical approach to the study of law. Arguably, law is a discipline in transition, with a culture where a small group still clings to a purely doctrinal approach, but a very large group (whether they describe themselves as socio-legal or not) are mixing traditional methods of analysis with analysis drawn from a range of other disciplines among the social sciences and humanities, while other small but significant groups are mainly concerned with the application of feminist ideas to law or in analysis of law which, like socio-legal studies, is interdisciplinary in nature, but tends to be more overtly concerned with critical theory.

Competing Paradigms—A Little Local Difficulty?

The existence of these fundamentally different approaches to law clearly brings with it the possibility of conflict between legal academics, of a kind which is not unknown in law schools. The conflicts resulting from the introduction of the critical legal studies movement into US law schools have been well-documented (Austin,1998; Tushnet, 1991). However, although I did not ask them directly about ideological conflicts, a large number of respondents commented on that possibility, only to reject it as a feature of their own department. Conflict of the extreme kind experienced in some US law schools appeared to be unknown among the English legal academics I interviewed. In most cases, respondents specifically described the culture of their department as 'pluralistic'; the norm was that different views were respected. Occasionally, however, tensions rose to the surface, and divisions, while not leading to schism, could be quite great. The attempted marginalisation of socio-legal scholars was certainly an issue in one of the law schools I visited:

> I think there is an element in the department that probably doesn't really have much time, or even respect, for that kind of teaching, which is reflected in their attitude. Not just feminism, but socio-legal in general. Hence the discussion about 'this wing of the department and that wing of the department'. It's almost as if people interested in that sort of activity have been hived off and can occupy their own little corridor, or whatever, rather than belonging to the department. Some black-letter people regard socio-legals as marginal, really.
>
> I think perhaps it's a certain arrogant attitude [on the part of these black-letter people], reflective of their own education, bringing their own perception of what should be regarded as hard law and what should be regarded as easy law. I think some people take the view that hard law is being immersed within the minutiae of the Companies Acts or something like that, so they see socio-legal as easy.
> (lecturer, early career, male, old university)

Resistance to socio-legal work on the part of students was also explicitly mentioned by some respondents:

> I feel this demand—it's implicit rather than explicitly set out, that well, just give us the basics, never mind all this challenging, why do we have property, why is land property? Why challenge any of that? Is it going to help us pass? If it is, then give it to us, if it's not, don't—and we can't find any of this stuff in the textbooks. So—and I think I'm looking over my shoulder at reviews and assessments and things like that. Although in fairness my external examiner is a challenger, so I don't have any worries in that direction.
> (lecturer, early career, male, new university)

> I think the attitude of students is that if it's anything that's not straight black-letter law, then it must be easy. The other thing that wouldn't help is that all those courses would contain a large element of coursework, so I think a lot of the dummies will take them anyway, just so they don't have to do exams.
> (lecturer, early career, female, old university)

> It strikes me that probably more than I would have expected are interested, but they're generally pretty negative—and I would think that probably reflects the type of people who come to university to study law, and their preconceptions of what law is. And also in the second year when they start learning that basically your life consists of moving on from here to a 'magic circle' firm, they want to study company law and commercial law, they're almost programmed that they shouldn't be studying those other subjects.
> (lecturer, early career, male, old university)

The existence of this sort of resistance fits in with the findings of the Law Society's Cohort Study of law students (Halpern, 1994). This was a longitudinial study of around 3,000 law students, built around the generation which graduated in the Summer of 1993. Among the topics explored were the relative views of law students and legal academics about the objectives of a law degree. It became clear that '. . . undergraduate law students have a much more vocational orientation to their degrees than those who teach them' (Halpern, 1994: 40). This was confirmed by my data, since the resistance of students to socio-legal and other more theoretical approaches which some respondents identified was not generally replicated among the legal academics I interviewed. Even those academics describing themselves as black-letter were in favour of departments having a pluralistic approach, encompassing both black-letter and socio-legal approaches. Their attitude is illustrated by the following respondent:

> [My approach is] black letter. But I think it's essential that a law school of our size should be able to embrace the whole spectrum. We each have a different role to fulfil. There has to be tolerance. I'm a bit suspicious of socio-legal courses, but having made that previous comment, and bearing in mind that lots of students will do things other than being lawyers, we've got to be academically tolerant . . .
> (professor, experienced, male, old university)

THE IMPACT OF FEMINISM

The other critique of black-letter law which I looked at in detail was feminism. As part of her examination of women legal academics in *The Woman Lawyer, Making the Difference* (1998), Clare McGlynn undertook a comprehensive survey of university law schools, to establish the extent to which courses particularly focused on considering the law from a gender/feminist perspective are represented in the legal academy. She found that twenty-four different law schools were offering such courses (McGlynn, 1998, App 2). She also found that just under half of all university law schools offered at least one course which included a gender/feminist perspective, the most common approach being the inclusion of feminist jurisprudence within a legal theory course (McGlynn, 1998, App 3). McGlynn comments that progress has been made towards the establishment of feminism in the legal academy, but it is slow (McGlynn, 1998: 16). Considering the impact of feminist legal scholarship, McGlynn comments:

What might usefully be added to such a discussion is the issue of how the teaching of such courses plays out in terms of prestige within a law school. Are there fewer courses of this nature because the academics who might be interested in teaching them do not wish to be viewed as less authoritative, or mainstream, than their colleagues? Or do academics fear the approbation of their students, who may view the teacher and researcher of 'soft' areas, like gender, as less authoritative, or deserving of respect? (McGlynn, 1998: 50)

In an effort to begin exploring these issues, I asked my respondents whether they were aware of a feminist critique of the areas of law in which they worked, and whether feminism impinged on their teaching. My data broadly agrees with McGlynn's. Just under half of the academics I interviewed said that they used a feminist approach in their teaching; there was no significant gender difference among these respondents. They were slightly more likely to be situated in old universities, but they were spread across a wide range of specialisms, including the 'core' subjects (ie, those which must be undertaken by students wishing to gain a law degree which qualifies as the academic stage of training for entry to the legal profession (Joint Statement, 1999). Indeed, it was the trusts lawyers who were keenest to tell me about their use of feminist ideas; several of them mentioned the 'Feminist Perspectives' series, published by Cavendish, as having been influential in leading them to use such materials:

> It certainly features as a critique in the material. One of the courses that I teach is looking predominantly at trusts in the family home, and obviously a feminist perspective in terms of property rights and how rights are acquired is an important area of that aspect of the law, so in that respect we would expect the students to read materials that come from a feminist perspective, as part of their judgment as to why the law is as it is, and whether it is achieving a just result.
> (senior lecturer, early career, male, old university)

In general, respondents regarded their departments as pluralist in outlook, tolerating feminism among a number of different perspectives represented among the staff. About half the respondents had a view about the reception of feminism in the legal academy. They split neatly in half when it came to attitudes to feminism and law. About half reflected the negative attitudes which McGlynn surmised might lie behind some peoples' reluctance to become involved in feminist work:

> I suspect some [colleagues] regard [feminists] with suspicion—the traditionalists who say 'What on earth are they doing?' But that's possibly because all they're seeing is the label, they've not actually seen what has been done.
> (senior lecturer, experienced, male, old university).

> I would have thought by some staff it would be very negative. I don't want to say that, but I think it is. I mean, I do hear it being pooh-poohed and I do hear derogatory comments being made, rather than saying 'Well, hold on, this is a different approach, let the students try it and see what they think.'
> [lecturer, mid-career, female, new university)

> I would say that among some of the older members of staff, I think [feminists] probably would be slightly derided, but I think that's an age thing. I think that it may also, by some people, be regarded as being a research bandwagon to jump on to, you know, if you want to be successful in writing, you take up a critical stance and apply it to areas nobody has applied it to. And I think there's, not cynicism, but an awareness that that can be done. But I think the majority of members of staff would be interested to take on board the critique—but probably wouldn't want it at the centre of their approach.
> (senior lecturer, early career, male, old university)

Similarly with student attitudes to feminist-inspired perspectives:

> It's badly received by students. Students invariably do not answer the feminist question on the exam paper. Never. Well, not never, but hardly ever. They regard it as difficult. Some of them are actually alienated from the subject itself—and that's not just the men, the women as well actually are alienated, they say 'I'm not a feminist, therefore I'm not going to engage in this topic.' But yes, they find it—I don't know, they don't engage with it particularly well.
> (lecturer, mid-career, male, new university)

> They're a bit suspicious of it. Some of the students are ok with it, but even some of the women are a bit impatient with it, as though it has been overtaken by events.
> (lecturer, experienced, female, old university)

These comments are unsurprising, in the light of the results of the Law Society's cohort study. Student resistance to approaches other than the traditional doctrinal one is well documented there, with 20 per cent of the cohort finding their course too philosophical and 13 per cent finding it too sociological (Halpern, 1994: 37).

Nevertheless, it is important to remember that these students held a minority view. Also, the negative attitudes attributed to some legal academics were balanced by just as many positive comments about the attitudes of staff towards feminist work. One male professor in a department which did not have a particularly strong feminist culture described feminist research and teaching without hesitation as 'highly regarded', and others reported an equally positive reception of feminist work:

> I think there probably wouldn't be a lot of difference, in how people were viewed—if they were good in their field, that would be the main criterion.
> (senior lecturer, experienced, male, old university)

> ... You suddenly find there's a whole new way of looking at things ... I like the idea that there's a whole range of approaches.
> (senior lecturer, male, experienced, old university)

> I think here feminists are highly regarded. We have regular staff seminars and the topic is regularly feminism in some shape or other.
> (lecturer, early-career, male, old university)

In terms of student reaction, both the Law Society survey and my data also reveal students who enjoy learning about a feminist approach to law, though these appear to be a small minority:

> ... Some students quite like it, because it allows them to show off different skills that they have, and some absolutely hate it, so I think it's very polarised among the students. I think some love it and some hate it.
> (lecturer, mid-career, female, new university)

Feminism may not have made as great an impact on the legal academy as some would wish, especially in terms of its acceptance by students, but it is far from marginalised. However, this is not to deny that some legal academics continue to have negative attitudes towards feminist work, nor that this may be a particular issue for women interested in making feminist work their specialism—a matter which is, as McGlynn points out, well-documented in the North American context, but not in the UK (McGlynn, 1998: 50). One point which several respondents made was that while they thought a minority of their colleagues might be suspicious of feminist work, that would be just as much the case with other non-black-letter approaches:

> ... I think there is an element within the department that probably really doesn't have much time or even respect for that kind of teaching, which is reflected in their attitude. Not just feminism, but socio-legal in general ...
> (lecturer, early career, male, old university)

The data which I have collected allows me to say with some confidence, however, that feminist legal scholarship has become more mainstream in recent years, with about half of my respondents using it in their teaching; use of feminist work is not confined to women academic lawyers, and it has spread beyond the confines of the 'obvious' specialisms, such as family law, to other areas of the curriculum, including the 'core' subjects.

THE FUTURE OF THE DISCIPLINE

Given the existence of a number of different perspectives which can be adopted to study law, I asked my respondents where they saw legal research going in the future, in terms of approach to law. Noone mentioned critical legal studies or feminism in their analysis of the future shape of the discipline; this appears to reflect the more marginal status of these two approaches, as compared with socio-legal studies. About two-thirds of the respondents believed that socio-legal work would become increasingly important. Respondents believing this were not confined to those who already regarded themselves as socio-legal, but included some who regarded themselves as definitely black-letter lawyers. They were also drawn from all stages of experience, and included fairly equal proportions of men and women, but were slightly more likely to be situated in old universities:

> ... I'm thinking 'Oh, the sixties haven't gone away', so it could be me, but I think there is a trend—the black-letter is well-rooted, but there is a trend away.
> (lecturer, early career, male, new university)

I think there has been an increasing broadening of different styles of legal research, and I think to some extent that will probably continue. I think the institution of law is changing—while there'll probably always be a place for black-letter law studies, increasingly that will be marginal to the institution of law, and people will increasingly realise that—it's a conservative discipline, and that change will be extremely slow, but nevertheless it will do so.
(senior lecturer, mid-career, male, old university)

Several people were clear that as far as they were concerned, the tide had already turned—and indeed, their comments are borne out by the data I referred to above, showing that pure black-letter law is a minority pursuit:

I actually don't think it *is* black-letter any more, predominantly. I mean, if you leaf through something like the *Modern Law Review*, it would be very difficult to find a black-letter article in the MLR. I think in all the good journals that the academic work is peppered with insights from other disciplines. I suppose that may be subject-specific. Probably if I was teaching property law and reading *The Conveyancer* it would be impossible to find theoretical work in there . . .
(lecturer, early career, male, old university)

. . . there are actually text books around which are starting to take a more critical approach than traditional textbooks have done, and if it is starting to reflect in teaching materials then that suggests that is where research might be going . . .
(lecturer, early career, female, new university)

Several respondents reflected that, with the increasing tendency of law schools to demand a PhD as a pre-requisite for an academic appointment, the trend towards socio-legal work is likely to accelerate:

I think, in terms of recruitment, because you recruit PhDs, and the pre-requisite of any PhD in law is to talk as little as possible about black-letter things, because you need to be original, and so you delve into sociology or whatever. Then you begin to appoint people who want to do that kind of work.
(lecturer, early career, male, old university)

An early career female academic in an old university, who described herself as being 'Pretty close to the black-letter end of the spectrum,' was confident about her perception of a move towards the socio-legal, but was not happy about it:

I think there is enormous pressure to move towards the more theoretical side of things. I think black-letter lawyers are getting more and more sidelined, and theory is becoming all-encompassing. You're only a proper academic if you're writing theory. It's sort of the importance of the work is indirectly proportionate to the number of people who can read and understand it. I'd say it was the Emperor's New Clothes really, with critical theory and that kind of thing, but I think there is enormous pressure, particularly on people starting out, to work towards the theoretical end, and the more theoretical topics in law, and stay away from the real grounding subjects—and the whole sort of sneering bit, the attitude is sneering at those who aren't doing theory.
(lecturer, early career, female, old university)

Only slightly less than a third of the respondents (from across the spectrum of institutions and experience) saw *both* doctrinal law and socio-legal work as continuing to play an important part in the future of academic law:

> I think black-letter will obviously continue, because, whether one likes it or not, this is a branch of academic life that does serve a very particular and defined market, and that market does require a certain number of highly skilled and technical people to come into it, and therefore I think that black-letter law will continue as a powerful discipline. But equally, I cannot see the socio-legal side of things declining.
> (professor, experienced, male, new university)

> I think that these two aspects [black-letter and socio-legal] will always remain. I feel that there will always be a need, and always be people commenting on, the position of the courts or how a particular statute is interpreted or should be interpreted—which is black-letter. But also there will remain a need, perhaps its significance will be greater in the future, as people begin to challenge some assumptions on which the rules have been based . . . for some empirical research.
> (professor, mid-career, male, old university)

A significant majority of respondents, however, believed that socio-legal studies would dominate the discipline in the future. Only a small group of the academic lawyers I interviewed thought that the future of academic law lay in doctrinal analysis. These included people at all stages of their careers, but were slightly more likely to work in new universities.

The implication of these findings, together with the other data discussed in this chapter, is that pure doctrinal law is certainly a thing of the past. While few people spoke in such direct terms as those which Bradney has used in his work, it appears that he may nevertheless be justified in arguing that:

> The academic doctrinal project which has dominated United Kingdom university law schools for most of their history, the attempt to explain law solely through internal evidence, is now entering its final death throes.
> (Bradney, 1998: 71)

In terms of the culture of the discipline, the results of my interviews give weight to the argument I raised above that law is a discipline in transition, coming from a tradition which was focused exclusively on legal rules, in which any attempt to introduce evidence about the social consequences or political origins of law was regarded as 'irrelevant', to a situation in which a knowledge of traditional doctrinal techniques of analysis is merely the starting-point for an exploration of legal phenomena using a variety of different techniques drawn from an increasingly wide range of disciplines.

POSSIBLE DIFFICULTIES AHEAD

While the general tenor of comments about the socio-legal future of the discipline were positive, a small number of respondents expressed some concern about possible difficulties which might lie ahead, such as the possibility of polarisation between those who continued to engage in doctrinal analysis, and those adopting a socio-legal perspective:

> I think the field is polarising, actually, that in some technical areas, the commercial areas and so on, there is a proliferation of extremely accomplished, very sophisticated black-letter law of a very high conceptual calibre. Whereas probably in most other fields, the drift is towards a socio-legal approach ...
> (professor, experienced, female, old university)

> ... What I think is that there is likely to be a greater schism between black-letter approaches, and theoretical approaches ... as getting funding becomes more important for academics who are engaged in research, it's the bodies paying the funding monies who are going to determine what research is done. And they seem to me to be increasingly not black-letter ...
> (reader, mid-career, male, new university)

Engaging in socio-legal or inter-disciplinary work is a significant challenge for academic lawyers trained in the British tradition, since doctrinal law does not engage with other disciplines. Even today, undergraduate course handbooks provide copious evidence that the law syllabus rarely includes any significant study of the theories or research methods which are regarded as fundamental by most disciplines within the social sciences. The lack of such a background, either in social sciences or in any of the other disciplines which might usefully be employed to examine legal phenomena, was seen as a big problem for the future development of the discipline by a significant number of respondents. In drawing attention to these matters, they were reflecting concerns which have been voiced both by the ESRC (1994) and by the Socio-Legal Studies Association (SLSA) whose recent Newsletters have carried several articles expressing concern about the research capacity of the socio-legal community (Witherspoon, 2002; Partington, 2002). The apparent lack of interest among academic lawyers in developing methodological expertise is reflected in the results of a survey of the socio-legal training available for postgraduate law students, carried out by the SLSA, which revealed a general lack of interest on the part of law departments in applying for ESRC recognition, despite the fact that a significant body of socio-legal work appears to be being carried out by postgraduates (Cowan et al, 2003). It was precisely these sorts of concerns which were voiced by some respondents:

> ... The thing that will stop interdisciplinary research is that most people are too lazy, or don't have the skills, to do interdisciplinary research. So what happens at the moment is you get a lot of articles—weak politics, weak economics, very poor social theory, and you just look at it and think 'It's not very rigorous', and I suspect in three or four years' time there's going to be a reaction against that. People will insist there's got to be a more rigorous approach taken if you're going to do interdisciplinary work. There are different types of research—but there's good research and bad research.
> (senior lecturer, mid-career, male, old university)

> I think the only problem with moving into more and more interdisciplinary stuff, especially in the UK, is that most lawyers are only trained in one discipline. And I think that probably affects the kind of research that you do. And it doesn't really help to get two people—one a lawyer and one an economist, for example—the product is probably better, but it's not as good as having one person thinking about it who has the intellectual equipment to deal with, or bring together, two disciplines. So although I do think that's the way it will go, I'm also a bit scared that the UK will miss out to North America and a whole load of other countries who do double degrees.
> (senior lecturer, mid-career, female, old university)

At the moment, there is a danger that some lawyers are merely dabbling in other disciplines, a matter which was raised by several other respondents:

> I went to a one-day conference a few weeks ago, and I was astonished at what some people—you know, even well-respected people, I was astounded at what they got away with—just cobbling together a few, what to me were intuitive reactions to a piece of legislation and slapping them together for fifteen minutes and that was it. I can't believe that in a philosophy conference or a literature conference you would be able to get away with such a superficial analysis.
>
> I also think there's a problem with the fact that law borders on other areas . . . at this conference there was one paper which drew very superficially on work in political theory—the person didn't have sufficient background in the subject to use it properly, they would never survive in a political theory journal, but because it was law, and they were just dipping in ad hoc to a couple of things, people were quite impressed by the sound of these words, but if you really knew about political theory you wouldn't have been.
> (lecturer, early career, female, old university)

It is arguable however, that provided it manages to overcome such difficulties, the increasing influence of socio-legal studies, with its focus on interdisciplinarity, together with an increasing awareness of theoretical concerns on the part of socio-legal researchers, will bring an increasingly intellectual flavour to academic law. In its *Final Report*, the ESRC noted that 'In general, socio-legal research has begun to address theory, and to apply it appropriately and sensitively to issues of policy concern' (1994: 37). If this trend continues, legal analysis is, in the future, likely to move much closer to the concerns of other disciplines in the humanities and social sciences. This view was reflected by the respondent who said:

> I don't get the feeling that there are a huge number [of socio-legals in my department], although those that there are have probably developed niche areas for themselves, and I think are probably quite well-regarded as a result. They are the ones who after all are more likely to get cited by a Court of Appeal judge or something of that nature, because they have some original thoughts, views, opinions on things. So I think they are probably looked upon more as the intellectuals and the black-letter people are looked at as, plodders is probably too negative a word, but the bread and butter kind of approach, I suppose.
> (lecturer, early career, male, new university)

Law and Theory

In terms of the future of the discipline, another matter raised by some respondents related to the long-running question of the relationship of academic law and theory, which underlies some of these responses. The position of theory in the doctrinal tradition is complex. It is not that doctrine completely lacks theory; legal techniques, such as the identification of the ratio of a case, the correct method of statutory interpretation etc, have been subject to prolonged analysis (see, eg, Bell and Engle, 1995; Cross and Harris, 1991; Goodhart, 1931). However, despite the existence of a large body of theoretical work relating to the operation of legal doctrine that explicitly raises complex and unresolved questions about doctrinal technique, it is rarely referred to by any of the legal academics who claim to be using that technique. The lack of any explicit reference to theory in much legal research and teaching has long been a criticism made of doctrinal law; the critical legal studies movement had its roots in intellectual dissatisfaction with those very issues:

> What is the guiding motivation behind critique of law? Above all, it is explicitly to refuse to accept legal doctrine on its own terms; that is, to refuse to accept it in the terms in which it justifies itself (as the unfolding of legal logic; as the self-evident embodiment of rationality; as the purely technical instrument of policies originating from 'non-legal' (political) sources).
> (Cotterell, 1987: 78)

Lack of explicit engagement with theory has also been a longstanding criticism of socio-legal studies, expressed as long ago as 1976 in Campbell and Wiles' seminal article 'The Study of Law in Society in Britain', in which the authors expressed their anxiety that socio-legal studies was in danger of being solely concerned with descriptive empirical research, and failing to fuse that work with that of 'the sociology of law', with its emphasis on constructing a theoretical understanding of the legal system in terms of the wider social structure (Campbell and Wiles, 1976: 553). These concerns are reflected in Cotterell's survey of the field, published in 1990 (Cotterell, 1990) and in the paper delivered by Niki Lacey to the ESRC Conference on socio-legal studies in 1993, where she argued that:

> Simply to bring together pre-existing, clearly-defined disciplines, categories and concerns . . . is problematic for two reasons. First, at the level of method, it suggests a cumulative or cross-disciplinary rather than a genuinely inter-disciplinary approach; research which draws on both sociological methods and legal techniques without subjecting either to critical scrutiny. . . . Secondly, thinking in terms of 'socio-legal' studies may encourage us to leave the concepts of the social and the legal—of society and law—under-examined, side-stepping questions . . . of the extent to which either is unitary or unproblematically definable.
> (quoted in ESRC, Review of Socio-Legal Studies: Final Report, 1994: 37)

To the extent that such concerns are still justified, the increasing influence of socio-legal studies will not, in fact, lead to academic law becoming a more intellectually sophisticated discipline, but merely to its incumbents becoming a more acquainted, in a haphazard way, with some ideas taken from other disciplines. These are the challenges which now face the discipline of law in its transition from an exclusive concern with doctrine to an increasing amount of interaction with ideas taken from other disciplines.

ANTI-INTELLECTUALISM OF LAW

Doctrinal law is often portrayed as essentially uncritical; 'Black-letterism concentrates on the law as it is, not as it ought to be, nor why it came to be as it is' (Adams and Brownsword, 1999: 29). Critical analysis, in the doctrinal tradition, is not entirely absent, but is confined to examining the logic or rational coherence of particular legal decisions or areas of law (Nicolson and Webb, 1999: 66). Law school, it has been argued, offers a 'trade school mentality', in which the hidden curriculum of the law school trains students '. . . to accept and participate in the hierarchical structure of life in the law' (Kennedy, 1982: 591). On this view, law is not an intellectual subject, in the OED sense of 'intellectual' as 'that which appeals to or engages the intellect.' This view of law as being a non-intellectual subject was certainly reflected in Becher's original analysis, when he presented what he termed 'a gallery of stereotypes', arrived at by asking academics about the impressions they had formed of colleagues in other fields (Becher, 1989: 28):

> The predominant notion of academic lawyers is that they are not really academic—one critical respondent described them as 'arcane, distant and alien; an appendage to the university world.' Their personal qualities are dubious: they are variously represented as vociferous, untrustworthy, immoral, narrow, arrogant and conservative, though kinder eyes see them as impressive and intelligent. Their scholarly activities are thought to be unexciting and uncreative, comprising a series of intellectual puzzles scattered among 'large areas of description'.
> (Becher, 1989: 30)

Over the years, academic lawyers themselves have often been, to say the least, self-deprecating. Professor Gower, writing in 1950, was forthright in saying that '. . . English teachers of law suffer from an acute inferiority complex' in relation to members of the legal profession (1950: 198). Professor Bridge, in an article entitled 'The Academic Lawyer: Mere Working Mason or Architect?' agreed with the opinion of one of his American contemporaries that 'Legal scholars have not been at the centre of intellectual ferment in the universities' (1975: 501). More recently, in a discussion of the influence of legal academics upon the judiciary, Neil Duxbury provides a number of telling illustrations of the academic lawyer as 'under-achiever', including Winstanley's comment, in his *Early Victorian Cambridge*, that '[T]he law school was generally recognised to be a refuge for those who were averse to intellectual effort' (Duxbury, 2001: 69–71).

This is a topic also addressed by Twining, in his Presidential Address to the Society of Legal Scholars 'Goodbye to Lewis Eliot; the academic lawyer as scholar' (Twining, 1980). Twining's judgment on the place of law within the academy is ambiguous:

> Over the long haul this perspective suggests that on the one hand the convergence of the law school with the university may serve to support a trend towards a greater commitment to research and scholarship; but on the other hand there are certain features in the environment which will militate against intellectually ambitious programmes or radical changes in perspectives within the mainstream of academic law.
> (Twining, 1980: 17).

Given that the current study is concerned with the culture of *academic* law, the relationship of law to things intellectual is highly significant. Universities are, above all, concerned with things theoretical and intellectual. 'One of the distinguishing features of higher education is that it is concerned with the elaboration of elaborate conceptual structures, or theories' (Barnett, 1990: 4) Or as Newman put it, 'the concern of the university is with a "philosophical" acquisition of knowledge, not merely knowledge which is confined to the pragmatic and useful, but knowledge which is "an end sufficient to rest in and to pursue for its own sake" ' (Newman, 1960: 78). To anyone adopting that (not uncommonly held) view of the purpose of a university, to have a discipline which is commonly regarded by its inhabitants as non-intellectual might suggest that the discipline in question (along with its inhabitants) does not really deserve a place in the academy.

With that in mind, I asked my respondents whether, in their view, you had to be intellectual (in the OED sense of 'given to pursuits that exercise the intellect', ie interested in and knowledgeable about a reasonably broad range of ideas) in order to be an academic lawyer. Almost all the respondents were clear that being an intellectual is not a necessary quality to be a successful academic lawyer. However, two-thirds of these people pointed out that although they thought you could succeed as an academic lawyer without being intellectual, the legal academics producing the best work *are* intellectual:

> No, I don't think so. I know quite a lot of people who've gone a long way as legal academics, but they're not at all intellectual.
> (professor, mid-career, male, new university)

> No, I know you don't. I have colleagues, and have met colleagues who are in probably higher positions than I'll ever attain, who—some of them have come very close to *saying* that they're not intellectual. Some of them are very open in the fact that they're black-letter and would see the potential shortcomings in that, and would admit that what they're doing is not much more than number-crunching. That's not an accusation I would level at them—that is the way these people have described themselves.
> (lecturer, early career, male, old university)

> . . . if you go in the [law staff common room] you just wouldn't mention the fact that you'd been reading a novel, or you'd gone to a concert or a play, in fact you play that

down and say that you went to the pub on Friday night and that's it . . . I think that teaching any subject in a university, then to do that well and with imagination, the more intellectual the better, but in terms of how I perceive the law department I find the atmosphere, and the people who are attracted to *legal* academia, less intellectual.
(lecturer, early career, female, old university)

Many academic lawyers are not only non-intellectual, but anti-intellectual. I would be very critical of many of them. You can do the job without being intellectual, but you can't be effective in the job or get satisfaction from it without being intellectually oriented.
(senior lecturer, mid-career, male, old university)

Academics are intellectuals by definition, but if you mean having a deeply enquiring, philosophical attitude, then, no, I think a lot of legal academics are unintellectual in that sense.
(principal lecturer, mid-career, male, new university)

There was some evidence from the responses that when respondents talked about legal academics not being intellectual, they had in mind traditional black-letter lawyers:

That's a sneaky question. No, I don't think you do [have to be intellectual] really. I think there is a certain level at which you can probably operate as an academic lawyer in a rather sort of narrowly technical way, which isn't actually terribly intellectual. [You mean in a positivist, black-letter way?] Yes.
(lecturer, experienced, male, old university)

Looking at the responses as a whole, they provide further evidence that law is a discipline in transition; although an intellectual approach may not have been highly valued in the past, leading to the conclusion, drawn by the majority of respondents, that you did not have to be intellectual to be an academic lawyer, it was nevertheless true that the teaching and research which was most highly regarded by respondents was that which came from those who they would regard as intellectual:

. . . In the way I see the subject, I'd say, yes, being an intellectual is important, if you're going to say anything worthwhile.
(lecturer, early career, male, old university)

I dare say it's possible [to be an academic lawyer and not be an intellectual]—there are people in post—but no, you couldn't be a good one, you've got to be scholarly and intellectual . . . I mean, apart from anything else, scholarship is for you as well, in a way it's the kind of reward that keeps you lively and interesting, with students, and for yourself.
(principal lecturer, experienced, female, new university)

. . . I think we should be striving to be scholarly—it's the nature of what we do, isn't it? We're striving to understand things all the time, aren't we, and, as I said earlier, I think doing law does tend to link in with a lot of other subjects and issues—so if you're trying to understand your aspect of the law as well as you can, then you've just got to be a rounded person, with an intellectual interest in other fields.
(lecturer, early career, female, old university)

> I think if you're going to be really good, you do have to be an intellectual, yes. I think there's room for plenty of competent non-intellectuals within the field. I certainly think you can be a good administrator, and a good teacher, and a competent researcher, and not be an intellectual. But ultimately, if you're really going to be a top legal academic, you have to be an intellectual.
>
> (lecturer, early career, female, old university)

CONCLUSION

The discipline of academic law, then, is in flux. The movement from an exclusively black-letter culture to a pluralistic one, peopled by lawyers adopting very different approaches to the study of law, appears to be well advanced, with half of my respondents describing themselves as adopting a socio-legal or critical legal approach, and feminism routinely used in teaching a wide variety of subjects. Although the other half of my respondents were somewhat reluctant to describe themselves as taking a socio-legal approach (perhaps reflecting the place which black-letter law still retains in the construction of the professional identities of academic lawyers), an examination of what is actually taking place suggests that in reality, doctrinal law is not what it used to be, with the majority of black-letter lawyers regarding the introduction of various policy-related matters as crucial to their analysis of legal phenomena.

One respondent neatly summed up the changing intellectual nature of legal academia:

> ... There have been moments, earlier in my career, when I sometimes found law faculties quite intellectually narrow. I suppose I've always just tried to solve that by making contacts outside my department, where necessary ... I think there is a certain narrow-mindedness. But I do think that's got better. If you look today at the relative status of things like socio-legal studies, compared to when I first set out, it's a much broader church, really ...
>
> (professor, experienced, female, old university)

This response neatly sums up the culture of academic law as reflected in the responses to my questions about the nature of the discipline. Academic lawyers adopting approaches other than the doctrinal would self-consciously see themselves as contributing to an intellectual drift occurring within their discipline, which is commonly acknowledged by the majority to have lacked a particularly intellectual orientation in the past.

4

The Legal Academic Career

CAREERS AND THE CULTURE OF ACADEMIC LAW

THIS CHAPTER SEEKS to shed light on the culture of legal academia and the professional identities of legal academics by examining various aspects of the legal academic career, from the initial decision to study law at university to the qualities and skills which contemporary legal academics think are necessary to be a 'good' legal academic, and those which make it likely that someone will become a professor. Academic identities, in the sense used here, go beyond the specifics of an academic as a person to a consideration of the situated academic who shapes and is shaped by his or her occupation (Taylor, 1999: 41). Bearing in mind Alvesson's idea of 'multiple cultural configuration' (Alvesson, 1993: 118), I am also focusing on the way in which legal academic careers are played out in the context of debates about the place of the discipline of law within the university, and its struggle to establish itself as an academic, rather than a vocational, discipline. The analysis here, as elsewhere in this book, therefore includes aspects both of culture and of identity.

READING LAW

One of the early questions in the interviews asked whether people had read law at university themselves, and asked them to explain why (or why not). The responses to these questions were very varied, with no particular pattern in terms of type of institution, gender or experience. Only three people had not read law as an undergraduate (though two of those had done the Common Professional Examination and had practised as solicitors). In terms of reasons for choosing to read law, broadly speaking respondents fell into one of five main groups. The two largest of these groups were composed of people who had studied law with the intention of becoming a lawyer and people who had studied law because it seemed as if it would be an interesting thing to do:

> I did a degree in law because I wanted to be a practising lawyer. I wouldn't have done the degree otherwise.
> (professor, experienced, male, new university)
>
> It was just something that I always wanted to do. I remember being quite committed, from quite an early age, to some form of legal career. I remember we used to fill in

74 *The Legal Academic Career*

> forms at school 'Put down the three jobs that you would like to do' and it was always 'barrister', 'journalist', 'teacher', in that order . . .
> (lecturer, early career, female, old university)

> . . . I went to a university open day, and a couple of my friends were thinking of doing law, and I went along to the lecture about law, and after that I came away thinking 'That's an interesting subject, that's something I could really get my teeth into'.
> (lecturer, early career, male, old university)

> When I decided to do law I knew nothing about the subject at all. I think I chose it because it had a certain, when I was 18, 19, mystique. I never took it with the intention of practising, and I would never practise law, but it seemed an interesting thing to do.
> (senior lecturer, mid-career, male, new university)

Two other slightly smaller groups were composed of people who had chosen to read law as a result of parental pressure, and people who had consciously decided to read at university a subject different from those they had studied at 'A' level. Parental pressure to read law is understandable; it is widely perceived as a vocational subject which will lead to 'a good job':

> I sort of fell into it. I wanted to read English Literature, and my Dad—I was 17 at the time and my Dad had quite a bit of influence on me—basically he had to pay for me to go through college and everything. And I had been told that law would probably be quite a suitable degree for me to do, and I had the grades that were necessary, and I sort of convinced myself, and my Dad was keen, and he was paying.
> (lecturer, early career, female, new university)

> I read law, basically, under parental pressure, to be honest. I wanted to change, and actually applied to change after two terms, to read philosophy, but the philosophy department turned me down. I can't say I enjoyed law or was any good at it until the end of the second year—then something clicked when I was writing an essay.
> (senior lecturer, mid-career, male, old university)

Law is particularly attractive to people who want to take up a new subject on entering higher education, because law schools will accept such a wide range of subjects at 'A' level, and historically this has always been the case. (Perhaps related to the fact that, as Hudson pointed out in *Contrary Imaginations*, while arts specialists are predominantly divergent thinkers and scientists predominantly convergent thinkers, lawyers can display either form of thinking (Hudson, 1966: 57):

> What I was really interested in at that time was music, but I knew I wasn't really good enough to do a music degree. I was fairly bored by all my 'A' level subjects, so law seemed like—I didn't really know much about it—but, 'Well', I thought, 'it looks useful and might be reasonably interesting, so why not?'
> (principal lecturer, mid-career, male, new university)

> Well, the subject interested me, and I wanted to do something different from what I had studied at 'A' level. Nothing at 'A' level sufficiently attracted me to want to continue it into higher education. I was fairly uncertain as to what I wanted to do as a career. I had thought in terms of going into the army, but had changed my mind about

that, so I wanted a degree which would open a number of doors, not necessarily legal doors, and I thought that the skills acquired through a law degree would be very beneficial.
(reader, experienced, male, old university)

The rest of the respondents had their own individual, not to say idiosyncratic reasons for choosing to read law, ranging from a perception that law was a high-status degree to a sudden decision to change long-standing plans:

> I think it was the status. I think it was the feeling that, you know, here I was, a girl, and there were very few girls in law [in 1969], and to be a law student seemed to have a different kind of quality to it than just being a student . . .
> (principal lecturer, experienced, female, new university)

> I'll give you the honest answer to this. Why I did law at university is because I made a sudden change in my decision. I had even filled in the UCCA form (as it was then) to study history. I was going to do history. The school was astonished. I was their star history student, and suddenly I went (and this is utterly ironic in context) 'What will I do if I study history?', the 17 year-old thought, 'I'll just end up teaching it'. And for some reason that didn't seem to me to be what I necessarily wanted to do with my life . . . It wasn't thought through, it wasn't counselled, I just went 'I'll do that'. Quirky independence of mind, I think.
> (principal lecturer, experienced, male, new university)

The original decision to study law was thus largely instrumental for a substantial number of those who eventually became academics. Even those who studied law because they arguably had an enthusiasm for the subject talked in fairly detached terms of their decision to study law being because it was 'an interesting thing to do' rather than in any more enthusiastic terms. Only one person described their interest in law as 'passionate'. Contrast this with the 'language people' interviewed by Evans, who talked in terms of 'happiness' and the 'fun' of studying a modern language (Evans, 1988: 75).

THE LEGAL ACADEMIC CAREER: VOCATIONAL OR ACADEMIC?

The two larger groups of respondents identified above neatly reflect the debate which has been a major feature of the literature on legal education since the nineteenth century, which I referred to in chapter two; is a university law school a place which trains lawyers or a place to pursue a liberal education in law? The answer to this question has considerable bearing, both on the culture of legal academia and on the construction of the professional identities of legal academics, since, broadly speaking, it reveals the orientation of those in the legal academy as either being towards the profession or towards the academy. In order to explore where the balance lies in this debate from the perspective of contemporary legal academics, I asked my respondents about their philosophy of education. Having found in the pilot study that most respondents felt unhappy with the term 'philosophy of education' (several of them telling me they didn't have such a thing), I asked instead, in the context of talking about teaching, 'What is your aim? What are you trying to do for your students?', questions which respondents in the pilot confirmed they understood, and felt able to answer.

There was a noticeable level of consensus among my respondents that their principal aim was to teach students to think for themselves. Respondents were concerned to ensure that students understood the legal materials they were dealing with (often described as a need to teach 'the basics'), but once that had been achieved, the objective which was singled out for particular mention by more than half of the people I interviewed was 'getting students to think'. In other words, these law teachers, from right across the spectrum of experience and from all types of institution, conceived legal education as a liberal education in the law. Other important aims were helping students to be independent learners, and gaining an enthusiasm for the subject, but it was critical thinking, above all, which was valued by the respondents:

> Essentially what you're trying to do is to give them a facility to think about their ideas about various topics which you decide they should think about. And that involves partly giving them some information. But information they can largely get for themselves—there's a large degree of getting very bright students to realise they haven't thought about things, to re-think things and decide whether they really believe what they thought they believed.
> (professor, experienced, male, old university)
>
> ... I'm trying to teach them to *think* and *read*—even novels, to relate to the wider environment.
> (lecturer, mid-career, female, new university)
>
> I'm probably trying to get them to think. That's the main thing I'm trying to do. I'm trying to get them to be able to develop the thinking processes which are necessary to enable them to approach any material ...
> (senior lecturer, early career, male, old university)
>
> First of all convey basic ideas, convey basic knowledge. Try to get them to actually think for themselves, to criticise and evaluate and make judgments about what they read, and that's a very difficult thing, to get them to say 'Well, I don't like this, I don't like what he's done there, that judge, *because* . . .'. So it's literally to try to get them to criticise other ideas and other views—and criticise my ideas. Sometimes I play devil's advocate and say 'Well, what do you think about that?' And hope that they will say 'Well, hold on, I don't like that *because* . . .'. So it's trying to take them to a higher plane in thought. Gosh, that sounds very idealistic, doesn't it? But that's what one is trying to do.
> (lecturer, early career, female, new university)

Imparting an enthusiasm for the subject was also picked out as an important teaching objective:

> I want them to learn things, and I want them to like to learn things, and I think the way to do that is to show them how much fun it is thinking about law, the different ways of thinking about it.
> (senior lecturer, mid-career, female, old university)

[My aim is to] make the subject interesting, try to stimulate them, get them interested in the subject. That is a fairly narrow set of aims and objectives, I suppose . . .
(principal lecturer, mid-career, male, new university)

None of the respondents mentioned preparing students for entry to the legal profession as one of their educational aims, (indeed, several specifically mentioned that they were *not* preparing students for legal practice); nor did anyone mention teaching vocational skills:

I hope I am turning out people who are learned in the law, which means they will be good technical lawyers, because I do not think you can call yourself a lawyer unless you do have technical knowledge, but I hope they will also be questioning, sceptical and critical lawyers. I am not turning out proto-barristers and proto-solicitors. If they want to go on and do that, that is fair enough, that is one of the things you can do with a law degree, though you don't have to do it . . .
(professor, experienced, male, new university)

I'm trying to make them think like a lawyer—I don't mean a lawyer in practice—to try and teach them the intellectual skills that are involved in thinking and in problem-solving. It's those that I am really interested in, rather than information about law, because they can find that in a book. Drawing them out to use their minds. Sometimes they go out of a tutorial looking quite tired, and I comment on it and say to them 'It's really a good thing, because you've been exercising your mind, and it's like any other kind of exercise, it's hard work — it can even be quite painful, but it's a good thing, because it means you've made an effort to understand something and struggled to get there' . . .
(lecturer, experienced, female, new university)

The insistence on critical thinking as the prime objective of legal education is particularly interesting in the light of previous pedagogic criticism of law teaching for its tendency to stuff students full of facts, and assess their competence in law by requiring them to regurgitate those facts in lengthy examinations. As Atiyah put it in the Introduction to the first edition of his *Accidents, Compensation and the Law*:

I do not think it is the function of a university merely to teach a student 'what the law is'. This may, perhaps, be the function of professional courses, but it seems deplorable for a university teacher to suggest that his only function is to teach a student facts. Most law courses are, I believe, already far too overloaded with factual content. Students simply have not time to think, they are so busy learning facts. Universities should surely be the one place above all others where new ideas are generated, where students can be expected and invited to think, and talk, and write about the equity or justice or policy (call it what you will) of the law.
(Atiyah, 1970: xvi)

Responses from those in my study would suggest that the modern law teacher is less concerned with teaching facts than with giving students the skills to analyse, question and challenge the law:

Make them think and make them think and make them think, pretty much. I mean, I'm trying to make them see that there is no answer, there are arguments, and I'm

trying to make them see different ways of arguing, different perspectives through which one communicates and so on. I'm definitely not into teaching the substance of the law as a primary thing. I mean, to a certain extent one does that, but it's secondary to teaching them to think.
(lecturer, early career, male, old university)

In revealing their orientation towards critical analysis, rather than vocational skills, these responses provide evidence that the culture of *academic* law is *academic* in nature, even if, as the last chapter revealed, its inhabitants do not generally regard themselves as particularly intellectual. As Martin argues in her analysis of *Changing Academic Work* 'The quality of critical questioning is at the heart of academic competence; it is the quality which allows pursuit of truth in research and should be seen as no less of an attribute in other aspects of academic work' (Martin, 1999: 97). Despite the views of those outside the law school (even in other parts of the academy), who frequently characterise law as vocational, law as taught in universities is not merely a preparation for the career of barrister or solicitor, but offers a liberal education in much the same way as a degree in history or sociology might do. It is frustrating for academic lawyers to find their subject characterised, for example, as 'vocational, but with a strong academic content' (Warnock, 1989: 12), since it is clear from my data that the majority of them would not themselves characterise their discipline in this way. As one respondent commented despairingly, 'Even in universities, there are people who think we're all in practice'. The fact that the discipline of law is not merely vocational or staffed exclusively by practitioners are key aspects of legal academic culture which, it seems, have failed to communicate themselves even to close observers of academic life. For instance, Becher and Trowler categorise disciplines using the Kolb-Biglan classification of academic knowledge; using this system, law is classified, along with subjects such as education and social administration as 'soft-applied', and the nature of knowledge within the discipline as 'functional, utilitarian, concerned with the enhancement of (semi)professional practice' (Becher and Trowler, 2001: 36). In their study, Becher and Trowler use academic law to represent the 'social' professions (with engineering and pharmacy representing the science-based professions) and comment that, 'The almost total neglect of these areas, in terms of any documentation of their cultures, may be connected with the fact that they are far from easy to demarcate from their surrounding domains of professional practice' (Becher and Trowler, 2001: 53). However, for the academic lawyers I interviewed, the demarcation between academic law and legal practice was well defined, and they had no doubts, in this regard, about the nature of their professional identities.

ACADEMIA AS SECOND BEST?

Given that all my respondents had the necessary academic qualifications to qualify as solicitors or barristers (and that some of them had embarked upon their law degree with the intention of entering legal practice), I was interested to find out what road they had taken which had eventually led them to an academic career. One possibility might have been that the culture of academic law (and the professional identities of academic lawyers) is affected by the fact that it is full of people who would rather be doing something else (ie, frustrated practitioners). However, only one respondent said that he would rather be a practising lawyer. It was nevertheless unusual for legal academics to make a positive and early choice to be an academic. Less than 20 per cent of the total regarded academia as their first serious career choice; most of these had done postgraduate work, sometimes including a period as a paid researcher on a funded research project:

> I suppose I decided I wanted to be an academic before I decided to do a Master's. The actual point is it happened almost by accident. I registered to do a PhD on a part-time basis, which meant I needed to do some paid work as well, and the obvious thing to do was to see if there was any tutoring work at the university, as it paid relatively well for a small number of hours. I did that, and a job came up which seemed just like the exact sort of thing I should apply for—so I hadn't quite envisaged getting a full-time lectureship this early, it just worked out perfectly. At least I haven't got to worry about what I am going to do when I have finished my PhD!
> (lecturer, early career, female, new university)

The largest group of respondents (more than half the total, spread across all types of institution and levels of experience, from both genders) had either seriously considered practice, or had qualified as practitioners (and in a minority of cases had worked as lawyers). However, they were clear that they regarded academia as a preferable occupation:

> ... I enjoyed the work, but didn't like the office environment, and I particularly didn't like the sense that I was under the control, and my time was under the control, of other people. That irritated me—and the presenteeism that goes with that—having to clock in early, with people noticing whether you're there or not there, rather than noticing the quality and quantity of the work you're actually producing.
> (lecturer, early career, female, old university)

> ... I thought articles was ok I enjoyed some of it. But they took a very long time to decide who they were going to keep on whenever articles finished, so I thought I had better think about what I would do if they didn't keep me on. And during that time the [academic job] came up ... I applied for it and got it. Then after that I was in fact offered a job at [a 'magic circle' firm] but I realised that by that stage I'd written a couple of short articles, based on things I'd been doing at the firm, and I'd enjoyed doing those things, and I realised I was enjoying doing that more than most things I was doing in the firm. I didn't go a bundle on lots of telephone calls and assembling great

masses of documents and meetings and so on . . . I had a row with the partner in charge of the group . . . I went to tell him I wouldn't be staying, and he was very put out. It didn't happen very often that people turned down [that firm] . . . They offer you articles at the beginning on the understanding that you'll stay afterwards if they offer you a job, and I had always thought that it was rather one-sided, because of course they wouldn't keep you if you wanted to stay but they didn't want you. And I said that to him, and he wasn't very pleased . . .
(professor, mid-career, male, old university)

It is unsurprising that many legal academics had contemplated practice before turning to academia. There is anecdotal evidence that while it is acceptable to qualify as a practitioner before entering academia, professional lawyers look with suspicion upon someone who has not made practice their first choice of career. For a law graduate who is undecided about where their future lies, it is therefore safer to try practice first. It is also the case that, as one of the respondents pointed out, until relatively recently, many university law departments regarded qualification as a solicitor or barrister as a relevant qualification for a legal academic:

[I was advised] that if I wanted to then follow an academic career, the professional route would not be a disadvantage, and that was true in those days. So I took that advice (which was certainly very good advice). I went into the solicitor's career path, got the Solicitors' Finals, did my articles in [my home town]—but I knew, even before I'd qualified, that I *did* want to pursue an academic career. And I was lucky enough to be able to use the professional qualification as the equivalent of a higher degree—because in those days (and I'm talking about the 1970s) some law schools (of which this was one) actually gave a preference to qualified barristers and solicitors. Nobody had a higher degree when I came into this law school. So following the professional route did not in any way disadvantage me—I think quite the reverse—whereas these days, of course, the career path is very different.
(reader, experienced, male, old university)

It was noticeable that several of the women who had been in practice specifically criticised the masculine culture of law firms and the Bar. Discrimination on grounds of sex and the masculinity of the professional culture of the legal professions are matters which are well-documented in the literature (see eg, Spencer and Podmore, 1987; Holland and Spencer, 1992; Hagan and Kay, 1995; Sommerlad and Sanderson, 1998; Malleson and Banda, 2000):

I did my articles, and didn't particularly like it. I didn't like the macho environment, I didn't like the long hours culture.
(lecturer, early career, female, old university)

By the time I'd finished my articles, I knew I didn't want to practise as a solicitor, I thought it unlikely that I would ever want that, because a lot of the work was deeply unchallenging, I think that's one thing—a trained monkey could have done quite a few of the things. I found also there was an awful lot of discrimination in practice. I found it not too difficult to take until we got a male articled clerk. I was the only one to start with, then when we got a man, he didn't have to sit in the typing pool, he was

immediately awarded an office, on his own, somebody to do his typing etc, etc. It was really obvious, but it was also 'Oh, Kevin has been in the police force, so he's useful to us'. Immediately useful in a practical way, whereas with my academic qualifications I was not immediately useful—but I was useful when the head receptionist went off sick, and I did a three-week stint in the front office—to be helpful.
(lecturer, experienced, female, new university)

Despite the fact that the majority of legal academics had not been clear about the career path which they wanted to follow, few of them had any regrets about their decision to study law. In fact, they were very positive about that decision. Asked if they regretted studying law, three-quarters of the respondents had no hesitation in saying 'No', often reinforcing their answer: 'Not in a million years' 'absolutely not'. The lack of clarity about the initial decision to read law or become an academic appears not to be unusual; Evans, in his qualitative study of *English People* quickly abandoned any idea of theorising the process of choice of his respondents, commenting that '. . . a decision is not usually a calculation at all but a judgement' and that this heroic quest is often reduced into a messy and arbitrary kind of 'muddling through' (1993: 19). Henkel notes that the academics in her study varied widely at the point at which they consciously began to construct an academic identity; on her timescale, legal academics appear to have started to form their academic identities at a relatively late stage (Henkel, 2000: 150).

THE QUALITIES/SKILLS OF A 'GOOD' ACADEMIC LAWYER

In order to try and find out what the legal academic culture values, I asked the respondents to identify the qualities or skills which they thought were needed by a good legal academic. The two sets of skills most commonly identified were analytical skills and communication skills (the latter being loosely used, in many cases, to encompass teaching skills). Legal academics across both sectors and genders, at all levels of experience exhibited a great deal of consensus about these two skills.

Analysis

When academic lawyers talked in terms of 'analysis', they talked about the need for curiosity, not accepting explanations without questioning them first, a quality which is related in particular to the practice of research:

Brains! (Which I haven't got). You do need intelligence, there's no doubt about that. And you need analytical ability . . .
(lecturer, early career, female, new university)

I think you need to be genuinely curious and not very accepting of an answer that someone gives you. So even when someone says to you 'Well, this is why it is', almost your automatic response is 'Why should that be so?' . . . and you need the skills to do

something with it, and that's probably much more technical . . . but if you don't have the first thing, you won't be a really good legal academic.
(senior lecturer, mid-career, female, old university)

On the research side, I think one has to have an interest in knowledge, in argument and debate and in knowledge for its own sake, rather than any instrumental reason . . .
(reader, experienced, male, old university)

You need to have an enquiring mind. You need to have a first-rate reluctance to take anything at face value. You need to be very sceptical; some might even say cynical . . .
(professor, experienced, male, new university)

What would go top of my list would be open-mindedness. I mean, hopefully it would be a quality for all academics, indeed all people in all jobs, but you do wonder. A kind of, how can I put this? Quizzical open-mindedness . . . It's not vacant open-mindedness, but it's about open-mindedness in the true academic sense. To hear competing arguments. Not just the ability to weigh them and synthesise them, but the instinctive desire to do that, if you know what I mean.
(principal lecturer, mid-career, male, new university)

Interestingly, imagination/creativity did not seem to be a quality that was highly valued as part of these analytical skills, since it was only mentioned by two of my respondents (one in an old and one in a new university):

I think you need imagination, because you need to produce something that advances knowledge. The aim is not just to regurgitate what the court said and explain it in a nice way. I think a good legal academic has to say something more imaginative . . .
(lecturer, early career, male, old university)

Communication Skills

Communication skills were strongly related to teaching, though several respondents also pointed out the need for written communication skills, particularly related to the publication of research. Enthusiasm was also a quality mentioned by several respondents:

. . . If you're going to be a good teacher—well, I'm firmly of the belief that good teaching . . . comes down to communication. I think teaching's all about communication, and from the feedback I've got over the years . . . one of the strengths they perceive me to have, one of the reasons they like my courses is my enthusiasm, so apparently if you look as if you care about what you're doing, you're interested in your subject, you're interested in your students and how they're learning, and you show some enthusiasm or inspiration, that actually makes you a good teacher . . .
(lecturer, mid-career, female, new university)

. . . You can be as organised as anything, but if you're not interesting when you're teaching your students, that's no good either. I think you need to be interesting and interested and enthusiastic. You need to have a passion for your subject, even if it's land law!
(lecturer, experienced, female, new university)

Several of the respondents in new universities mentioned the very broad ability range among the students they taught, regarding this as a particular reason why communication skills, particularly the ability to explain difficult concepts clearly, were particularly important for academics:

> ... Also, you're taking in a broader spread of quality, in students [than years ago] so you need the skills to deal with that—and these tend not to be things that one is taught, or even has any real support in acquiring, these you just pick up as you go along, so I think being able to learn pretty quickly helps as well.
> (principal lecturer, experienced, female, new university)

> I suspect that the qualities you need in old universities are different from the qualities you need here. Here, we recognise that many of our students begin their studies at a lower skill level (and I mean intellectual skills as much as anything else) than many of the students at an old university. So we need here to have a much greater clarity in our basic approach than is probably needed in an old university. Teaching on the LPC I get a good picture of how students from old universities differ from our own students. Teaching in some universities, you expect students to be self-motivating, you expect them to understand long words. Whereas our students ... you need to work very much harder to communicate fundamental ideas ...
> (principal lecturer, mid-career, male, new university)

> [You need] The ability to understand difficult concepts and make them accessible to people who, I'm sorry, but even if they read the judgment some of my students wouldn't understand those concepts, so you've actually got to sort of dilute it down for them and put it in simple language and simple concepts ...
> (lecturer, early career, female, new university)

The skills which are identified as important by legal academics correspond with some of the key skills identified in the literature on higher education, with core aspects of the academic job. Martin comments, for example, on the almost legendary emphasis given by academics to independence of thought and individualism (Martin, 1999: 94–95), and Barnett identifies critical thinking as 'a defining concept of Western universities' (Barnett, 1997: 2). In terms of teaching, communication skills are frequently stressed in teaching manuals; Brown and Atkins, for example, identify the key skills of lecturing as 'explaining, presenting information, generating interest and lecture preparation, while key skills in small group teaching are 'explaining, listening, questioning, responding and summarising' (Brown and Atkins, 1988: 19, 68). In the context of legal education, Le Brun and Johnstone also emphasise the importance of good communication skills, including non-verbal as well as verbal performance (1994: 104). Legal academics' perceptions of the skills needed to do their job are thus congruent with those identified in academia as a whole.

84 *The Legal Academic Career*

Organisational Skills

While there was a great deal of consensus about the importance of analysis and communication, it was noticeable that the academics in old universities also regarded the ability to be organised (good at time-management, self-disciplined, able to multi-task) as just as important as the other two skills, whereas this was hardly mentioned by academics in new universities:

> ... I think you need to be diligent, conscientious and organised—the demands of the job are such that if you don't have those kinds of skills and qualities you'll be forever chasing your tail and never finding time to get anything finished.
> (professor, experienced, male, old university)

> You have to be very dedicated, sometimes almost single-minded. I think you have to be very good at managing a lot of things at the same time. I think you have to be organised ... You have to be interested in your subject, very adaptable, hard-working, good at dealing with stress and pressure—well, at least able to deal with it, able to prioritise—everything seems to need to be done at once, and you have to work out what really does need to be done at once—and you have to be a researcher, and have those critical, analytical qualities ...
> (lecturer, early career, female, old university)

The difference in responses between respondents working in old and new universities may be because of the noticeable difference in culture between those two parts of the sector, with new universities being somewhat less collegial in nature, in the sense of being a *collegium* of scholars running their own affairs, due to the fact that they often have permanent administrators/managers (who may or may not be former academics) performing a significant number of the administrative tasks which in old universities are undertaken by the academics themselves. Several respondents in new universities explained that they had permanent heads of department, who did no teaching, and just did administration, for example. This phenomenon appeared to be unknown in old universities. This difference in culture was clearly reflected in the results of Leighton et al's study of legal academics in 1995, which showed that 'Being a member of an academic community' was given a much higher priority by respondents in old universities than in new (Leighton et al, 1995: 51). When I asked my respondents about their involvement in administration (discussed in more detail in chapter 5) they all said that they were involved in some administrative tasks, and in individual cases, both in old and new universities, this involvement could be significant, especially relating to student admissions. However, the administrative burdens of academics in new universities predominantly related to teaching and to student-related matters such as admissions, generally carried out by most academics in both sectors, while those in old universities also mentioned the burdens of sitting on large numbers of departmental/faculty and university committees as well. It may be that additional requirements to attend meetings and to carry out the administrative tasks that accompany them, made legal academics in old universities place a particular emphasis on time management skills. Court, in his analysis of the use of time by academic and related staff in old universities, based on a survey carried out for the Association of University Teachers (AUT), points to the effect of the 'audit culture' in increasing threefold the amount of administrative tasks carried out by academics in old universities between 1963 and 1993 (Court, 1996: 257). Whatever the precise explanation, legal academics in old universities were clear in valuing such skills.

Persistence

Perseverance/persistence was another quality singled out as equally important by academics in old universities, though not mentioned by those working in new universities. This was a quality which was invariably related to research. Behind the emphasis on this quality lies the pressure to publish—it is not enough to have good ideas, they must be transformed into publications:

> I've known many people in legal academia who were very good on ideas, but could never actually seem to turn them into anything. So they're actually far more able, I think, than I am, I would have no question about that. But actually, they don't seem able to translate their ability and insights into the kind of material that is regarded as being valuable . . .
> (lecturer, early career, male, old university)

> Not getting stalled—not getting stalled when your time isn't structured. I worked with one colleague who eventually left to go to the Bar, who was one of the most imaginative, intellectually brilliant people I've ever worked with (and they are not the only person I've met who was like that)—they just didn't like that 'being alone in the library' thing, so I think you've got to be able to put up with that solitary—you've got to *like* that solitary [aspect of the job].
> (professor, experienced, female, old university)

> I think you have to have a lot of patience to keep chipping away at something. You have to really very much be interested in what it is that you're doing, because otherwise you start writing a PhD or a book, even a long article about law and if you weren't really interested in it there's no way you'd get it done.
> (lecturer, early career, female, old university)

> . . . I think it helps being a bit obsessive on the research front, I really do; I mean, getting things done matters, doesn't it? Nobody's going to come and stand over you. I mean, it's really unpleasant these days, with the RAE, if you don't do research, and it's going to make an impact on your career, but nobody is going to stand over you and make you do it, so being pretty disciplined and self-starting and good at motivating yourself I think is very important . . .
> (professor, experienced, female, old university)

Both the ability to organise one's time, so as to make space in which to carry out research, and the determination and drive necessary to see an idea through to eventual publication are very important in a competitive research environment.

86 *The Legal Academic Career*

Evans noted in *English People* the difficulties involved in fitting research activities into an institutional framework which requires a range of activity. Research, he argued, is not institutionalised in the same way as teaching and administration. 'The institution expects it to be done in the margins by ambitious, committed individuals' (Evans, 1993: 88). There are, of course, gendered aspects to the commitment required in academic life. Since women frequently undertake the major responsibility for unpaid caring work, this 'second shift' can impose a structural barrier to their occupational progress, particularly if academic staff are increasingly required to undertake research in their 'non-work' time (Goode, 2000: 252).

GETTING ON

In order to try and explore further the qualities which are valued within the culture of the legal academy I asked respondents 'Thinking about all the legal academics you know, what do you think marks somebody out as likely to become a professor?'

Research Output

Three-quarters of the respondents, of both genders, spread across both sectors and at all levels of experience, had no hesitation in identifying the publication of significant amounts of research as the primary factor which marked somebody out as likely to become a professor of law in due course:

> Research. Although this institution says it is also going to try and reward good teachers, even at chair level, but you still have to do the research, and I don't know how they're going to strike the balance.
> (professor, mid-career, male, new university)

> A high level of publication. That's it, as far as I can see—and I don't mean quantity. It must be a high level of well-regarded publications. There are people who produce quite a lot, but it's hopeless—that's no good. But you can be a hopeless teacher, as long as you're not absolutely the pits, but you can certainly be a pretty mediocre teacher, and a mediocre, if not hopeless, administrator, and still obtain a chair, even in a good university, provided you have good research output.
> (lecturer, early career, female, old university)

> Research—especially RAE research—people who do research which is respected— because professorships are associated with that type of research, rather than teaching, as such. Professors tend to be about research, and if they're teachers as well, that's incidental.
> (lecturer, mid-career, male, new university)

In the context of the academy, this finding is unsurprising; Halsey's extensive survey of British academia revealed that rates of publication are significantly related to the chances of becoming a professor (Halsey, 1992: 207). In this regard, academic lawyers are not any different from academics in other disciplines.

Informal Contacts

Nearly a quarter of the respondents thought that the ability to network, or 'knowing the right people' also played a significant part in securing a chair. Legal academics holding this view were twice as likely to be situated in old universities:

> Probably the older I get, the more cynical I get . . . because I can see across the legal academic community people who have really soared through the ranks, and one of the reasons for that has been their ability to network and connect with the people that you need to connect with. (So that's probably no different from any other profession, but I think I had a naïve view when I entered academia that that might not be the case. But perhaps the academy is as tainted as every other sphere of life) . . . I do see people who I consider to be very bright who are not even readers, whereas some people have got chairs and I think 'Why have you got a chair?' And I've seen them in action, and I know why they've got a Chair, because they're very good at networking.
> (lecturer, early career, male, old university)

> . . . I had a long chat with [one of our professors] about professorships, and how you get one . . . and you obviously have to have worked incredibly hard somewhere along the way; underneath that, of course, it seems to me that you have to somewhere have fallen in with the right people . . . so you've got to put yourself about a bit, I suppose, you can't just sit in your ivory tower producing your work, you've got to be out and about, attending conferences, giving papers, getting known and so on . . .
> (lecturer, mid-career, female, new university)

> My observation of the process is that it's—I think I'd use the word 'corrupt', actually, and I don't mean that in the sense of individuals being corrupt, but I think the system which produces appointments, by and large, is corrupt, systematically corrupt, I think. My feeling is that there are appointments being made on a rather 'clubbable' basis, really, and chairs being advertised which are clearly written for particular individuals, and that's surprisingly defended by VCs and senior academics everywhere, whom you'd expect to be more—who have kind of good liberal track records on all sorts of other things, but on that issue seem to think that this is perfectly acceptable . . .
> (senior lecturer, mid-career, male, old university)

Respondents holding these views were echoing the views of Becher and Trowler's law respondents, who emphasised the particular importance, in academic law, of close informal contacts and personal recommendations in career advancement. Becher and Trowler contrast this with other disciplines, where, they say, the majority of respondents held the view that 'It could be useful to have a well-regarded patron in applying for one's first appointment or two, but after that, one was expected to be judged by one's own efforts' (Becher and

Trowler, 2001: 79). The culture of law appears unusual, then, in its acceptance of personal contacts as a 'normal' part of career advancement.

Gender, of course, plays a significant role in terms of the development of informal contacts, so that a finding that law is a discipline in which such contacts play an important role has implications for equal opportunities. As McGlynn comments in her analysis of women legal academics:

> [Being an academic] remains a career which is sustained by systems of peer review and professional support from those in senior positions. Thus, advancement can depend on the support of senior members of a department and university who will determine, among other things, teaching requirements, nominations for important university committees, research support, sabbatical leave and promotions. Peers in the wider academic community will be responsible for invitations to conferences, to contribute to collections of essays, to collaborate on funding applications and the like. These 'gatekeepers' tend to be men, although slowly there are more women occupying positions of power and influence. And, as in all aspects of public life, the gatekeepers tend to fashion change in their own image.
> (McGlynn, 1998: 50)

It is not only in relation to gender that the informality of the culture is problematic. Heward et al, looking at difficulties faced by minority ethnic academics in law, make very similar points in relation to the difficulties faced by the subjects of their study, providing numerous examples of ways in which informal processes of networking and personal recommendations are crucial in determining recruitment and selection in law (Heward et al, 1997: 214).

Ruthless Ambition

Nearly half of the respondents regarded ruthlessness or ambition as being qualities which are characteristic of those who will hold chairs in law departments. Nearly twice as many women as men mentioned this as being a distinguishing feature of those who would be likely to get a chair. Often, these qualities were associated with 'not being a good citizen':

> Ambition. Ambition, irrespective of ability—all the best people don't become professors. I think you can almost identify it at an early age, the requisite characteristics which might help somebody. Ambition, self-esteem, not being over-concerned about the students' side of education in any real sense, whatever you might say. And single-minded.
> (lecturer, experienced, female, old university)

> A certain ruthlessness in not performing other tasks which perhaps should be performed, but which one can survive without doing. And I think there is a tension between research and teaching, and particularly between research and administration. And my suspicion is those who will become professors are quite good at resolving the tension in their own favour.
> (reader, mid-career, male, new university)

The ability to delegate tasks to other people. From what I can see of others, the people, to me, who are likely to become professors are the ones who don't take quite so seriously some aspects of the job, or manage to avoid some of the unpleasant, time-consuming aspects of the job, like administration—or they have the title, but they delegate the tasks, by and large, to someone else, or they rely on secretarial support. From the people I've seen who have been promoted, very few seem to be all-rounders, who devote equal amounts of time, energy and skill to all three aspects of the job. They're people who have generally committed themselves to the research aspect of the job, and have not devoted as much time and energy to the teaching or admin side of it. It irritates me, because I think other people then have to pick up the load, which then scuppers their chances of a good academic career . . .
(lecturer, early career, female, old university)

Disquiet, particularly on the part of female respondents, with the relationship of these stereotypically masculine qualities to success in the legal academy, reflects broader concerns in the literature that there is a continuing problem with equal opportunities in the academy (Collier, 2002: 7). There is an extensive literature detailing the empirical evidence about, and analysing the possible reasons for, the apparent marginalisation of women within universities (see, eg, Aisenberg and Harrington, 1988; Bannerji et al, 1991; Brooks, 1997; Howie and Tauchert, 2002; Morley and Walsh, 1995, 1996; Thomas, 1990). Researchers have also, more recently, begun to explore the implications of the university as a 'gendered organisation', subject to the complex interconnections that exist between '. . . men's practices, academic practices and managerial practices' (Hearn, 2001: 70). The perception that 'ruthless ambition' is a necessary quality for career advancement is a stark reminder of the gendered nature of academic life.

In terms of the legal academy in particular, Thornton has drawn attention to the 'congruence between bureaucratic power and masculinity' and the way in which 'benchmark men represent the core of the university "club" ' (Thornton, 1996: 108). She constructed a typology of 'acceptable' roles for women legal academics, suggesting that their acceptance in the law school is contingent upon them falling into one or other or a combination of these roles, such as the 'dutiful daughter'. All of these roles are '. . . characterised by conventional notions of the feminine, in that they emphasise appearance, sexuality, deference, docility, diligence, care and self-sacrifice' (Thornton, 1996: 112). Collier has recently drawn attention to the range of work on the 'masculine culture' of the law school, which throws light on matters such as the marginalising effects of homophobic and homosocial cultures, the dissociation of women from authority, a routine association of women with normative gendered ideals such as 'caring', and the characterisation of assertion on the part of women as 'aggression', which in turn has adverse effects in terms of promotion (Collier, 2002: 9). In analysing the effects of recent changes in higher education, Collier argues that in contemporary law schools, as in other parts of the academy, '. . . a masculinist culture has not only been maintained, it has arguably been strengthened by the thrust towards corporatism' (Collier, 2002: 24). Wells, reporting the results of her study of women law professors, has also noted the importance of the culture of law schools, and found that her respondents identified two particular law schools as harbouring particularly negative organisational cultures in relation to women. 'There may well be some others', she notes 'including among the thirty or so law schools without a single woman law professor' (Wells, 2002: 24).

In discussing the nature of career progression in the legal academy, several respondents also reflected some of the issues pointed up in Aisenberg and Harrington's qualitative study of female academics in America, which threw up some particularly interesting results about the difference in attitude between men and women to the politics involved in career progression. Although they found that sometimes women were unaware of the 'rules of the game', women also displayed an extreme reluctance to accept that playing games is necessary to gain advancement. They held tenaciously to the idea that people in academia gain advancement primarily through merit. 'And by merit they mean true merit that includes quality of mind and moral commitment as well as performance in writing and teaching'. Aisenberg and Harrington dubbed this form of behaviour the 'merit dream', and comment 'The point here is that the hold of the merit dream is so strong that even women who recognise its falsity find it difficult simply to set it aside and play by the accepted rules (Aisenberg and Harrington, 1988: 53–54).

The precise ways in which gender plays out in the law school have yet to be uncovered, but the reliance on informal contacts and the strong perception of the need for stereotypically masculine behaviour in gaining promotion suggest some areas of the legal academy which might benefit from further examination.

Being a Man

Interestingly, in the light of the previous discussion, just 10 per cent of the respondents (the majority of them female) commented that gender was a significant factor in marking people out as likely to become a professor:

> In my own mind, I suppose, I make a difference between career development for men and for women . . . I can see male academics around late thirties age, with a reasonable research record and having done a fair amount of teaching, being promoted to professor. I don't see it with women. I don't know why that is. I know very few female professors. I have only worked in two departments, which each had one female professor, and they're both people who had done an awful lot of research, they have published widely. But I've seen men be promoted to professor almost just by serving time and doing reasonably well. That's not to devalue the male professors that are out there, because many of them are extremely competent, but I'm just not sure that the same rules necessarily apply . . .
> (lecturer, early career, female, new university)

> Probably the cynical answer is gender, the ability to network, and scholarship—but I wouldn't put scholarship first.
> (lecturer, mid-career, female, new university)

The small number of respondents who drew attention to gender as a factor in career success suggests considerable lack of awareness on the part of the majority of legal academics about gender inequality as reflected in the literature (of which there is an increasing amount specifically devoted to the position of women legal academics in the UK, several examples of which are discussed above; see Collier, 2002; Cownie, 1998, 2000b; McGlynn, 1998; Thornton, 1996; Wells, 2000, 2001, 2001a, 2002; quite apart from the substantial literature in the US, Canada and Australia). The apparent lack of awareness of gender issues displayed here is particularly interesting in the light of the finding in chapter 8 of this study that, when asked *directly* about the position of women legal academics, two-thirds of respondents indicated that women are disadvantaged in pursuing a career as a legal academic, when compared with men. The differences between the two sets of responses suggests that awareness of gender issues is not very deeply embedded into the culture of academic law, and that most academic lawyers have to be specifically directing their attention to the subject before they readily identify gender as problematic.

The Administrative Route

In one of the new universities I visited, although research was seen as a theoretical route to a chair, respondents were unanimous in saying that in their institution, people became professors if they could do administration:

> I assume by that you mean a proper professor. I mean, they give professorships to administrators here. In this institution, it's the ability to push paper around and be a yes-man or woman, which has nothing to do with scholarly activity. There are *some* chairs given to people for scholarly activity, but they're very much in the minority. The majority are just bureaucrats.
> (principal lecturer, experienced, female, new university)

> ... I'm afraid that the title has become, in the new universities, imbued with mediocrity, as far as I'm concerned, and when I look at some people who have taken that title in new universities, I don't see what qualities they have, other than that, I suppose, they can shuffle bits of paper around ...
> (lecturer, early career, female, new university)

These responses point up a particular difference between old and new universities. In new universities, for example, the heads of law schools are frequently holders of that post on a permanent basis, so that, as Leighton points out in her analysis of new university law schools, 'Essentially, those aspiring to leadership in a new university school have joined a well defined management structure. Appointment to headship in a new university has meant self-identification as an administrator or manager' (Leighton, 1998: 97). Similarly, in some new universities, professorial appointments are made as essentially administrative, rather than academic appointments, and this was the case in one of the new universities in which my respondents worked. This has long been acknowledged as a difference between old and new universities (Becher and Kogan, 1992: 111).

SUCCESS

Mary Henkel's work shows that reputation is a key feature of academic identity (Henkel, 2000). This is as true for legal academics as for those located elsewhere in the academy. Reputation (being regarded as a leading figure in a specialist area) was much more important than status (being a reader or professor) for a large majority of the academics I interviewed. Having explored their opinions about what it takes to become a professor of law, I then asked 'What, for *you*, would be success in your career as an academic lawyer?' Three-quarters of the respondents identified academic reputation as at least one of their own personal measures of success. This was slightly more the case for academics working in old universities than for those in new universities, which is unsurprising, given that some individuals in new universities did not undertake any research, whereas all those in old universities described themselves as 'research active'. More interestingly, it is a view which is twice as strongly held by early-career and mid-career academics as compared with experienced academics, although there was no significant difference relating to gender. This finding provides more evidence for the argument I have put forward elsewhere that law is becoming a more 'academic', intellectually-oriented discipline, whose inhabitants place more emphasis on research and publication than was formerly the case:

> What I'd count as success, I suppose, is—I think everything depends upon recognition by others. In terms of scholarship, when I produce a piece of work that is regarded by other academics as useful, valuable, and so on, then I have been successful.
> (senior lecturer, mid-career, male, old university)
>
> . . . I'm sure that some people are really good at getting a sense of success from good students and so on, and I, of course, get enormous pleasure if the teaching's gone well—and I certainly would feel unsuccessful if I thought I was a poor teacher. But the honest clue to what makes me feel successful is research reputation.
> (professor, experienced, female, old university)
>
> I suppose it's partly promotion, getting up the hierarchy. I think it's also closely tied in with publications, though. Having a lot of publications that are well respected. You want to make a bit of a mark, don't you? I mean, the first time you get something published—I felt that I had made just a little tiny mark, you know, that after I'm dead, there's still that one thing that lives on.
> (lecturer, early career, female, old university)

The other personal measure of success which was identified as significant by nearly half of the respondents was related to feeling that one had done something positive for one's students. This was a view held across all levels of experience, by men and women equally, though twice as many people holding this view were located in new universities. In this respect, my data is broadly in agreement with that of Leighton et al, who found, in their study of law teachers, that significantly more law teachers in new universities than old regarded teaching an 'essential' or 'important' aspect of their work (Leighton et al, 1995: 50):

> I think to me the greatest measure of success is to see the students mature during their three years with us. To see how they blossom, particularly when they perhaps started off not particularly strong, but somehow the penny drops and they transform themselves. The greatest success is when you have got a student at the end of the final year, when you can have academic discussions on essentially equal terms, and that's what gives me a kick most of all, that I played some part in what I think is the most important stage of one's education. I think the degree is so important. I mean, it really turned me round. I was a fairly laid-back sort of person, who managed ok, but didn't really get any great kick out of anything intellectual until I did law. I mean, it was absolutely marvellous. You know, Paul on the road to Damascus. It changed my life.
> (professor, experienced, male, new university)

> . . . To me, success is the feedback I get from graduates who talk about the benefits they derived from my classes when they were students. I think I'd put that above everything else. I mean, I value seeing my work in print, but I sometimes wonder how long it has a currency . . . whereas our teaching does have a long-term individual impact upon those whom we teach.
> (reader, experienced, male, old university)

> Success as an academic is when a student says 'Thank you, I understand that' and when you can also say inside, 'Yes, I know you do.' So that is it for me, when a student says 'Thank you, I have enjoyed this,' 'Thank you, you've opened my eyes, ' 'Thank you, you've helped me.' Those are the success things that I enjoy . . .
> (professor, experienced, male, new university)

> I think it would be how my students thought of me. I think I would value that more highly than how some outside person thought about something that I'd written, and so that is a very personal answer . . .
> (reader, experienced, male, old university)

Only about a third of respondents (spread across both sectors and the whole range of experience, with no difference related to gender) identified both teaching and research reputation as equally important measures of success:

> I have been thinking about this recently, because one or two people have said that if you are ambitious you have got to move about a lot when you first start and go to different places if you want to be head of department. I can't imagine being head of department to be honest, I don't measure the question that way. I think it is more important that you become respected in the area that you research in, and that people think your work is good quality. That your peers recognise the work you do, I think is a measure of success. Also, just doing things, perhaps related to the teaching side of it, like starting up a new course you think is really worthwhile and different. I think

those things are more important than having the title professor or having the biggest office in the building or teaching at Oxford.
(lecturer, early-career, female, new university)

Being a professor, having a respected book (or two) and being remembered by students—some students, it's never going to be all of them, for sure, but enough students who say, as someone said to me last night, actually, not someone I taught, but someone who's just graduated, and I said 'How did you go?' and she said 'I got a 2.1, and it's all because of you, you persuaded me to do this degree.' It's that kind of thing, when students come to you and say 'You changed my life.' So it's respect in the eyes of your academic peers, and respect in the eyes of your students, so that you can say you've done a good job.
(principal lecturer, experienced, female, new university)

Having a chair was seen as important only to a very small minority of respondents (most of whom were male, working in old universities), and even then, publishing work which was well received by the academic legal community was seen as more important. Nearly as many people expressly said that having a chair was not, in their view, an aspect of success. Men formed the majority of this group too, noticeably those at the start of their career; they were situated in both old and new universities:

For me, I'd certainly like to have a chair one day, at an institution where I'd feel happy and proud to have a chair. So that's part of what's important, but also to be able to look back and think that I've written some things that I'm still very happy with. And, probably to a slightly lesser extent, that they've had an impact. I don't mean being cited by the House of Lords—because that's not really important to me—but that it's to some extent changed the way my subjects are thought about and written about.
(lecturer, early career, male, old university)

... In fact, I don't think I'd be too disappointed if I didn't get to chair level. I'd be quite happy to retire as a reader, or whatever, as long as I was kind of known as somebody who'd contributed something in my field, produced good work, and, you know, people would remember me when I'd retired.
(lecturer, early career, male, old university)

I think success would be a really good publications record, having written things that you were quite pleased with, and were proud of. Salary isn't something I would value highly, and I must say, neither would I be judging success in terms of titles, although they do have an importance, and for people who deserve them I think that is great, and good for them. But I get a sense that sometimes there are some curious appointments. When you talk to people from other departments, they can all identify somebody who is a professor who perhaps isn't as deserving as other people who have been passed over. So I wouldn't put academic success in terms of whether or not you become a professor at the end of the day.
(lecturer, early-career, male, new university)

Only two people mentioned having their work cited in the House of Lords as among their personal view of success, and one more person mentioned having the regard of the legal profession as among his measures of success. This is interesting, in view of the fact that Duxbury argues that citation of academic articles by the judiciary is still regarded as important among English legal academics (Duxbury, 2001: 61–62), although he concludes that, 'The day when English judges feel slighted by jurists, rather than jurists by judges, is not entirely beyond the imagination' (at 115). However, the lack of emphasis placed by the respondents in my study upon recognition by the judiciary or legal profession suggests that those institutions are not such a significant influence upon the culture of academic law as might have been thought.

CONCLUSION

We know from evidence discussed in the previous chapter that the general consensus among legal academics is that you do not need to be intellectual to be a legal academic. However, the ability to analyse and an enquiring mind are highly valued as qualities of a 'good' academic lawyer. Perhaps the academic lawyer's position is best explained by one of the respondents, who focused on the need for rigorous interrogation of a problem, rather than being, in his terms 'incredibly bright':

> For research, I don't think you have to be incredibly bright—I mean to have a sharp, immediate wit, what you need are things like curiosity and passion—to think 'Hang on, that's an assumption.' I expected to go to the Bar for a year, but found I wasn't very good at it—I didn't have that slick, quick patter, and I know I wouldn't be any good as a barrister, but I think I do OK as an academic, and the reason for that is that I was always ready to read the article beyond the last article, saying 'Well, hang on, is that the end of the debate?'
> (senior lecturer, mid-career, male, old university)

In the end, it is academic rigour which is valued; the ability to 'read the article beyond the last article' in the search for the truth about legal phenomena.

In terms of career progression, the abilities which appear to be rewarded by the prevailing culture are being single-minded about research (often at the expense of being a 'good citizen'), being male, and the ability to network effectively. However, when it came to people's personal measures of success, research reputation and peer esteem were the key features, making legal academics considerably more similar to other members of the academy than some people might have predicted. Legal academics fit centrally within Henkel's observation that 'the project of identity' is centred in the dynamic between individuals and their disciplines (Henkel, 2000: 189). My data suggests this is as true for legal academics as it is for other members of the academy.

5

The Experience of Being a Legal Academic

INTRODUCTION

THE FOCUS OF this chapter is the way in which the respondents view their occupation as legal academics. What are the shared attitudes and assumptions about being a legal academic? Is this an occupation people feel proud of, or do they merely regard it as a way in which to 'keep the wolf from the door'? What are the most (and least) enjoyable aspects of the legal academy, as far as its inhabitants are concerned, and what does that tell us about what is valued, tolerated, disregarded and positively disliked in this culture? How much effect does belonging to this cultural group have on the private lives of its inhabitants? Is it meaningful to talk of achieving 'work-life balance', or is that not attainable within the cultural expectations of the legal academy?

These issues go to the heart of an examination of the culture of legal academia, in that they are quintessentially issues which, if we can understand them, allow us to 'construct a reading of what happens' (Geertz, 1975: 18). Since the majority of matters discussed in this chapter clearly form constituent parts of academic identity, in terms of a socially-constructed self-hood (Jenkins, 1996: 20), this is also a chapter which particularly clearly reflects the utility of Bourdieu's idea of 'habitus', conceptualised as 'the distinctive modes of perception, of thinking, of appreciation and of action' associated with a particular collectivity, such as an occupational group (Delamont and Atkinson, 1995: 96). Habitus is a useful concept here because it provides a mediating link between the individual and the systematic or social, providing a sufficiently dynamic theory to allow one to move between 'culture' and 'identity' and examine the relationship between the two (McNay, 1999).

PROUD TO BE A LEGAL ACADEMIC?

In order to try and throw some light on the way in which inhabitants of the culture of legal academia view themselves, I asked my respondents if they were proud to be a legal academic. The answer was overwhelmingly positive, from people located in both old and new universities, of both sexes, and across the whole range of experience. Many respondents were quick to point out that displaying pride in being a legal academic was not an activity they habitually engaged in. 'I don't go round shouting it from the rooftops.' 'I wouldn't ever put it that way.' Nevertheless, privately, the great majority of the legal academics I interviewed *were* proud to be doing the job they are doing. Only a very few were neutral on this question. For most, being a legal academic appeared to have a positive effect on their self-esteem. Only one person said they were not proud (because 'I don't think anyone with the title lawyer should be proud of themselves; it's a parasitic job.'). In displaying a generally positive attitude towards their occupation, the responses of the legal academics I interviewed reflected the attitudes of academics around the world reported in the Carnegie Foundation's international survey of the academic profession, published in 1994, which found that '. . . overwhelmingly, [academics] say they would become an academic if they had to do it over' (Boyer et al, 1994: 14). Respondents in my survey were, however, more positive than the subset of English academics in the Carnegie survey. Enders and Teichler, considering characteristics of European academics using the data from the Carnegie survey, found that English academics were considerably less satisfied than their European colleagues with various aspects of their jobs, and that there was a higher proportion than in any other country analysed who would not opt again for academic work (Enders and Teichler, 1997: 367). It is worth noting that the legal academics in my survey also displayed considerably more positive attitudes towards their job than were revealed in Rose's analysis of 103 occupational groups. Rose examined feelings of happiness/depression as they related to job satisfaction, and found that academics feature in the ten least happy occupations (Rose, 2000: 7).

For nearly half the respondents, their pride was related to the idea that being a legal academic is a worthwhile thing to do, both in terms of a contribution to the intellectual life of society, and in terms of the contribution to education which academics make:

> . . . Well, you know, it seems to me worthwhile, teaching students and doing research—you know, I do have a very strong sense that scholarship is a very worthwhile thing to do. I have moments of self-doubt about it, when I think 'How many people are going to read this very theoretical article I've just written?' . . . but I suppose I think that having a serious cadre of intellectuals in the country is important . . . I think it does, you know, it really matters that you have high-level intellectual debate. It matters for all sorts of secondary things like literary and artistic production, politics, just sort of general social conscience.
> (professor, experienced, female, old university)

> I suppose I'm rather old-fashioned in thinking that academics have a useful role to play . . . in holding up a mirror to the way the world works, and suggesting ways that it might work differently, and in helping us to understand the system we've designed to govern ourselves and arrange things. So I think having a specialist body of people who think about those sorts of issues is important . . .
> (professor, mid-career, male, old university)

> Yes I am [proud]. Partly because I believe education is *so* important. I know it's not a very fashionable view now—saying you're a teacher in some circles is tantamount to saying you've got some form of horrible condition. But I actually think it's a very important role. I come from a family of teachers, and I really do think it makes a huge difference... I really believe there's an awful lot of work left to be done [even at degree level], and you can actually help people to reach their potential, and so I'm proud and pleased to be able to do that, which I know sounds very self-congratulatory—I'm not always sure I do it well, but I think it is an important role, and one that is not always recognised enough...
> (lecturer, early-career, female, new university)

For about a quarter of the respondents, pride was related to the fact that they perceived themselves as belonging to a high-status profession:

> Yes, I am proud. If you've been a historian, and then you go into law, there's a great difference in the way you're received. Anyone can do history, but law gets respect—often misplaced, I'm sure, but it does get respect...
> (principal lecturer, experienced, female, new university)

> Yes, I am proud. I think you're seen as something different to a professional lawyer, and just generally I'm proud to belong to academia as a whole. I mean, I think it's a good thing to do, and I would be horrified if government underfunding meant there was less opportunity. So yes, even though I fell into it—the reason I hadn't gone into it earlier was that it seemed to me to be a very high-status thing, and I didn't really set my sights that high.
> (lecturer, early-career, male, old university)

> Yes, I am proud. Peculiarly, although people seem to dislike practising lawyers so much, it seems to me that HE generally, and certainly legal HE, has retained its status. I am often astonished by the fact that while teachers have been slagged off so much, and doctors and many other professions have had an enormous drop in status, it seems to me that being an academic is still surprisingly respectable, and valued. So in that sense, yes, I feel comfortable, socially, about what I do.
> (lecturer, early-career, female, old university)

Frequently, these respondents did not directly explain that their pride was related to membership of an elite, preferring to imply such membership, by saying that it was the sort of job where socially you played down being a university lecturer, in order not to embarrass others or appear to be pulling rank:

> ... I certainly feel that status goes with being an academic, although I don't usually qualify it by saying 'legal'. In fact, to be honest, when I meet people, I often simply say I teach, and hide the fact that I'm a university academic, because of the wariness that some people feel when they encounter a university lecturer. Some people are intimidated—in social settings it can be awkward, depending on what setting you're in. So if I was travelling on holiday, say, I'd just say 'I teach'—though I wouldn't lie if someone asked me further...
> (reader, mid-career, male, new university)

> I feel I have to moderate what I say to people depending who my audience is—what I've found in particular is that if I'm talking to a labourer or someone like that, if I say

'Oh, I'm an academic', I might as well be talking French, so I often say I'm a teacher. But people who understand the nature of academia—then yes, I do [feel proud] to a certain extent—I always think it's nice when you get these forms—I'm filling one out at the moment, and you get this question 'What level are you?' and you can put academic or whatever.
(lecturer, early-career, male, old university)

Several respondents talked about the fact that others whom they met did not understand what a legal academic was (usually confusing them with practising lawyers). This confusion can be tricky to negotiate:

Yes I am, I think I'm quite proud. I think people probably have misconceptions about what it is and that it's perhaps grander than it is, and certainly that it's better paid than it is, and I suppose sometimes I have to be careful not to be saying 'Oh, yes, but I don't make much money' or that sort of thing, when people sort of say 'Oh, you're a lawyer', and they think you're Mr Moneybags . . .
(lecturer, mid-career, female, new university)

. . . I am a little embarrassed sometimes, because people automatically have views and preconceptions about you, and I sometimes think if you mention the word law people assume you are an expert in everything, and there usually then follows a practical point of law which I can never provide advice on, and then you start to feel uncomfortable, because you feel that initially they looked on you quite favourably, but now they've decided that you don't know anything, and you have lost any credit you might have had in their eyes.
(lecturer, early career, male, new university)

In terms of pride, about 20 per cent of respondents contrasted their position as legal academics with the position of practising lawyers. They varied in the way in which they characterised the relationship between legal academia and the legal profession. Just under half of this group were particularly aware that legal practitioners often appear to hold legal academics in little esteem:

If I meet people at parties and they ask me what I do, I don't say I'm an academic lawyer, I say I'm a university lecturer, and I'm happy with what I do. But I don't think it really has the same social value or social kudos as saying I'm a company lawyer in London . . .
(lecturer, early career, female, old university)

Yes, in the sense that it's a successful career that's not open to other people, and in that sense I do feel proud that I've been able to achieve that, and I do enjoy it. I'm also very conscious that among the secular world, the world out there that's involved in legal practice, it's seen to be irrelevant . . .
(lecturer, early career, male, old university)

The majority, however, had far more self-confidence about their chosen career, and several respondents expressly made the point that they regarded their job as something much more worthwhile than being a solicitor or a barrister:

. . . I think it's particularly important to have people who think and reflect about the law and the legal system in a way which practitioners don't often have the time to do.

That's not to say there aren't any thoughtful people in the profession, there clearly are . . . but I think by and large most practitioners are naturally concerned with the immediate demands of their clients, and don't have time to reflect on the law in a more general way. And I think the reflection on the law in a general way is important, . . . because I think it contributes to the broader understanding society has of the way the world works . . .
(professor, mid-career, male, old university)

I'm prouder than I would be if I had to say I was a practising lawyer, yes, a lot prouder. Because I think the image of the legal profession is the lowest I can ever recall. I mean, I have to say I don't go round telling people I'm a legal academic, volunteering the information—but if was asked, yes.
(principal lecturer, experienced, female, new university)

Yes, [I'm proud to say I'm a legal academic], because I think it carries a certain standing, and there's like a recognition hopefully that you've made some reasonable contribution in some particular field or another, that might not be possible if you were in legal practice.
(senior lecturer, experienced, male, old university)

In describing their perceptions of the academic job as 'worthwhile', legal academics are reflecting on both the social and intellectual value of their job. Being a legal academic is a vocation—badly paid, but, for the most part, hugely rewarding. In a collection of essays on the relationship between teaching and research, Frost comments:

> Although teaching in academia might not yet be accorded the institutional and professional significance given to doing research, I think that when teaching is done well, it contributes to learning where it counts the most—in the hearts and minds of others, of the students with whom one works. To teach others so that they learn to be more competent, to be wiser, to be better human beings, is what it is all about. To be remembered for having spent oneself in the service of learning and of improving the human condition through teaching would be a worthy epitaph, I think, for an academic.
> (Frost, 1997: 110)

These are sentiments which neatly sum up the attitudes of the legal academics I talked to. Equally, many of them derived their sense of self-worth from their involvement in research, which appears to be allied to their view of the university's role in society as a critical friend, 'speaking truth to power.'

JOB SATISFACTION

As will be apparent from some of the material referred to at the beginning of the preceding section, the job satisfaction of academics is highly contested in the literature. Thorsen, for instance, details a range of studies which have identified a range of stress factors in academic life, including having insufficient time to keep abreast of one's field, having too much to do, conflicts between teaching, research and administrative duties, as well as the long hours spent on the job

(Thorsen, 1996: 474). Her own study of five hundred Canadian academics produced similar results. Everett and Entrikin, examining academics in Australia, found a sustained increase in alienation and dissatisfaction among academics in a range of institutions, though the *rate* of dissatisfaction differed according to the type of institution involved, rank, gender and discipline (Everett and Entrikin, 1994). In Britain, Paul Trowler's qualitative study of academics at 'NewU' revealed some individuals who were sinking under the pressures of contemporary academic life and are merely remaining passive in the face of apparently overwhelming odds (Trowler, 1998: 115). Halsey, in his major study of academics in the early 1990s talks of academics seeing themselves:

> ... as an occupational group losing its long-established privileges of tenure and self-government, pressed to dilute its tutorial methods, hampered in control of syllabuses, and restricted in its research ambitions by chronic shortage of funds.
> (Halsey, 1992: 269)

Yet some commentators, such as Adams (1998) and Henkel (2000) are noticeably more upbeat; we will return to them later in the chapter.

In relation to legal academics, commentators are equally divided. Collier has drawn attention to the increasing 'performativity' required by law schools, which has 'become increasingly important in recruitment and promotion practices and in institutional determination of career "success" or "failure" (Collier, 2002: 15). He has also argued that '... both legal practice and the legal academy associate visible displays of ability to work long hours with an individual's personal commitment to the institution, and development of an appropriate 'professional attitude' (Collier, 1998: 32). Collier's arguments are made as part of his analysis of the arrival of the 'corporatised university', with its features of managerialism (bringing with it the possible 'proletarianisation' of academic life) and its demand for 'ideal workers', unfettered by family or other responsibilities (Collier, 2002: 30). As part of her analysis of Australian women legal academics, Thornton, too, notes the 'increasing erosion of collegiality' and analyses the contemporary university as '... a modern corporation organised along bureaucratic lines' (Thornton, 1996: 106). She points to the appointment of '... powerful Deans of mega-faculties' who are 'now appointed, not elected, to "manage" staff and students, and contain unruly elements' as an obvious feature of the 'top-down' style of management which she sees as prevalent in law schools and which 'serves to reaffirm the linkage between masculinity and the apex of the bureaucratic pyramid'(Thornton, 1996: 129).

On the other hand, there are those who are more optimistic about the future of the law school, and the working conditions of legal academics, myself included. Writing about the state of university law schools in 1996, I examined (together with my co-author) 'whether autonomous academics have become managed employees' (Bradney and Cownie, 1996). Our conclusion was that, while we acknowledged in the context of university law schools the relevance of Foucault's 'disciplinary society', we also noted Foucault's insistence that alongside the exercise of power inherent in such a society, there is also resistance. While not being over-optimistic, and acknowledging that collegiate governance of universities by and for academics remained at risk, we were nevertheless able to point to a number of factors (including burgeoning online resources, the availability of email to facilitate contact with others who are sources of support outside the immediate working environment, resistance to demands from the legal profession and the positive reception of new types of legal scholarship) which provide evidence that the march of managerialism is not a completely unproblematic one. Recently, Bradney has gone on to make this point even more forcefully. In his book about the state of the contemporary law school, *Conversations, Choices and Chances,* he argues that 'though there have been attempts to bureaucratise and corporatise the university, they have been resisted and can continue to be resisted . . . [t]he liberal law school remains a possibility in the twenty first century' (Bradney, 2003a: 201). We are not alone in our more optimistic view of legal academia. As Bradney points out in his book, Weidner has recently described being a legal academic in the US as 'one of the last great jobs in the world' (Weidner, 1997). In the UK context, Twining argues that,

'. . . more than most academics, lawyers have some grounds for optimism: the subject-matter of our discipline is ubiquitous, important, intellectually challenging, and accessible; it has a rich mass of constantly renewed primary sources that have to date been generally underexploited by scholars, including legal scholars. It is constantly fed by problems and materials from outside the discipline—what some people call 'the real world'. Its economic base is reasonably secure because of high demand, alternative markets for legal education, association with a generally profitable and powerful occupational group, and because it has relatively low overheads, even if it is not quite as cheap as its traditional image. The community of legal scholars is strengthened by the contributions of practising lawyers and judges , at least some of whom can genuinely be said to be learned. There are signs that law is becoming more part of the intellectual mainstream. Above all, the modern English law school is a very recent creation, which has only recently been assimilated into the university and is only just in process of coming of age . . .
(Twining, 1997: 353)

In the context of the debate about the nature of the legal academic job, I was interested to find out where the law teachers I interviewed would stand. In order to get as spontaneous a response as possible, I decided to ask them two questions at the beginning of the interview, before the respondents had had time to draw many conclusions (correct or otherwise) about my research agenda. The first was 'What do you like most about being a legal academic?', and the second was 'And what do you dislike most?'. The answers to these questions have provided a rich source of data about how legal academics view their occupation, throwing light both on the construction of their professional identities and on the culture of academic law.

AUTONOMY

When asked what they liked most about being a legal academic, the factor identified most often (by just over half of the respondents, in a group spread across the range of experience, but containing slightly more women than men, and slightly more likely to be situated in old universities) was autonomy, or the freedom to organise one's own working life. In identifying this aspect of the academic job, legal academics were once again showing their proximity to the mainstream of academic life. Surveying research over a thirty-year period in Australia, Adams notes that 'All surveys found that academic freedom, expressed in various terms such as flexibility, independence, professional judgement and so on, was a highly-ranked item in academic satisfaction' (Adams, 1998: 426). Henkel (2000: 257) comments that one of the most prominent aspects of academic identity which her major study uncovered was academic freedom. This included being free to choose one's research agenda and follow it through, and '... being trusted, and being given the space to manage the pattern of one's own working life and to determine one's own priorities.' 'The importance of these things' writes Henkel 'was one of the most dominant themes of our interviews.'

> ... the space and time free from too many short-term pressures to pursue my own interests, ideas, thoughts—we're talking research here, but in the broadest possible sense of the word. I don't mean RAE or anything that may necessarily end up that way, but the ability and time to think things through properly and work it out, which is a privilege to the extent that you still have it compared to a lot of jobs, and it shouldn't be knocked...
> (principal lecturer, experienced, male, new university)

> I think I like the flexibility of it. I like the fact that I organise my own day, and work on what I want to work on, and that I work the hours I want to...
> (lecturer, early career, female, old university)

> I suppose I really like the individual freedom. It's a job where you can, to a large extent, do what you want, work on questions that interest you. You can spend a lot of time reading books—I like reading books, and at times, certainly not all the time, but at times it can just seem like one of the best jobs in the world, because you can be sitting in the garden in the summer reading what I think are very interesting books, and being paid for it—it's a pretty good deal. It's not always like that, but that's what's really good.
> (lecturer, early career, male, old university)

> ... I particularly value the autonomy—that I can plan and organise my own work, in my own time, and other than having to be at lectures and classes at particular times, whether I work at home or in the office is very much under my control. I'm good at planning, and time-keeping, and I resent other people doing that for me, because on the whole they don't do it as well as I do.
> (lecturer, early career, female, old university)

> The freedom, probably—freedom to work on what you want, more or less—it's pretty much unbounded, isn't it, although the RAE sort of affects it—but it doesn't really matter what it is, does it? So you can sort of choose the area, and I think with a lot of jobs you can't do that, can you?
> (senior lecturer, mid-career, male, old university)

> What I like most about being an academic is the freedom to pursue a subject that interests me, and has interested me since I was a student. To decide which particular aspects of it I might pursue, to decide what approach I take. I think academics have a relatively high degree of control over their professional environment, although I think that degree of control has reduced over the years, but at least in terms of their academic work, and in terms of what they actually do with students, I think they still have a fairly high degree of autonomy, especially for employees.
> (professor, mid-career, male, old university)

Comments such as these would fit in well with the more optimistic commentators on higher education. Adams, for example, in her examination of the effects of policy changes in higher education on Australian academics, notes that 'Although increasing workloads and demands for accountability are sources of irritation and complaint for academic staff, the intrinsic rewards and satisfactions of the academic role have, so far, remained as constant consolations despite the erosion of work conditions' (Adams, 1998: 432). At the end of her extensive examination of academic identities in the face of recent policy changes in higher education, Henkel's conclusion is that, faced with huge amounts of change, academics have adopted a range of '. . . more or less conscious strategies to conserve academic identities, collective and individual' (Henkel, 2000: 261).

VARIETY

The other significant factor, also identified by nearly half of the respondents, was the variety of tasks involved in being an academic, and in particular the ability to do *both* teaching *and* research. This was a view expressed by those in both old and new universities, by slightly more women than men. It was a factor which did not, however, seem to be valued by the respondents in mid-career, who were fairly evenly distributed between those singling out autonomy, teaching, or research as the thing they most valued about their job:

> Well, the freedom to do my own research, and it's being a bit like having two different jobs—I'm not sure I could have coped with being a sort of freelance writer—because when I get to the end of the vacation, or say when I'm on sabbatical (which, of course, one longs for), often it's really hard motivating yourself, making your own structure, that kind of thing. So usually, certainly by the end of summer vacations, albeit with some nostalgia, I'm quite looking forward to a different kind of life, where the day's mapped out, and you can tick things off lists, you don't have to be seamlessly creative. But then, of course, by the end of term I've had enough of that, and having to go into work . . .
> (professor, experienced, female, old university)

I do enjoy my job, there's no denying that. I think I like the freedom to organise my own life and time, and what I teach, and what I write, and the fact that I can do them both. I also like the feeling that one sometimes has that you make a difference to the students' lives.
(principal lecturer, experienced, female, new university)

I like the mixture of work that I do—research, teaching, and, dare I say it, admin. I actually enjoy the fact that my job is very diverse.
(lecturer, early career, female, old university)

There are two elements to it that I particularly enjoy—a blend of teaching and research, and they give very different pleasures. I would find it very difficult to do 100 per cent research. Teaching widens your mind, gives you adrenalin highs, and provides nice breaks between researching. Conversely, doing 100 per cent teaching I think would lead me to become intellectually closed—research provides new avenues for thinking...
(reader, mid-career, male, old university)

The variety of tasks and the flexibility with which you can approach them. So as regards variety you have the teaching and variety within that—small and large groups, undergraduate, postgraduate, and the different personalities of the students, and the pastoral dimension, personal students—I like hearing about their lives, their hopes and problems. Then you've got research, and working on your own or in libraries, and I like that. And the year is varied—you have intense periods during the term, and deadlines, but there is a difference between term and vacation—your time is limited in term, but I like the fact that you have a different pace during the summer. Also travelling, going abroad and linking up with other academics, and this sense that you're in a community that's not just localised. I could go to Canada, and meet some academics there, and we'd feel we had something in common, and we could work on projects together, even though they're in Canada. I like the possibility of travel.
(lecturer, early career, female, old university)

In stressing their interests in both teaching and research, legal academics are reflecting attitudes found across the academic profession. Halsey reported in *Decline of Donnish Dominion* that despite all the changes in their conditions of work, academics in his study remained firmly attached to the tradition of simultaneous interest in teaching and research (Halsey, 1992: 184). It is a relationship which is much discussed within the literature (see, eg, Rowland, 1996; Brew, 1999). The traditional relationship between teaching and research appears to be under threat from current government policy, with the 2003 White Paper on *The Future of Higher Education* making determined efforts to split the synergy between the two which is so cherished by many legal academics, along with others in the academy:

> It is clear that good scholarship, in the sense of remaining aware of the latest research and thinking within a subject, is essential for good teaching, but not that it is necessary to be active in cutting-edge research to be an excellent teacher.
> (DFES, 2003, para 4.31)

The data I gathered from my respondents suggests that a significant number of legal academics would resist any such attempts to divorce teaching from research.

THE WORST OF TIMES?

In order to throw further light on cultural values, the second question I asked all the respondents was what they disliked most about being a legal academic. Predictably, the aspect of academic life which was identified as being a negative part of the job was bureaucracy/administration, with nearly two-thirds of respondents identifying this as the thing they disliked most. These people were men and women spread across all levels of experience, but it was noticeable that nearly twice as many of the respondents giving this answer were situated in new universities, rather than in old universities. The differences between old and new universities which emerged in this context were similar to those I discussed in chapter 4, where respondents were talking about the skills required to be a legal academic. In that context, it was noticeable that it was only respondents working in old universities who emphasised the need for time-management skills and the ability to multi-task. Here, it was a matter of respondents meaning different things when they talked about their dislike of 'bureaucracy'. In new universities, dislike of bureaucracy was frequently linked to dislike or criticism of 'management' (whether departmental or at university level). This was a matter rarely mentioned by people working in old universities; their dislike was of 'administration', ie administrative tasks which have to be carried out by academics. The difference between 'management' and 'administration' is subtle, but crucial, since it is an indicator of a cultural difference between old and new universities. Legal academics in new universities seem to be affected to a greater extent by the 'managerialism' which, here as elsewhere in the public sector, has involved an increased concern with 'results', 'performance' and 'outcomes'; hence higher priority is given to the 'management' of people, resources and programmes, compared to the 'administration' of activities, procedures and regulations which one might find in old universities (Pollitt, 1993: 49):

> Well, probably in line with many other people, I dislike having to sit down and do all the paperwork—that's always going to be the case, because there's a huge amount of it, and an increasing amount of it. I don't mind so much the essential paperwork surrounding courses—it's just the sheer volume of paper—it's just trying to make sure the systems are in place, so, for example, every time I communicate with a student by email, I have to keep a copy of their email and my email. And with a large number of personal tutees, I seem to spend a good few hours each day just printing and filing and trying to find more files to stick all the stuff in . . .
> (lecturer, early career, female, new university)

> Administration—I'd be amazed if anyone said anything else—ie anything which I don't think is directly related to the input of teaching—so for example, research feeds

into teaching, preparation feeds into teaching—but supervising enrolments, doing course administration, typing letters to fifty students saying 'Can you be here on this day at this time?', chasing up exam marks. None of those to me—well, really they could all be performed by a bright seventeen-year-old—that's what I really don't like.
(reader, mid-career, male, new university)

... We aren't properly supported with administrators and secretaries, we end up doing everything, and it means—I think the really frustrating thing is it means you can't do your job properly, and in particular you can't do the research .. It's partly the sense of injustice, which comes round to the whole way the department is managed—and I disagree with lots of the decisions that are made, but on the other hand, it isn't just the head of department—he's being squeezed by decisions which I wouldn't have made at a higher level and so on. So I just think we're being asked to be Jacks of all trades, and then when we aren't excellent at any one of them that happens to be prioritised we get slammed for that, and it's just self-perpetuating and very disheartening at times. Like you said 'What have you done on your X paper?' and I have done absolutely nothing since I saw you at the X conference, and yet I came away from that conference really buoyed up and anxious to do it, and I come here every day and it's just sorting out students who've got into a muddle with the department, and sorting out their lives—it's all to do with administration.
(principal lecturer, experienced, female, new university)

I dislike the fact that, it all ties in with management, with internal politics, with a lack of apparent awareness on the part of many senior people about how the rest of us work, about different workloads ... we seem to have a whole host of people in management positions now, and fewer and fewer people doing teaching, and yet still the place isn't brilliantly managed ... It's pressures not just put on by our VC, but by HEFCE or whoever it is, that then impacts on the way we get treated ... it's that feeling you get sometimes where you feel you've got a lot of responsibility, or you're in the front line, you're having to deal with the students, but you can't actually solve their problems ... so I just try and focus on the things I *do* have control over, and try and make those operate a bit better ... and then, you know, do my bit where I can to try and voice concerns.
(lecturer, mid-career, female, new university)

The participation of universities in the phenomenon of 'new public management' has been well documented in the literature (see, eg, Becher and Kogan, 1992; Kogan and Hanney, 2000). The hallmarks of new public management are concerns with 'quality' and 'consumer responsiveness', which sit alongside concerns with economy and efficiency (Pollitt, 1993: 189). It is the effects of such concerns, when imposed on universities, that have led Collier to argue, in the context of law schools, that the processes of corporatisation (to which, he has argued, law schools are subject just as much as any other part of the academy) will lead across the sector to 'a diminution of autonomy and a greater rigidity in academic labour' (Collier, 2002: 30). It is with such effects on the academic job that the respondents, particularly in new universities, were concerned.

Respondents in old universities were not immune from the changes in academic life lying behind these concerns. Their experience was generally, however, slightly different in quality, in that it was the huge increase in the amount of administrative tasks which they were expected to do themselves which concerned them, rather than being 'managed':

> ... I do find it a chore being in a meeting that's been organised, and it isn't going anywhere, and you can't see why you're being involved in that kind of work—and there's a fair amount of that about.
> (professor, experienced, male, old university)

Audit/Accountability

Respondents in new universities also highlighted their dislike of audit/accountability measures (which were often associated with seemingly constant change). These matters were much less frequently mentioned by people working in old universities. The differences in response here again appear to reflect differences between the sectors in their management structure and their attitude to accountability. Audit is something the whole sector has experienced, but it appears to impact differently on the two sectors:

> I think the administration, and the extent that these days you have to have a piece of paper to prove you've done something, whereas previously it was taken on trust. And I suppose the change has come about because of one or two bad pennies.
> (professor, experienced, male, new university)

> ... I regard spending time on things like TQA as presently formed as an utter waste of time, and not at all conducive to student well-being or anything. So I loathe that kind of bureaucracy ...
> (professor, experienced, female, old university)

> I think what I dislike is that we seem to be moving away from the important things, teaching and trying to help students in their understanding of the law, and more towards form-filling and changing rules and regulations every year ... Every year there is a new form of modularity, or so it seems, and that is a nuisance. You are constantly gearing up to this review or that review, and that can become a bit unsettling and unfortunate ...
> (lecturer, early career, male, new university)

> Bureaucracy. I just do not like the way that we have turned into educational corporations providing commodities for which we have to account all the time. And endless bits of paper. Box-ticking exercises. Audit, review, call it what you will, it is all the same. It's a constant process of being checked up on, which I find corrosive.
> (professor, experienced, male, new university)

The effect upon those working in law schools of the various types of audit which have recently been introduced into higher education will be the subject of detailed discussion later in this book. Suffice it to say, in this context, that both the Research Assessment Exercise and the Quality Assurance exercise (focused on teaching quality) have been the subject of sustained criticism by commentators on legal education. Brownsword has pointed up a number of concerns, including some related to the actual methodology of the audit of teaching, the increasing pressures on academic staff and institutions, and the deleterious effects of the replacement of a culture of collaboration between law schools with a culture of 'unfriendly competition' (Brownsword, 1994: 539–40). Bradney has also criticised audit in terms of its 'commodification' of the academic enterprise:

> Attention becomes focused on those things that can be audited. Audit has thus moved from being the verification of the quality of learning and teaching by the use of objective measures to being a process by which education is commodified, where things are judged to be of value in the educational process if they can be measured, even though those measures are in no way measures of learning and teaching quality. Measurement then becomes more important than education.
> (Bradney, 2001: 439)

The concerns which have been expressed by commentators on the legal academy were accurately reflected in the responses of the legal academics I interviewed.

'Pressure'

In old universities, alongside concerns about increasing amounts of administration, respondents identified a wide range of other matters as being negative aspects of the job, including the politics of academic life, the constant pressure (especially to publish) and marking. Given the larger teaching and assessment loads which can often be found in new universities, it was surprising that more people in old universities than new mentioned marking, although because of the increase in student numbers over the past decade or so, the presence of assessment in a list of the negative aspects of academic life is not in itself surprising. The other factors mentioned by respondents situated in old universities appear to reflect the very competitive nature of old university law schools, where there is constant pressure to research, and as a result, some individuals behave in ways their colleagues find particularly distasteful:

> The people. The egos. The self-inflated egos. Yes, I guess the attitudes that permeate academia. Because a lot of people think their jobs are *so* important, it is *so* crucial, and they're going to work twenty-four hours a day. Plus the competition. There's no collegiality any more. Everyone's competitive and everybody is criticised at every stage. Also, people combine peoples' work with the individual, directly. So someone may be a wonderful person, but they don't like their work, so they're a crappy person. And you can be a crappy person and do good work—it works both ways, but people don't separate one from the other. So to see the way people have been insulted, in a book review, in an article, or face-to-face—it blows my mind!
> (lecturer, early career, male, old university)

> You'll hear all sorts of mundane stuff about administration and so forth. But I don't think for most academics, certainly at universities that do well in research terms, the administrative loads are excessive. It irritates me, sometimes, some of the moaning

about certain parts of the job. I [also] think research is a very self-obsessed process, it's difficult to cut off, I don't think it's good for relationships and friendships. There's something very, very narcissistic about it and that I don't particularly like . . .
(reader, mid-career, male, old university)

The inward-lookingness of the academic community, and the rather petulant back-biting that goes on. I think academics are, how can I put it, vulnerable to being very self-regarding and not really linking up what they do with the wider world and society.
(senior lecturer, mid-career, male, old university)

Several academics working in old universities referred to the pressures of life in the legal academy as being the thing they disliked most:

The pressure to publish—the Sword of Damoclese hanging over my head constantly.
(Lecturer, early career, female, old university)

At times it can just seem a real drudge. You can be reacting to things with very little control over them—lots of things come across your desk that you have to deal with very quickly, and at times you just feel you have more or less no free time, everything overruns and you're just bogged down in it. It's a job that's always running over the weekends and the evenings—a lot of the time that doesn't particularly bother me, but sometimes you just feel it's got a bit out of control. I mean, I come in here on a Saturday often, and a whole load of my colleagues are in too—and it's not just because we're all boring people with no lives. And I suppose combined with the general fact that we're not being paid enough to kill ourselves, that's the worst part . . .
(lecturer, early career, male, old university)

. . . The pressure is to do with this idea that you've got to produce a certain number of pieces for the RAE, and therefore that while you might have an unproductive year for whatever reason, it seems that only the product matters, as opposed to the process or the quality, even though the quality is supposed to be assessed, but what I mean is that perhaps what you publish in one journal would be less well accepted, even though it is a good piece, at least, that's the impression I'm given. It matters more where you publish it than what you say—though technically we're being told that's not the case. That kind of pressure I find difficult . . . while I enjoy research sometimes I dislike it because of that pressure and because of that expectation that promotion will only come if you publish on a regular basis in certain journals.
(lecturer, early career, female, old university)

In making such comments, legal academics are reflecting the pressures felt throughout academia. Halsey draws attention to the pressure to do 'more research than I would like to do' increasing steadily over time (Halsey, 1992: 185), and Ryan comments 'The focus on research is now obsessional, far beyond reasonable measure in the life of learning' (Ryan, 1998: 31).

WORKING AT HOME

For the great majority of respondents, there was no clear division in their life between work and home. When I asked them if they worked at home at all, they said that they worked at home regularly; this was true across the spectrum of experience, institution and gender. Most people said they worked at home in order to avoid interruptions, and most used it to do research, although a significant number also carried out other tasks, such as administration or teaching preparation, in the evenings, when they felt they were too tired to do research:

> Yes—there's not a big division between working here and working at home—it's part of the job, it doesn't bother me. I sometimes think this place—and I expect it's the same everywhere—couldn't survive unless we did work at home, certainly at some times of the year. There's no way that exam marking would get done if people didn't do it at home . . .
> (principal lecturer, experienced, female, new university)

> It's wonderful—I absolutely love it. Again, that is the sort of thing that makes the job, that makes me willing to sacrifice £30,000 a year. I feel it makes my home life viable.
> (lecturer, early career, female, old university)

> Yes, I feel fine about it—it's part of what being an academic is—it's a necessary part of academia, because it's important to get away from students and administrative pressures sometimes, so you can read something uninterrupted . . .
> (lecturer, early career, male, old university)

Several people mentioned that they felt much calmer at home, and found time spent working there more productive:

> Yes, I don't resent it, I quite like it. Because there's no interruptions, I feel far more relaxed, I suppose, than I do at work, less threatened. That sounds awful, doesn't it, but I do feel safer, I suppose, and my mind is far more restful. So if I want to do any original work at all it tends to be at home, where I can have deep periods of concentration, no interruptions, and also I'm more relaxed . . .
> (lecturer, early career, female, new university)

> Yes—I choose to—it's—if I'm doing anything academically serious, it's much easier, I find it better, to do it at home, partly because you don't get interrupted, also because I think the office has such an 'office' feel—it's busy, and so on, and to do proper scholarship I need to retreat from that, and with the internet you *can* work at home.
> (senior lecturer, mid-career, male, old university)

Most people said they enjoyed working at home, with only about a fifth of respondents saying they rarely worked at home. Most of the latter group preferred to keep a marked separation between home and work, although one or two had personal circumstances (eg, several small children and no study) which simply made working at home impossible:

> I rarely work at home—because my home life and my work life are actually quite separate, and although there's a lot of stuff that I would tell my partner about what's happening at work, and she would with hers, I don't know—I think it would be fairly tedious to kind of bring too much of the work baggage to home, and vice versa—most people would regard it as fairly tedious to bring your family issues and problems to work, and I think it works the other way round as well.
> (senior lecturer, mid-career, male, old university)

... there are all sorts of distractions at home—the kids are constantly asking me to do something, or asking questions, and they don't understand that I don't want to be interrupted—so it's better not to work at home ... and when they come home from school they want to come in and see me—and, of course, I want to see them, too—except I don't want to see them because I need to do other things—so it's no good really.
(professor, mid-career, male, old university)

The extent to which legal academics work at home reflects the 'indeterminacy' of the academic job to which Collier has drawn attention (Collier, 2002: 21). While, as some respondents mentioned, having the freedom to work at home can be one of the positive aspects of being an academic, it can also be a two-edged sword, putting pressure on individuals who feel that the demands made upon them require almost constant attention to some aspect of the academic job, with a consequent deleterious effect on any notion of 'work-life balance'. It is the latter issue which I explored next with the respondents.

WORK-LIFE BALANCE

The question I asked in this context was 'Do you find it easy to balance the demands of work and the rest of your life?' Responses were evenly divided across the two sectors, and between men and women, between those who found this balance easy, and those who did not. Significant differences in responses are revealed when considering responses according to level of experience. Here, it was clear that as the legal academic career progresses, work-life balance becomes more of a problem. Nearly three-quarters of early-career academics said they found maintaining a work-life balance easy. Mid-career academics were evenly divided on this question, while more than three-quarters of experienced academics said that they did not find it easy to maintain a balance between work and the rest of their lives. There may be a number of explanations for this. One is that the early career academics falling into this group may not have had many responsibilities outside work. However, looking at their family situations, one-fifth of them had a partner and children or other dependents living at home, three-fifths had a partner but no children, and a fifth were single. The group of people who said they found the maintenance of an appropriate work-life balance problematic had almost exactly the same spread of family responsibilities. It seems, therefore, that increasing difficulty with work-life balance may be related more to increased responsibilities at work, career pressures and so on, than to the demands emanating from peoples' personal lives.

Work-Life Balance? Not a Problem

Looking first at the respondents (50 per cent of the total) who regarded the maintenance of work-life balance unproblematic, their responses fell into three categories. For about a quarter of these respondents, the family took priority:

> In a way yes, because I think it is easy in the sense that a lot of the time there isn't a decision to make—the decision is made for you. We have two young children, and therefore there are times when, obviously the weekend used to be an opportunity to do a fair amount of work, now if you can get something done that is a bonus. That's the way it is, and that's the way it's got to be, and that's the way you want it to be. My partner is an academic as well, so we are both in the same boat, and obviously we have to be careful that she needs as much time as I need to be able to do work things. Family life is so important, you don't want to lose that. I would hate for them to grow up thinking 'We didn't see much of Mum and Dad, but here's a book they were involved in.' There are times, admittedly, when you would like to be able to get on with something, but I think as time has gone by, we have adjusted ourselves to the idea that you can't, and that's that. It's pointless getting frustrated by it; we chose to have children, and you should never resent them for encroaching on time that you might otherwise spend working . . .
> (lecturer, early career, male, new university)

> Most of the time it's ok . . . I'm not involved in anything which grossly intrudes on work. But I also made a decision fairly early on that I would work reasonably hard at my career, but I would not let it take over my life. In a way, I'm glad I did that, because there is an increasing expectation that you'll be around more, and if you aren't, you're [seen as] not sufficiently committed. I do take some work home, and I might work at home, just to get more done, but I don't let work take over my life.
> (lecturer, experienced, female, old university)

Another quarter of those who said that they had no difficulty with work-life balance were people who related this to the fact that their partner had a similarly demanding job (so wished to prioritise work to a similar extent):

> Yes, I find it easy—but I think that's because I have arranged my life to deal with the demands of academia. Partly also my family circumstances fit in, in that my partner is a teacher—and she's probably more manic about working in the evenings and at weekends than I am, so she's in no position to fall out about it, and actually it's more likely to be me that's saying, you know, 'Can we go for a walk now?' at the weekends.
> (professor, mid-career, male, new university)

> . . . I am quite lucky, in that my partner has to take work home as well, so we both spend some of our evenings working, and if that wasn't the case I think it would be difficult. It is difficult to switch off sometimes.
> (lecturer, early career, female, new university)

But the largest group (about half of those who said they found work-life balance unproblematic) attributed their positive attitude to the flexibility of the academic job (which allowed them to avoid clashes between personal life and work, because work could be shifted to evenings or weekends, allowing time for dentists' appointments, child-care or other personal matters to be carried out during the conventional working week). It was noticeable that more of these people were situated in old universities than in new ones:

> Well, it's easier than some professions anyway, in that if there's a crisis of some sort at home, you can just say 'I'm not giving my lectures' and you can go and deal with it.

Or you can take the kids to school, and pick them up, because you can organise your timetable to allow that, normally. So that's the good side. And one often works at weekends and in the evenings—that's one of the things I like about the job. If I have a paper to do and yet I want to take the children to the seaside or whatever, you can go off and take them to the seaside and then just work late or at some other time. So you can shift your work around like that.
(senior lecturer, mid-career, male, old university)

... in the main, I think it's been fine, because the university's fairly understanding of how we work—you're not necessarily expected to keep particular hours. Provided that you're delivering teaching and research, they're reasonably happy about how you structure your life. I think the hardest thing is that my wife also works at the university, but she's an administrator ... and my time is much more flexible than hers ... I can take time off when I want, when it's convenient for me, but she can't ... if I feel like working at the weekend, I do, and then I take compensatory time, whereas my wife can't ...
(lecturer, early career, male, old university)

However, about a quarter of the group who identified themselves as finding work-life balance unproblematic specifically drew attention to the ambiguous nature of the flexibility which they associated with being a legal academic, in that, while it allowed them to avoid problems with work-life balance, it was also associated with the all-pervasive nature of academic work. These respondents were aware of the problems of indeterminacy associated with being a legal academic, but appeared to be able to overcome those problems in a way which they found satisfactory:

Work is always there—I mean, it's never ended, is it? There's always work. So that's the down-side of it, I suppose, that there are always unfinished bits of it—it's sort of endless, really, isn't it? There's so many things that you want to do. But I think it's a big plus that you are flexible.
(senior lecturer, mid-career, male, old university)

I suppose I *could* feel that I should work all the time, and that's a disadvantage of academic life—even though you can organise your time flexibly you might feel 'I should be working now' on a Saturday—I mean, I don't at the moment, because I feel I've worked very hard this year, so I don't feel guilty if I head off somewhere on Friday and don't come back till Monday. I feel I deserve that. But if I was working in a more competitive place, say in a competitive university in London, where I've heard that it's very competitive, where someone's breathing down your neck all the time to get articles out, where you're trying to better yourself all the time, then—well, I suppose I'd have to say I'm not interested in that, I don't want that, you know; I wouldn't want to work at the expense of a personal life ...
(lecturer, early career, female, old university)

I do balance it, but only because I'm absolutely ruthless in terms of what I will do and what I won't do. I do find it difficult. I mean, I think to be a success in modern academia, you are expected to work eighteen hours a day, every day, seven days a week. Now I take the view that I'm simply not paid enough to live my life in that way, and although I love my job, I don't love it that much, so I work a good day, if I've got something to do the next day then I'll work in the evening, if I haven't, then I feel no

obligation to work late. I work longer hours than most people in normal jobs, and that's fine for me. But I think there's certainly pressure that you should be working all the time. And I think if you feel that pressure, if you're not prepared to say 'Well I'm not playing that game,' I think for someone who has ambition it must be impossible to balance work and life. But then maybe ambitious people don't have such a problem, because they prioritise work above life anyway. As far as I'm concerned, I work in order to enjoy my life, and so I won't let work take over to such a great extent ... If it gets too much, I'll just turn round and say 'Sod it. I'll be a gardener.' But I think a lot of people feel under more pressure than that.
(lecturer, early career, female, old university)

The importance of flexibility to legal academics was pointed up by Leighton et al, who found in their survey of law teachers that 88 per cent of their respondents regarded the opportunity for flexible working as an 'important' or 'essential' aspect of the job (Leighton et al, 1995: 56). This was particularly true for female respondents—but, as Collier argues, there is growing reason to believe that the physical and psychological costs of academic life bear particularly heavily on women (Collier, 2002: 21).

Problems with Work-Life Balance

Turning to the other half of the respondents, those who found maintaining work-life balance problematic fell into two categories. Half of these people found the workload so great that it did not allow them to maintain what they regarded as an appropriate balance between work and other activities:

It *is* time-consuming—that is, if you want to do everything that you are expected to do, and do it properly. It's a huge task. It means that you have to work extra hours, in the evenings and at weekends.
(professor, mid-career, male, old university)

I'd be a liar if I said it was easy ... One of the attractions is the sense that you can manage and control your own time, traditionally, to a certain extent. But the danger with that, of course, is that it washes too easily into what you might call your private life, if you are not careful. What's the commonest thing to find in prefaces to books? The apology to the wife/partner/children/dog that you neglected while this manuscript was being completed. It's almost invariable. It's not easy. I'd like to think I know when it is all getting too much. But I'm not sure that if it was getting too much I'd go and take a holiday or watch a film or do some gardening. I hope that I get it right ... [The problem is] that the work never stops in one way. There is always something you could be doing. That's the real problem.
(senior lecturer, experienced, male, new university)

The remaining half of this group of respondents found work-life balance problematic because for them, academia is in the nature of a vocation. The resulting effect on their lives was similar to the previous group of respondents, in that work permeated the majority of their existence:

> No I don't. I think that being an academic is a vocation, and a consequence of that is that you become obsessive about it. So you never really leave your work behind . . . I'm constantly thinking about [my area of law] in some way or another . . . and that can be boring for the people I live with. It's useful to have your reveries punctured by people making domestic demands on you. I think if I lived on my own, I'd turn into some sort of nutcase. Although, of course, domestic commitments prevent you pursuing things . . .
> (professor, mid-career, male, old university)

> . . . I find that my academic work leaks into my evenings and weekends, in a way which is quite disconcerting for those around me, in that I'm constantly thinking about it. I do find it difficult to take a weekend off, not to do academic work at all, unless I have specifically arranged to go somewhere in advance and do something specific. So I do in some respects feel 'on call' . . . in some respects it does take over . . . I actually have to impose space, rather than that happening naturally.
> (Lecturer, early career, female, new university)

The nature of academia as vocation was also stressed by two respondents who said that they could not divide their lives up into 'work' and 'life', because it was a meaningless division for them:

> I don't accept the distinction between your job and the rest of your life, and I never have done. It's not what I've aimed for. I believe . . . things should be a whole, and I think it is possible to integrate . . . there's a continuum between everything that's done. I think academic life—probably particularly academic life—demands huge amounts of time from you . . . but I don't think it's about balancing demands, I think it's about this being the thing that most interests me.
> (professor, experienced, male, old university)

> Academia really *is* my life—it's perhaps part of the nature of the job that you perhaps don't need to make such a separation. I have however in recent years been conscious that it can come to dominate too much, and I think it's important that people have time that isn't determined by the academic agenda. Some people may disagree about that, but I try to have one day a week that's my own, in the sense that I don't do university work . . .
> (professor, experienced, male, old university)

Similar beliefs about the nature of academia were also mentioned by two other individuals in the course of talking about work-life balance:

> I never stop, actually, and that's a problem. I read from the first thing in the morning to the last thing at night. I think that's the problem, really, there's no end. It's very difficult to be disciplined enough to stop. And I think that probably ties in with the fact that academia's a vocation, rather than just an ordinary job, and that it's something that you feel you've devoted your life to, scholarship and the pursuit of knowledge. So I guess it becomes a seamless web, and your whole existence . . .
> (lecturer, early career, male, old university)

> I'm not very good at taking holidays. We have a cottage, which is lovely, and we go there quite a lot. But part of the quid pro quo, of course, is that we always take work with us. The result is, of course, that I actually very rarely, except possibly at Christmas, take more than a couple of days off at a time. I don't work full-time when

I'm at the cottage—but that's interesting, actually, because . . . I used to be able to stick to my thing of working in the morning and taking off in the afternoon. Quite often now, the morning will extend to 1.30, and then I'll do another couple of hours in the afternoon . . . So I suppose, to answer your question, it's hard to balance, and if I didn't love the job so much, it would really get on my nerves. If I was less research-obsessed, it would get me down.
(professor, experienced, female, old university)

Commenting upon the difficulties which accompany the indeterminacy of the academic job, Collier argues that the model of academic performativity which now takes precedence in academia is premised on what can be seen as '. . . distinctly masculinised forms of labour' and that it is in relation to issues of work-life balance that the implications of the masculinisation of academia is most marked. The dominant culture produces '. . . a self-surveilling performative self on the part of the academic' (Collier, 2002: 20). Clearly, the achievement of an acceptable work-life balance in this situation is very difficult.

However, Bradney's view of the difficulties inherent in the indeterminacy of the academic job are somewhat different. Bradney acknowledges the danger that in the light of the analysis put forward by some commentators, talking about the academic job in terms of a unity of 'vocation' and 'avocation' (ie, doing what one loves) may be seen as '. . . no more than a romantic piece of false consciousness, a whimsical affectation that fails to address the less than pleasant realities of everyday academic life' (Bradney, 2003: 195). Nevertheless, even while acknowledging that 'universities and their law schools are sometimes clearly exploitative', Bradney urges us to conceptualise the debate in different terms. The life of an academic, in his view, should be a seamless whole. This means there will be times when domesticity prevails, or when the demands of creativity (or more mundane academic tasks) take precedence. What matters is that, in the final analysis, work-life balance should be a matter of individual choice; the important thing, in Bradney's view, is to ensure that we have the kind of law schools where such choices are possible (Bradney, 2003: 203).

The decisions made by individuals about the maintenance of work-life balance in their lives are personal ones. However, it is clear from the data which I gathered that it is an issue which is intimately connected with the culture of academic law, and the ways in which legal academics construct their professional identities.

CONCLUSION

Overall, legal academics are very positive about their choice of career. They are proud to be doing this job, and that feeling of satisfaction is based on a value-judgement—that it is a 'worthwhile' way in which to spend their lives. As with all academics (Henkel, 2000), autonomy was a key part of professional identity, as was the importance attached to the ability to carry out *both* teaching *and* research. Legal academics share with others in the academy a strong dislike of things which impinge on their autonomy ('bureaucracy', 'audit', 'accountability') and they also expressed worries about changes in the culture resulting in feelings of increased 'pressure'.

This chapter has provided detailed insights into the perceptions of legal academics about the lived experience of being part of the 'academic tribe' of law. It provides additional evidence for the thesis which has begun to emerge from the data that the culture of academic law and the professional identities of academic lawyers, are more closely bound up with the other tribes which inhabit the academy than might otherwise have been thought.

6

Teaching and Research in the Legal Academy

BOTH TEACHING AND research lie at the heart of the culture of academic law and are examples *par excellence* of the 'lived experience' of legal academics. Teaching is about students learning to construct knowledge in the context of a particular culture (Le Brun and Johnstone, 1994: 71–75). As an activity, teaching is also an important part of the professional identities of academic lawyers. Le Brun and Johnstone write that their book about teaching law is '. . . about some of the dilemmas we face and decisions we take about the directions we take in our lives' (1994: 400). Yet research has traditionally been seen as the high point of the culture of academia; the university is '. . . the key knowledge institution of society' (Scott, 1984: 21). Research is also fundamental to our understanding of 'who we are' as legal academics (Jenkins, 1996: 4), and therefore also a key component of professional identity. 'The disinterested pursuit of knowledge is the highest achievement of the academic, and that which differentiates him or her from the other knowledge mongers' (Kogan and Henkel, 1992: 112). Barnett captures particularly well the way in which research has traditionally related to both culture and identity. 'Research is the fulcrum of the academic community. It is the point on which the academic community turns, and it is by their research performance that academics take on their professional identity and are judged by their peers' (Barnett, 1990: 135).

A great deal has been written about many aspects of teaching and research, both as they exist in the university as a whole, and as they are played out in law schools. I do not propose to replay the well-known debates, but rather to try and uncover the place of teaching and research in the culture of academic law, and in the construction of the professional identities of legal academics.

TEACHING

All except one of the legal academics I interviewed said that they enjoyed teaching. Reasons for enjoying teaching were variously expressed, but centred on the satisfaction gained from helping students to learn, especially when academics could sense excitement or enthusiasm on the part of the students:

> I suppose it's the sense of achievement when you come away from a class and you have managed to convey something to students that they might not otherwise have understood. Or you might have got students interested in a subject that they previously might have found boring.
> (lecturer, early career, female, new university)
>
> ... I enjoy it when the penny's actually dropped with somebody—it can take a long time, but it's worth it.
> (professor, experienced, male, new university)
>
> ... I love teaching first years, there's a real naïvete, a fresh-facedness, which is engaging. Also, their minds are much more pliable. Provided you put it in suitable terms, they can engage with the most phenomenally complex things. Second years, in some ways, are the most difficult to teach. Something happens to them in the summer—they're the most bolshy. Third years I find very engaging—I find most third years are pretty good lawyers by then, and intellectually the most engaging ...
> (reader, mid-career, male, old university)
>
> ... And I do, in the end, think it changes lives. I model my teaching on the best teacher I had in my law degree, who was a real mentor to me—it was just terrific. So I know how I responded to her, and I'd like students to respond to me that way.
> (principal lecturer, experienced, female, new university)

Despite saying that they enjoyed teaching, several respondents said that they disliked teaching the same subject repeatedly to a large number of small groups:

> For the most part, I do enjoy teaching. But I don't enjoy having ten groups in the same subject, because there are only certain ways you can cut the tutorial—there are certain topics that have to be dealt with, and only a certain limited number of ways you can do it—so I feel people who get me late in the cycle suffer ...
> (senior lecturer, experienced, male, old university)

Several others drew attention to the stress involved in teaching:

> It's quite stressful—often just the stress of spontaneity in face-to-face contact, or it's the worry 'I'm going to get caught out,' not knowing something—and I know it's silly, and I know it's actually ok—you can't know everything, and it's not a good thing to convey the impression that you ought to know everything, but ...
> (lecturer, early career, male, old university)
>
> Lecturing is daunting—Equity is perceived as boring, so I have a 'difficult' group, and I have to discipline them like a school teacher—and you are very conscious of them looking at you, and you wonder whether they're thinking about what you've got on, your clothes ...
> (lecturer, mid-career, female, new university)
>
> I find it hard work. I'm always conscious that I could do it better. I don't think that I'm as good a teacher yet as I want to be. I've had no training, so I'm always conscious that I could probably be an awful lot better if I ever had any time to do some training to help me to be better. So in some senses I find it frustrating.
> (lecturer, early career, female, old university)
>
> [I don't enjoy it if I've given a bad lecture]. I get quite upset about it, when I feel I was rambling on, and I didn't have a grasp of my subject, and somehow the students

weren't interested. It actually happened in a lecture yesterday—a few students walked out—it was the end of the course, so it was just an overview lecture, and maybe they just weren't interested, but I took it personally, and I was not very happy . . .
(reader, experienced, male, old university)

Overall, two-thirds of the respondents liked both lecturing and small-group teaching, with the remaining third split evenly between those who preferred lecturing and those who preferred teaching small groups. These preferences were more marked in old universities, where nearly three-quarters of respondents liked both forms of teaching. There were no significant differences in attitude related to experience or gender in either sector. Lectures and tutorials were seen as offering the opportunity to engage in different kinds of teaching activity, with the lecture characterised as a performance, a time to show off knowledge, or control the agenda:

I am an innate showman, so I do enjoy lecturing.
(professor, experienced, male, new university)

. . . as long as you've got a good rapport with your students, it's a fun fifty minutes. And I enjoy that—you know, we wouldn't be lawyers if we didn't like the sound of our own voices. It's just a bit of a giggle . . .
(lecturer, early career, female, old university)

. . . With land law, I enjoy making it clear and accessible, and interesting (as best I can). So, yes, I love it, because I get a lot of positive feedback from the students. But there is that whole power thing, you know, you're there holding forth, and you're in control, and you're controlling what goes on. It's very structured—I like that . . .
(principal lecturer, experienced, female, new university)

Tutorials, however, provided an opportunity for interaction with the students on a more individual basis. Several respondents mentioned that the experience of teaching tutorials could be quite extreme—in the sense that, because of their more intimate nature, they could provide a very positive teaching experience, or a very negative one. It was common for people to point out that the tutorial experience was heavily dependent on the students involved—if they are well-prepared and engaged, it tends to be more enjoyable than teaching silent groups where engagement is minimal:

Lectures are so boring—they're no fun for the person who's giving them or the students—just a mindless transfer of information from one person to another without either person thinking about it. I much prefer something with interaction, a session where you can actually see what the students have done, see how clearly they understand the subject, allow them to explore little points they spot for themselves.
(professor, experienced, male, new university)

. . . and tutorials, again it's a performance, but it's a much more intimate one, and you're much more able to give students individual guidance and really push things through. On the other hand, a bad lecture is just simply dull. A bad tutorial is excruciating, and that depends on the bunch of students you've got in the tutorial group. So tutorials can go from the 'Wow, what a great fifty minutes' to the 'Oh my God, I've got another forty nine minutes of this' . . .
(lecturer, early career, female, old university)

Student-centred learning was frequently perceived as the ultimate goal in tutorials, with respondents often referring to the satisfaction they felt if they could achieve this, or their frustration if it did not take place:

> I like teaching very much, particularly small-group teaching. Because of the interaction, and because I like tutorials to be student-led. I like it if I can get all the students to participate, at least to some degree. You can really get quite a dialogue going. Sometimes in a really good group, I can sit back and let them engage in the debate . . .
> (reader, experienced, male, old university)

> I really enjoy lecturing, and I really don't enjoy doing tutorials—I find them really hard to co-ordinate. Whatever the skill is of being a good tutorial leader (and probably a good interviewer, actually), I don't have it. I find that when asking a question, I sort of have the answer in the back of my head, and if people don't give me the answer I'm expecting to hear, I sort of steer them round to it. I find it very hard to get that situation where a conversation is going on, and you just withdraw and let the students talk and think 'Well, this is brilliant.' It's happened once or twice, but apart from that, I find tutorials really hard work . . .
> (lecturer, early career, male, old university)

It is well-known that universities tend to under-value the teaching function of academics (Becher and Kogan, 1992: 114). Nevertheless, teaching remains an important activity for academic lawyers. In this respect, legal academics are once more confirming their place within the mainstream of academic life. They are similar, for example, to the majority of respondents to Halsey's survey, who also placed considerable emphasis on the importance of teaching (Halsey, 1992: 187).

LECTURING AS PERFORMING

> In the pilot study for this project, so many of the respondents referred to lecturing in terms of 'performance' that I decide to explore this concept further. I asked whether the respondents would describe lecturing as 'performing' at all. They were unanimous in agreeing that lecturing could be characterised in this way, and proceeded to elaborate enthusiastically about why this is an apt description of the lecturing process:

> Yes—because all those people are staring at you, watching you do your thing.
> (lecturer, early career, male, old university)

> . . . I still remember when I first became a university teacher, and went on a little course about university teaching, and I remember the research we had to read which said how the actor who knew nothing about the subject was rated much more highly by the students than the expert academic. And I've always had that in mind. There is a certain degree of performance involved . . .
> (reader, experienced, male, old university)

In many ways, the lecture appears to be the ultimate example of the 'impression management' thesis that Goffman put forward in *The Presentation of Self in Everyday Life* (originally published in America in 1959). A lecture theatre is certainly a social setting, in Goffman's terms, since it is a 'place surrounded by fixed barriers to perception in which a particular kind of activity regularly takes place' (Goffmann, 1990: 231). It is a highly artificial situation, in which one individual apparently controls the behaviour of many others; the conventions are such that the lecturer speaks, the audience listens (quietly or not, depending on the success of the performance).

Goffman suggests that if we are interested in analysing social life in terms of impression management, we should look at the techniques of impression management which are employed. In relation to lecturing, the 'setting', or the physical layout, decoration and so on of the lecture theatre (whose very name is associated with performance), is supplied with equipment such as white boards, overhead projectors and screens for powerpoint presentations, all of which assist the lecturer in presenting a picture of knowledgeable expert whose role is to transmit information, ideas and so on to the less knowledgeable audience. Sometimes, dramatic impact (and authority) is increased by the presence of a dais or raised platform for the lecturer to stand on, not to mention lecterns, spotlights and microphones:

> It has got everything to do with performance. I accept a lecture is not necessarily the best way of getting a lot of information across, but at its best it is unparalleled as a way of getting inspiration across, and that has always been my style of teaching. I don't honestly believe that any of us ever really effectively teaches anyone anything. What we do is enable them to teach themselves. That, at the higher education level, is what it's all about. So you inspire people, you make them interested, you make them say 'Good Heavens! He is interested in that, so why can't I be interested in that—I'll go off and read that' . . .
> (professor, experienced, male, new university)

The respondents in my study also drew attention in their responses to matters which Goffman characterised as 'personal front', ie '. . . the items that we most intimately identify with the performer himself . . .' (Goffman, 1990: 34). Included here are posture, speech patterns and bodily gestures, as well as manner—confident, amusing, boring and so on. 'If the individual's activity is to become meaningful to others, he must mobilise his activity so that it will express, during the interaction, what he wishes to convey' (Goffmann, 1990: 40). This aspect of the performance is particularly interesting, because respondents stressed that the reason they engage in performance in the context of a lecture is pedagogic:

> Oh, yes, I think it is a performance, really—especially to a big group. Less so with a small group, but I think you have to have a certain histrionic talent in order to hold the attention of 200 testosterone-charged first-year students, who aren't actually very interested in the doctrine of consideration. You've got to have a certain presence to get them listening—and interested, that's the more difficult bit, to get them interested in it.
> (lecturer, experienced, male, old university)

I'm afraid I do, yes, because I think it's an act. I believe that certainly you don't show what you feel, if you're upset, you don't tell them, you don't let it affect your performance in relation to the students, it's not fair on them. I mean my policy is to tell a lot of jokes, that sounds really pathetic, but there's that aspect, and I do think it's generally a performance, trying to give them silly little examples, especially in land law, to make the ideas accessible, so this is all a performance which is, I hate to say it, largely thought out beforehand, before one goes in. It's not a scripted performance, I don't tend to script things, but you sort of have in your mind various little stories to tell them, and it is a performance . . .
(lecturer, early career, female, new university)

A small minority of respondents stressed the dangers of getting too carried away with the idea of performance, at the expense of content:

I have thought a lot about this. I think if it is *just* performing then it's not very good, bluntly. Maybe just occasionally that's unfair. I am trying not to be too pious about this. Even if you avoid true performing you have to project. You have to be more of yourself than you normally are . . . It doesn't have to be complete performance. You have to project. It isn't just a conversation, is it? . . . I think you do get people who are just performers and just showmen. In some situations it might work, but I think you have got to be a little wary of them . . .
(principal lecturer, experienced, male, new university)

I would argue that lecturing falls into the category of performance which Goffman characterised as unproblematic in terms of dramatisation, since the act itself vividly conveys the qualities and attributes claimed by the performer (he instances policemen, prizefighters and surgeons) (Goffman, 1990: 41). The very act of 'lecturing'—appearing on the dais, delivering a formal speech, filled with considerable amounts of technical 'jargon', accompanied by explanatory handouts or powerpoint slides, tells the audience that they are dealing with a legal expert here. It is a self-conscious act on the part of the lecturer:

Lecturing *is* performing—in the sense of 'being on stage'—you've got an audience, and it has to be perfect—you can't afford to slip up.
(lecturer, mid-career, female, new university)

I like the lecture, because it does give the opportunity for a performance, because you can think about what you're going to do and how you're going to do it, you can concentrate on extracting some kind of reaction from the class. I find it quite fascinating to watch the lecture group as a whole and see what they're responding to and what they're not responding to. I think a good lecture should be a good performance with a serious purpose.
(professor, mid-career, male, old university)

Several respondents noted that the ability to perform was very much part of their professional identity as lecturers, though not of what they regarded as their 'personal' identity. This aspect of being a law lecturer is not only a good example of Judith Butler's ideas of 'performativity' (Butler, 1999), it is also an aspect of Hall's 'identification', the idea of identity as a construction, a process never completed, but always 'in process' (Hall, 1996: 2). Identity, in this view, depends upon context; it is inevitably constructed within a particular culture. Here, in the context of the university and the law school, people construct an identity for themselves as 'law lecturer'—which they then abandon in other contexts:

> Yes, it is a form of performance. One way you try and make lectures less boring is by sticking in a little bit of repartee, just so there is an amusing moment whereby the students can actually remember a point that you're trying to make. So to that extent, yes. I'm absolutely hopeless at that sort of thing, but it's certainly a performance—and strangely, it's a professional performance, in that you just walk in and do it as if it's water off a duck's back—but then if you're asked by your best friend to be best man at his wedding and you have to stand up in front of an equally large number of people—I just remember how frightening that was. You sort of think to yourself, 'Don't be stupid, you stand up and talk to people every day of the week'—but it's not the same.
> (professor, experienced, male, new university)

> Definitely a performance, yes, definitely. I think I'm a completely different person when I'm in a lecture theatre. I sort of think it's not really me. A lot of my friends, who I grew up with, say 'I can't believe you do that sort of thing, that's not you, you're quiet and sort of academic-y, you don't go and talk to 150 people for 50 minutes'—but I do. So yes, because I'm not really that outspoken, or particularly extrovert, or even really that confident. So yes, I do feel I become a different person, and it is a performance. I feel I have to at least project a kind of image of being confident and knowing what I'm talking about, I kind of make sure that the students are confident that I know what I'm talking about.
> (lecturer, early career, female, old university)

> Yes, I think it is. I think it all comes down to preparation beforehand. I'm not naturally gregarious, so I need to have the confidence that I have prepared beforehand, even though I won't read it, I'll know what I'm going to say. And of course, that's something that's terribly time-consuming, but that's time that I'll put in, because it's too frightening to me to be unprepared—it's a bit like learning the lines beforehand.
> (lecturer, early career, female, old university)

> Yes, when I'm lecturing, I suppose it doesn't actually come naturally to me; it does to some people, but it doesn't come naturally to me, talking in that way to a huge number of people. And I feel I have to be a bit of an actress, so it's not quite [me], it's being [me] in that role ...
> (professor, exper.ienced, female, old university)

It is noticeable that the law lecture has in common with the theatrical performance an element of contrived spontaneity. There were many comments, both explicitly, and by implication, which showed the value that academic lawyers place on giving a 'natural' performance in a lecture, in the sense that any suggestion that a lecturer would merely read out a set of notes was dismissed out of hand:

> ... when I'm preparing lectures, I put as much effort into the style of the presentation, and the way the presentation's done, as into the content of the presentation. Because I've always felt that you could be the best lecturer in the world in terms of knowledge,

> but if the students aren't listening to you, you're wasting your time. So what you've got to do *is* like performing, you've got to get the audience to pay attention to you, ... I know when I was an undergraduate I had some brilliant teachers, who I didn't learn anything from, simply because they stood and read from a text—and I wasn't listening to them.
> (lecturer, early career, male, old university)

> ... the last thing you want as a student is somebody who literally comes into the room and just appears to be reading from a set of notes, doesn't really look up, doesn't digress. So, yes, I think there is a performance element to it, certainly.
> (lecturer, early career, male, new university)

> Oh, well, yes, if it's me you're asking, I think it's highly theatrical. For me—well, I'd never look at a video of me lecturing, because I might flail my arms about, I might pause for effect to make a point, and also, because I have been lectured to or been to speakers who've been very unanimated, very monotonous, and I struggled, even if I was particularly interested in the topic...
> (lecturer, early career, male, new university)

The fact that some legal academics had trained as lawyers was also not far away from this discussion. One respondent told a story, illustrating how he had used his rhetorical powers (given additional weight by his former incarnation as a solicitor) to persuade his students that they were really interested in conveyancing (which, as a property-law subject, falls within a group of subjects commonly characterised as 'boring' by students):

> My first conveyancing lecture, a few weeks ago, I decided I'd follow the example of my external examiner. He said to me 'I don't know why students find conveyancing so dull, but they always do. I start off by going in to the first lecture, and telling them what a wonderful subject conveyancing is, and how exciting it is to be able to do it and learn about it.' So I thought I would try that for once. And I found myself putting on a good performance, which I thoroughly enjoyed, saying how good it was to do conveyancing, how it was really the most useful thing possible for the students to learn, it was their passport to a really happy and successful life as a solicitor—I was astonished at the end of the hour to find that they'd all believed me...
> (lecturer, mid-career, male, new university)

Another respondent explained that lecturing gave her the chance to be like the barrister she might have been, had her financial circumstances been different:

> I think it's a big act, and this is why when I said to you earlier that I wanted to be a barrister, in some senses it's the next best thing, because it's all part of the same performance...
> (principal lecturer, experienced, female, new university)

Characterisation of lecturing as 'performing' is not a completely original idea. Evans, in *English People*, notes the element of 'theatrical display' in lecturing (Evans, 1993: 55). What is interesting, however, is the wholehearted enthusiasm with which legal academics agree that lecturing can be characterised as 'performing', and the ways in which they can articulate precisely the techniques they use to give the illusion of a 'natural' performance (an achievement which is highly valued), whether it is their use of rhetoric or humour, or their sensitivity to the reaction of the 'audience'. Arguably, this is discipline-related; Morison and Leith's analysis of *The Barrister's World*, for example, while stressing that oratory is not as prominent in barristers' working lives as might appear from the media, nevertheless provides plenty of examples of 'performance' in relation not only to court appearances, but to other aspects of a barrister's professional life, such as negotiation (Morison and Leith, 1992: 121–32). Aspects of 'performance' in the legal profession are not confined to the court; as Goodrich has pointed out, the pronouncements of judges set out in the case reports with which many academic lawyers work so frequently are shot through with rhetorical devices (Goodrich, 1986). My data suggests that performance is a fundamental aspect of the culture of academic law and 'being a good performer' is a major part of the professional identities of academic lawyers.

TEACHING AS PART OF PROFESSIONAL IDENTITY

Overall, being a good teacher is an important part of the professional identities of legal academics. When I asked them 'Is it important to you to be a good teacher?' they all said yes, although about 10 per cent qualified that by saying that it wasn't as important to them as being a good researcher; this latter group were mostly situated in old universities, these responses reflecting the former binary divide in the higher education sector (Fulton, 1996):

> The day I cease to be a good teacher is the day I'll want to get out.
> (professor, experienced, male, new university)

> Yes, I'd be happy if I was a better teacher than I am. And I would be very unhappy if I was not a competent teacher. And if I have a class that goes badly, I feel miserable afterwards, though I don't let it stay with me. And if I have a class that goes well, I feel quite elated. So it's important for me to be a really professional, competent teacher. But if you asked me with my hands on my heart is it as important to me as it is to be a really excellent researcher, the honest answer is no.
> (professor, experienced, female, old university)

Teaching was seen as an important part of professional identity not only in new universities, where some respondents were not involved in research, giving the teaching role primacy, but across both sectors and all levels of experience:

> I think it is an important part of my own self-image. I'd think if I suddenly wasn't [a good teacher], it would be very difficult for me . . .
> (principal lecturer, experienced, male, new university)

> It's very important—because I'm not doing research at the moment, so I feel I'm a teacher . . .
> (lecturer, mid-career, female, new university)

> Yes it is. Partly, I'd feel I was really failing in my job if I wasn't giving the students something to take away.
> (lecturer, early career, male, old university)

The ability to teach was seen as an important part of professional competence; respondents said how upset they felt if teaching did not go well, and they emphasised how unpleasant it would be to be perceived as a bad teacher by students:

> Fairly important, I think, though no more than fairly. I think I would be absolutely gutted if students said 'God, no, she's absolutely dreadful, she doesn't know her subject, and she can't put any of it across to us' . . . I know that you're not going to please everyone, I don't have a problem with that, but if there was a general consensus among the students that I was just absolutely hopeless, I would be pretty devastated.
> (lecturer, early career, female, new university)

> For me, it is important. I mean, I'd be alarmed if I didn't have student questionnaires with a range of reasonably favourable comments. I'd be worried if I was seen by students as not being a good teacher, and I'm probably inordinately pleased when I'm seen by students as being a good teacher. I take great pleasure in the favourable comments on student feedback.
> (professor, experienced, male, old university)

The positive attitudes towards teaching displayed by legal academics should give heart to those commentators who have expressed some concerns about the attitudes of legal academics to teaching. Webb, for example, has characterised the quality of legal education as being a largely 'hit and miss' affair, plagued by uncertainty on the part of law teachers about both their functions and their methods (Webb, 1996: 24). Elsewhere, I have myself expressed concerns about the apparent disinterest on the part of law teachers in underpinning their teaching with knowledge of educational theory or philosophy (Cownie, 1999). Enthusiasm about being a good teacher cannot fully address such concerns, but it can provide some grounds for optimism that calls for improvement in the teaching of academic law may not go entirely unheeded.

THE INSTITUTIONAL ATTITUDE TO TEACHING

Being a good teacher was an important part of the professional identity of academic lawyers, regardless of the fact that when I asked whether they thought good teaching was valued by their institution, half of the respondents thought that it was not. The distribution of opinion about institutional attitudes to teaching were markedly different as between old and new universities, with two-thirds of respondents working in old universities saying they did not feel that teaching was valued by the institution, while the position was reversed in new universities, with more than two-thirds of respondents there saying they thought their institution did value teaching. Institutional attitudes to teaching thus provide another example of different cultures operating in old and new universities.

Where respondents felt good teaching *was* valued by their institution, this was based on a range of criteria, including allocation of resources to teaching initiatives, inclusion of teaching in promotion criteria, and emphasis by the institution on staff joining the Institute of Learning and Teaching (a factor only mentioned by respondents working in new universities). Even among those who felt teaching was valued, there was, however, a considerable degree of cynicism:

> I think it is, but I think that sometimes the way people try to show it is counterproductive, because they sort of rub people up the wrong way. At the moment there's this, what is it called, Institute for Learning and Teaching. I think people think they are being coerced into it, and it's another thing that seems to involve filling in a lot of very complicated forms, seemingly for no obvious purpose. If that is supposed to show how important teaching is, I don't think it's a very constructive way of doing it.
> (principal lecturer, mid-career, male, new university)

> ... More money has been put into it. There has been more attempt to get teaching quality enhancement funds pushed around. There's an institution called the Teacher Fellow that they have set up, to give parity of esteem to people who are heavily committed to research in teaching, as well as the practice, so that's good ... but I honestly wonder how much importance has been given to it over the years compared with other things that bring in money.
> (principal lecturer, experienced, male, new university)

> I think the institution does value good teaching. The problem is, the institution values umpteen other things as well, and you're subject to constantly conflicting demands and pressures ...
> (professor, experienced, male, new university)

> I think it does, though I think what they value more is pass rates, to be honest. If you can get the students to pass, and obviously the better the marks, the better it is. They value that, but I am not sure they look at how you get them there. It doesn't matter how you've taught them, as long as you get the result ...
> (lecturer, early career, female, new university)

> It is very important, but that's because of the QAA rating system, and league tables. I think it's probably more important to the institution now that there are these league tables than it was when I started, when it tended to be assumed that it was something you'd pick up, and if you didn't, then it didn't really matter. The culture has definitely changed.
> (reader, experienced, male, old university)

Respondents generally looked to the reward system, in terms of promotion, for evidence as to whether teaching is valued. Where respondents felt that teaching was not valued, they pointed to the fact that promotion is based solely on research criteria:

> It's valued on paper, they send all the development stuff round, they reinforce various best practices, they require a lot of paperwork to be churned out to prove that you're doing best practice, but when you look at promotions—it's all based on research. When you look at the people who are fingered as being better or worse—it's always based on research. So the priorities, in practice, are all geared towards research. I mean, look at the examples of the senior members of staff here—they're all researchers, not teachers.
> (lecturer, early career, male, old university)

> It's not particularly important—because the emphasis is on research, and it doesn't matter how good you are on teaching, it's what you've done on the research front that'll make the difference.
> (senior lecturer, experienced, male, old university)

> Yes, it is formally rated equally with research in terms of promotion to a principal lectureship. That's the formal situation, and certainly we've had people who've got promotion on the basis of being good teachers and good administrators. The reality, however, is that you stand a better chance, I think, of success, if you can also present yourself with some decent publications.
> (professor, experienced, male, new university)

Several respondents pointed out that although teaching is not valued, this did not mean you could be a bad teacher. Bad teaching, it was felt, might hold up promotion, or lead the institution to impose other pressure to try and achieve improvement:

> It's fairly obvious that it's not as important as research. As far as I can work out, in terms of promotion, the emphasis is on research . . . If you want to be a senior lecturer, I'm sure bad teaching would hold you up to some extent, but not that dramatically.
> (lecturer, early career, male, old university)

> No, you don't have to be a good teacher, but you have to be an acceptable teacher. Certainly I never get the impression that institutionally teaching is a priority—it's very, very much a research-led institution. But I do honestly think that if you weren't a good teacher, somebody somewhere would show concern about it.
> (lecturer, early career, male, old university)

Other respondents emphasised the difference between institutional rhetoric and reality, and the element of lip-service involved:

> . . . I think a lot of the right noises are made about the importance of teaching, but ultimately we're looking to other concerns of universities.
> (lecturer, early career, male, old university)

> . . . there's lip-service paid to the importance of teaching, but I think everybody understands that it's your research output that will determine how long you will be on lecturer A or lecturer B and so on.
> (lecturer, early career, male, old university)

> Not at all. They have an approach which is the following: that you mustn't be a bad teacher, but actually striving for excellence in teaching (I mean, this is my take, they would deny this)—striving for excellence in teaching isn't much rewarded. Provided the students don't complain too much—nothing is done.
> (reader, mid-career, male, old university)

As far as the culture of law schools is concerned, teaching appears to be very important for the professional identities of individual academics, with many putting considerable emphasis on their need to be 'good teachers'. However, institutionally, in old universities particularly, teaching was not valued in terms of promotion. Even in new universities, where teaching was seen as valued, respondents commented that good teaching could only get you so far up the promotion ladder—to a principal lectureship; after that, research or going into management were generally seen as the routes to a chair. Evidence from the US would suggest that such cynicism is probably well-founded. Academics in the US have been subject to prolonged pressure from both legislators and students to devote increased time and effort to teaching, but a recent survey conducted by the Carnegie Foundation for the Evaluation of Teaching found that research remains the path to promotion (Huber et al, 1997).

RESEARCH IN THE LEGAL ACADEMY

Turning to research, I asked the respondents whether they were involved in research, and if so, whether they enjoyed it. In old universities, all the respondents were involved in research, and all except one person said they enjoyed doing research. In new universities, two-thirds of the respondents were involved in research; they all enjoyed it. There were slightly more men than women in this group. This result was not surprising; in one new university, the majority of respondents told me that they thought some women in their department were unfairly burdened with administration, to the extent that research became an impossibility for them; this particular institution providing an example, *par excellence,* of Margaret Thornton's thesis that women academics are accepted in law schools provided that they play a 'handmaiden' role (1996: 112); Celia Wells' study of women law professors also confirmed that women believe that they take on more pastoral work in law schools, not only because staff and students think this is something women do better than men, but because women themselves appear to take these roles more seriously than men do (Wells, 2002: 16). However, in the other two new universities in my study, this gender difference was not so marked.

Reasons for enjoying research were varied; the most common was that it offered the possibility of satisfying intellectual curiosity:

> Yes, because you learn more. Probably the only things I do research on are the things I don't know about, and I want to know more about. And I think that's probably the most fortunate aspect of being an academic. In very few other jobs do you get just to pursue your intellectual curiosity . . .
> (senior lecturer, mid-career, female, old university)

> . . . I think the best thing is being able to set up a project myself, follow it through, and also to be able to discuss it with colleagues, and get feedback on it, in a fairly supportive structure . . .
> (lecturer, early career, female, new university)

> . . . I enjoy particularly something that's totally new, or I'll enjoy exploring *why* they're doing this, what they say they're doing, and whether the rules do what they say they do or something else. I enjoy looking at the way certain cases make one rethink what the system's meant to be doing, and where it fits.
> (senior lecturer, experienced, male, old university)

I like finding out things I don't know—a sense of the curious, I suppose.
(senior lecturer, experienced, male, old university)

Others expressed their enjoyment in terms of complete enthusiasm for the business of research:

It is the most important thing to me personally—the reason why I get out of bed in the morning. I wouldn't want to do purely research and no teaching, I think that would lead to a hermit-like existence, but purely in terms of my personal motivation and so on, research is the most important thing—I mean, it's what I'd do anyway, even if I wasn't paid for it.
(principal lecturer, mid-career, male, new university)

Truthfully, if I couldn't do it, I'd just leave academia—I may as well go off and be a solicitor . . .
(lecturer, early career, female, new university)

. . . there's nothing I enjoy so much as being at home with my books, and going to conferences is great, and I love writing, I love finding out new things, it's a pleasure, it's not a drudge at all . . .
(principal lecturer, experienced, female, new university)

A few respondents also drew attention to the hard work involved in research:

I do enjoy it. I enjoy reading, and I enjoy trying to think though problems. I find writing very hard—the actual setting-down. I don't know whether I'm a bit of a perfectionist, but it takes me a very long time to actually write up articles. And I find that quite difficult, the actual sitting down and writing. But thinking up ideas and reading works of scholarship and just thinking about them, I enjoy all those aspects.
(lecturer, early career, female, old university)

I enjoy it like I enjoy going for a run—in terms of, when I'm actually doing it most of the time I'm thinking 'What on earth am I doing? This is really hurting me.' But I can see the benefits of it, and I get a buzz having done it. But it can be an incredibly painful process.
(lecturer, early career, male, old university)

It's very painful at times, and it's the most difficult part of the job, but I do enjoy it. It's intellectually demanding—it's the struggle to develop original ideas, hopefully at a reasonably high level, within a reasonably short time-frame—because you never quite have the time to let those ideas really develop. Writing is difficult; trying to write really well is very hard work—I write and re-write and write and re-write—and one still ends up not happy with it. And the amount of material that's out there seems to grow and grow, and to keep on top of what's going on is one of the most stressful aspects of research.
(lecturer, early career, female, old university)

As Becher and Trowler note, it is a common finding of studies which examine the motivation of academic researchers that a prime motivating factor is the desire to develop a reputation in their field and to contribute significantly to it (Becher and Trowler, 2001: 75). Research is, for many academics, a key part of the 'psychological contract' which underpins their job (Murlis and Hartle, 1996:

48). Given that the majority of respondents were involved in research, their enthusiasm for the pursuit of knowledge about law also has implications for the culture of the discipline; it is '. . . inquiry, not income generation [that] is the essential business of the law school' (Brownsword, 1996: 2).

THE RAE EFFECT

One of the changes in academic life most remarked upon by the respondents (and discussed in the next chapter) is the increasingly important place of research in the culture of academic law. Many respondents attributed this to the effect of the RAE. There has been considerable criticism of the RAE, and particularly its effects on individual academics (Talib, 2001). On the other hand, there are those who point out that in the discipline of law, the RAE has also had the (desirable) effect of increasing the emphasis upon research and enabling law as a discipline to move further towards the centre of the academy (Bradney, 2003: 186).

I was interested, therefore, to explore the attitudes of my respondents to the RAE. I asked those who said that they carried out research (all of the respondents in old universities and two-thirds of those working in new universities) whether the RAE had affected their research at all, and if so, how that effect had worked out. Overall, two-thirds of the research-active respondents said that their research had been affected by the existence of the RAE. Nearly all the relevant respondents working in new universities agreed that this was the case, but only about half of the respondents working in old universities did so. Within old university law schools, it was noticeable that early-career academics were three times as likely to say that the RAE had affected their research as academics at other stages of their careers. Women were twice as likely as men to say that their research had been affected by the RAE, with virtually all the women regarding their research as having been affected, but only half the men doing so. Many people described the RAE as an ever-present consideration when they were thinking about their research. The main effects, identified by about a third of the research-active respondents, were that the existence of the RAE affected where they published, the type of work they published, and that it provided a constant pressure to publish. The RAE is, of course, having the same sort of effects upon legal academics as it is upon other academics. Talib has documented the increasing pressures of the RAE, showing that the effects increase with every exercise (2001). Henkel comments that while at one level the RAE affirmed the centrality of research to academic identity, it went well beyond that, for research output was not merely part of the individual's struggle for recognition in the discipline and a major part of career advancement, but also became part of the collective departmental and institutional competition for reputation and resources (Henkel, 2000: 135). In terms of legal academics, my interviews confirmed Vick et al's findings that the RAE has particularly noticeable effects upon early career academics; they also noticed some differences in the effects upon male and female legal academics (Vick et al, 1998).

The need to publish research which satisfied RAE criteria (at least as perceived by those overseeing research in each department) meant that some respondents had changed the type of journals in which they published, largely abandoning publications primarily intended for legal practitioners in favour of refereed academic legal journals. There was also an increased emphasis on the production of monographs:

> I write for practitioners as my main research output . . . I was appointed on the basis of my professional links, but I'm not sure that I would have been able to start writing with the emphasis on professional links now. I see it as important as part of what I call the 'broad church' research profile—but I was told I had to be careful or a lot of my style of publication would not fall within the ambit of the RAE—to which my reply was 'I don't care', because I am in a position to say that. But it was very—one felt denigrated, and I felt not valued . . . I did give up one book purely because I was told the next edition would not count for RAE purposes. And I do regret that—because that book is on what is now a very popular topic . . . but, well, these things happen.
> (reader, experienced, male, old university)

> . . . there was more pressure to write things that were seen as capable of being submitted for the RAE, and less support for things that were clearly (or at least in the view of the people making the decision here) non-RAE-able . . .
> (lecturer, early career, male, new university)

> . . . I'm probably more likely to write a monograph than I once was, because it's seen as needed. And I think that's RAE-inspired. Undoubtedly the RAE has had an effect, because it's meant the research committee go round saying 'Well, what are you going to do?'—in a gentle kind of way, but they're making sure people are going to produce things. And I think I shall publish more in refereed journals, which I haven't really cared about, particularly. I wanted to write a monograph anyway, but I'm probably more likely to do it more quickly, to try and get it in for whenever the next RAE deadline is . . .
> (senior lecturer, mid-career, male, old university)

The increased emphasis on academic, rather than practitioner publications, is something which has also been noted by other commentators (see, eg, Hicks, 1995). Vick et al note a widespread belief among academic lawyers that the effect of the RAE has been to make writing for practitioners a 'second rank activity', and that '. . . there is a general perception that the law panel's assessment procedures are weighted against professional and legal practice publications . . .' (Vick et al, 1998: 558). The evidence from my interviews, together with the data from Vick et al's survey, underlines the academic drift within the discipline of law which I have identified at other stages of my analysis. Not all respondents were comfortable with this phenomenon:

> I think sometimes an unfortunate by-product is that whatever you think of black-letter analysis, there is a place for it within the law school, and I actually think the RAE has kind of downplayed the importance of that sort of research, so that there's a bit of a

snobby attitude towards anything that might be practitioner-oriented. I sometimes think there's something very unhealthy about any form of closure, and any sort of patronising attitude towards any particular type of scholarship. I'm not a black-letter lawyer, I hate that type of analysis, I don't like reading it—but I think it would be arrogant in the extreme for me to presuppose that my way of doing things is the only valuable way of doing things.
(lecturer, early career, male, old university)

Several respondents mentioned the fact that the RAE had affected the type of research output they produced, so that they were disinclined to engage in projects which took a long time, preferring instead to write shorter pieces, so that they were sure to be able to satisfy the demands of the RAE:

... Because of that need to put in the four pieces, there has been a definite disinclination for me to pursue other ideas I might have had of doing a major piece of work which might take perhaps seven years to complete. It's definitely inhibited any ideas I might have had along those lines.
(professor, experienced, male, new university)

... I am aware that the research other people have done that I think is of value would not have been achievable under the RAE structure, and I do feel that I am pushed into working on a more short-term, quick-result basis than I would prefer, if I were to be given completely free rein ...
(reader, mid-career, male, new university)

It was noticeable that most of the women who spoke about the way in which the RAE had affected their research spoke in terms of the *pressure* to publish. This particular aspect of the existence of the RAE seemed to be of considerably more concern to women than men:

Has the RAE affected my research at all? Is the Pope a Catholic? The overwhelming requirement is for me to ensure that I produce four pieces of international quality work within the relevant period. That hasn't, for me, ever been an issue, so in a way, that's my starting-point. That is my absolute minimum requirement. Everything else is on top. In my career, that's probably the most fundamental thing that's mattered to me ...
(lecturer, early career, female, old university)

I think you'd have to be pretty self-centred, these days, to be in an academic department and not care about the RAE. Like here, for example, if anybody didn't have four pieces, and they said 'Well, this is my big project, I want to do it, it's really important to me,' I think they'd be regarded as being not a team player. For example, all the new people, even if they've not been in academia that long, they're all busting a gut to have really excellent things. So I don't think that's an attitude you could have and be liked.
(lecturer, early career, female, old university)

... the clear impression is that only certain types of research are valued, and that mainly, you should think about the RAE before you do the research, and think 'What use is it going to be, in RAE terms?' You can't simply do whatever you think, you have to have an eye on the RAE, rather than just doing whatever you want and sorting it out afterwards.
(lecturer, experienced, female, old university)

Yes, it has, because as a new lecturer, rather than being able to take the time to develop your own writing and your own interests at a sort of normal speed, you are under immediate pressure to be writing things that can go straight to publication. So it has undoubtedly had an effect. And it's also that much harder to write, if you think you *have* to have something out by X or by Y . . .
(lecturer, early career, female, old university)

Like much that goes on in the legal academy, it may be that the RAE impacts differently upon men and women, and that it does so in ways which we do not yet understand. The effect of gender upon the culture of academic law and the professional identities of legal academics will be addressed in a later chapter, but in the present context, it is interesting to note Collier's observation that '. . . the assessment of the worth of various academic practices has been increasingly subject to the gaze of a more masculinised university centre through a dominant culture which emphasises not only visible outcomes, but which produces a self-surveilling performative self on the part of the academic' (Collier, 2002: 20). This analysis reflects recent developments in the sociology of organisations, where Joan Ackers' analysis of 'the gendered organisation' is particularly influential (Acker, 1990, 1992). Louise Morley, writing about women and the role of publication as a performance indicator for academic career development, quotes Young-Eisendrath and Wiedemann, two Jungian analysts, who highlight the pressures women may face in relation to performance indicators such as the RAE:

> Because her self-esteem is directly connected to male evaluations, a woman constantly monitors her legitimate value in terms of internalised male judgements . . . she always falls short of the standards she applies because she is not a member of the privileged group; she is not a man.
> (Young-Eisendrath and Wiedemann, 1987: 88, quoted in Morley, 1995: 126).

The RAE would appear to be an inherently gender-neutral process, to which all research-active academics, male and female, are subjected; but as Acker's work has emphasised, the particular power of bureaucracy is in its neutral appearance; on the contrary, she argues, these apparently neutral structures are inherently gendered (Acker, 1990, 1992).

EVALUATION OF THE RAE

The other question I asked respondents about the RAE was designed to throw light on the place of the RAE within the culture of academic law, and find out whether it is highly regarded, or largely discredited, whether it is seen as playing a useful role in the development of the discipline, or as largely irrelevant to the way in which law is researched and studied. I therefore asked the same group of research-active respondents what they thought of the RAE system. They were evenly split, between those who saw the RAE in completely negative terms, and those who, while acknowledging the many disadvantages of the system, nevertheless thought that it had some positive qualities (these groups were not significantly different in terms of institution-type, gender or experience).

The factor which was most often cited as an advantageous effect of the RAE was that it had encouraged much more research within the discipline of law, making research more highly valued within the culture than had previously been the case:

> . . . I think there's no doubt that having it there has made people more professional about doing research, it's raised the priority of research, which for the sector has probably been a good thing—for the whole sector, because I think it's probably been good for the old universities as well to have the competition with the former polytechnics...When the new universities came along, they probably thought 'My God! We can't possibly do worse than polytechnics! We've got to do something or somebody's going to close us.' So I think it gave a massive boost to research . . .
> (professor, mid-career, male, new university)

> . . . I'm very sceptical about the RAE as a process. I suppose where I'm a bit ambivalent is that I think in the context of law schools one of the consequences of the RAE has been to give research, and those who are serious about it, a bit of clout which they previously lacked, at least in certain places, and I think that is a positive by-product.
> (senior lecturer, mid-career, male, old university)

> . . . I think it was valuable in the first place in that there was a degree of dead wood in university law departments. People who had found—and it is, it's a very nice life if you can get into it—and they had very much settled into it, and they were teaching—they were perhaps very good teachers—but in a sense they were being paid for more than just teaching. Oh my God, I sound like a Tony Blair government minister! So in a sense the RAE gave you the chance to find out who were the valuable staff, and who weren't, and in a sense I think it reinvigorated legal academia, and promoted things like law and society research.
> (Lecturer, early career, male, old university)

However, those positive effects were generally outweighed by the negative effects. The main negative effect of the RAE which was identified by respondents was that they saw it as operating in a very divisive way within departments, leading to considerable unhappiness on the part of individuals who were not entered for assessment:

> . . . The part I really don't like is that it differentiates as to what makes a good academic and what makes a bad academic. The people that aren't producing the RAE research are sort of bad academics—even though they may be fantastic teachers, fantastic administrators . . . all these people are talking about how research is so important, and how they wish they didn't have to teach—one may make the observation that teaching is part of the job. That's the problem with the RAE. It says that people who are valuable at teaching and administration aren't valuable . . .
> (lecturer, early career, male, old university)

I think the RAE system is appalling. I think it's a scandal that the system doesn't require every member of staff everywhere to be submitted, because I think it then turns

into a lottery. I've been a little bit involved in the process, and it causes immense distress to staff who are not returned.... Also, it gives an incentive for people to oversell themselves, and it causes quite a number of people to consistently talk up their work...
(lecturer, early career, male, old university)

Respondents also drew attention to a range of other disadvantages which they regarded as resulting from the RAE. These included doubts about the credibility of the exercise because of cynicism about the methodology, a feeling that too much poor-quality research was published, and dislike of the 'transfer-market' in academics:

I think it must encourage a lot of research to be done for the wrong reasons. I mean, it seems to me there's quite enough research being churned out by people like me who actually want to do it, without pressurising people who don't want to do it to churn out more of the stuff...
(principal lecturer, mid-career, male, new university)

... And then what you get is it's used by people to wangle these amazing jobs in the window of opportunity just before the RAE. And I can't understand why—the best law professor in the world is only going to be an A. It's not so much the RAE I object to—it's the way institutions react to it, and individuals within the institutions, and these transfer-fee salaries—something that will probably happen even more with top-up fees. So I see this as something that's had divisive effects, within institutions...
(reader, mid-career, male, old university)

Several people also drew attention to what they saw as the detrimental effects of the constant pressure to publish which exists as a result of the RAE, which was especially a matter of concern in relation to early-career academics, not only from the point of view of stress, but in relation to the effect upon collegiality:

I think the RAE has very much changed university life, and not necessarily for the better. My experience as a young academic was that you had three years' probation, and during that time you wrote a casenote, which probably wasn't much of a problem. You were given plenty of time to develop confidence in writing, plenty of time to develop your teaching interests, and to find out how universities worked. Now, as soon as somebody is appointed, the pressure is—you must publish, you must do this, you must do that—and the waiting-list for journals goes up, and the pressure is put on younger colleagues to concentrate on publishing rather than dealing with teaching or dealing with students. It throws the three elements of the job out of balance.
(senior lecturer, experienced, male, old university)

I kind of hope there won't be too many more RAEs, because it just places great demands on people, and teaching's just kind of being neglected as a result, yet that's one of the main reasons why we're here. It makes the profession much more stressful, simply trying to fit everything in.
(lecturer, early career, female, old university)

The RAE was also seen by some respondents as being another form of 'managerialism'. Contribution to one's discipline as judged by one's peers has traditionally been a central aspect of academic identity (Henkel, 2000).

However, that traditional, voluntary research activity is very different from a centrally-organised bureaucratic system of review. Morley points out that 'while purporting to provide consumers with a basis for selection, performance indicators also provide powerful managerial imperatives' (Morley, 2002: 128):

> I think it's just a joke. It has allowed the worst kind of academics to gain the most power, and has caused all these distortions towards theory, towards completely pointless articles, to chopping down rainforests for a million more monographs that no-one will read. And it's caused an enormous amount of resentment and difficulties within faculties. I find it very difficult to see anything really positive about the RAE.
> (lecturer, early career, female, old university)

The ambiguity towards the RAE inherent in the responses to this question is similar to that uncovered by Vick et al; their data, like mine, leads to the conclusion that overall, the influence of the RAE has had a negative effect on the working lives of academic lawyers (Vick et al, 1998: 560). One comment, they write, seemed to encapsulate the view of a substantial proportion of non-professorial staff 'the RAE makes for low morale, inter-departmental competition, anxiety and low productivity' (Vick et al, 1998: 551).

In a related study, Campbell et al found that the majority of their four hundred respondents indicated that they had been subjected to pressure to change their research and/or the type of publications they produced in order to meet the perceived demands of the RAE (Campbell et al, 1999: 476).

The negative effects which respondents to my questions noted were very similar to the effects which Henkel identified, in her study. The rigid external timetable imposed on the production of research, the almost constant review of personal research agendas, and a new culture of competition, which has a divisive effect upon collegiality, are but a few of the reasons which lie behind Henkel's conclusion that 'perhaps more than any other policies, apart from the growth of student numbers and the restrictions on resources, the RAE had become part of academics' assumptive worlds' (Henkel, 2000: 138).

CONCLUSION

Academic lawyers enjoy teaching; they enjoy helping students to learn, and they are concerned if they feel that their teaching has not gone well. Overwhelmingly, they regard lecturing as a 'performance', and they are able to articulate in considerable detail the ways in which they 'dramatise' their lectures. The importance of teaching as part of the professional identity of academic lawyers is reflected in the fact that their desire to be 'good' teachers appeared to be independent of the value placed on teaching by the institutions in which they work. Research has come to play an increasingly important part in the culture of academic law, and the type of research which is valued appears to be changing, with less emphasis upon research which is oriented towards practitioners.

There is a corresponding emphasis upon research in the construction of the professional identity of the majority of academic lawyers, though this varies somewhat as between those working in old and new universities. Overall, insights into these aspects of the lived experience of academic lawyers have uncovered further evidence that this is a discipline in flux.

7

Inside and Outside the Academic World: Administration, 'Networking' and the Impact of Higher Education Policy

INTRODUCTION

IN HIS SEMINAL article on 'Culture and Identity in Higher Education Research', Jussi Valimaa argues that it is very important, when analysing the culture of academic communities, to take account of the 'significant others' with whom individual academics may interact (Valimaa, 1998: 132–33). In this chapter, I acknowledge the strength of Valimaa's observations, by exploring the relationships of legal academics with a number of 'outsiders', including colleagues working in other law departments, professional organisations and the legal profession. I also explore the effects upon legal academics of the changes in academic life engendered by various government policies. This chapter, then, is a prime example of what Knorr-Cetina and Cicourel would regard as the importance of looking at both 'macro' and 'micro' influences upon a culture (Knorr-Cetina and Cicourel, 1981). The chapter starts at the 'domestic' level, by investigating the attitudes of legal academics to administration, and the 'housework' of academic life, before moving gradually outwards from the law school. In this chapter, as in others, the interconnections between 'identity' and 'culture' rapidly become apparent, particularly as we consider the tensions between the individual's desire for collegiality and the culture's emphasis upon research.

ADMINISTRATION

I asked the respondents what the attitude of people in their department was to administration, and whether they thought administrative tasks were evenly spread among members of the department. The overwhelming majority of respondents thought that administration was not evenly distributed; only about 10 per cent thought that it was, and all except one of these people were early career academics working in old universities, in departments where the stated policy was that early-career academics should have a light administrative load.

Apart from that minority, the general view of administration (regardless of gender, experience or type of institution) was that it was a necessary evil, whose burdens are unevenly distributed among academic staff because some people were very good at getting out of doing it. Respondents pointed to a number of strategies for avoiding involvement in administrative tasks; appearing to be incompetent was a common one, as was being very 'difficult' if asked to do administration, so that heads of department took the line of least resistance and gave the task to someone else. 'It tends to get landed on people who will perform effectively and with no fuss.' Administration, in other words, seemed to bring out the worst in many people:

> Admin is regarded as a chore, which gets in the way of things you want to do. It's perceived to be for the benefit of the whole, and when it comes to having a limited amount of time, we're selfish, and prefer to get on with our own things . . .
> (professor, experienced, male, old university)

> Some people are very skilled at avoiding it, which is a very shrewd move on their part . . .
> (lecturer, experienced, male, old university)

> I have found a wonderful way of getting less administration, which is to be totally incompetent—if one's incompetent, one gets less. That's what I do, and I think my colleagues have more than I do, and I don't have a problem with that. I don't mind administration which goes with one's courses, but it's the rest . . . if I'd wanted to be an administrator, I'd have gone off and worked for Marks and Spencer.
> (lecturer, mid-career, female, new university)

> It is formally taken account of, and you know you must do *some*. But some people do it very minimally. We had someone who was supposed to chair a committee—that was his admin—and it never met, so nothing ever happened . . .
> (senior lecturer, mid-career, male, old university)

Being good at administration was seen as being a bad move:

> It's a good idea not to be good at it. There's no doubt about it, everyone here could actually do most of the admin jobs.
> (professor, experienced, male, new university)

> . . . it's not evenly spread, and there is the usual institutional problem that people that are bad at administration have it taken away from them and are not given anything in place of that work. People who prove that they can competently perform and function tend to get asked to perform more of the same . . .
> (reader, mid-career, male, new university)

> . . . If I was advising someone coming into academia now (though I sometimes think they've got the message already)—I'd say there are certain admin jobs you should never touch—for example, admissions. And anything to do with the lower level (in terms of status) jobs—anything to do with pastoral care. Anything which doesn't obviously have a high-powered managerial aspect to it. The ideal admin job would be minimum work and maximum credit—and some people have an unerring habit of picking those jobs.
> (lecturer, experienced, female, old university)

Administration, 'Networking' and Impact of Higher Education Policy 145

> ... When I first went to [X university] one of my colleagues said to me (and I'm paraphrasing), 'There are two kinds of academics—the shits and the suckers. You look to me like a sucker, and I'm telling you that the sooner you learn to be a shit, the better.' And he was joking—he was the last person who could be described as a shit—he was an incredibly conscientious person. So it was advice offered on the 'Do as I say and not as I do' principle. But I think that's a big difference among academics, people who perceive doing a certain amount of departmental administration as shit work—and it's often quite unseen, sitting on boring committees, or being on time writing student reports, or just being there when your students need to see you—some people see that as just oppressive, and something one should get out of as much as possible, and certainly one should not do more than one's fair share.... And I think that's a difference among academics—I think a disproportionate number are like that—I think most of them are very dutiful at some level, but there are some people who aren't—and I think that's probably a tension that's been exaggerated by the research culture.
> (professor, experienced, female, old university)

There was some pointed criticism of management strategies:

> ... it's not evenly spread ... and we probably don't work hard enough at finding out what bits of administration each individual would be good at and then plugging them into it ...
> (professor, experienced, male, old university)

> ... so you have people allocating administration, and they're doing it on the basis of who they can remember, and who they think has an ability, and who they hate, and all those kinds of criteria that people have ...
> (professor, experienced, male, old university)

The negative attitudes to administration expressed by legal academics are unsurprising. It is a well-known fact of academic life that carrying out administrative tasks generally earns no 'brownie points' (Park, 1996: 48). Generally, little attention is paid to this aspect of the academic job; '... administrative skills are expected to develop spontaneously, through experience and observation' (Johnston, 1996: 105). There is also evidence from elsewhere in the academy which supports the views of some of my respondents that one result of increased pressure produced by recent government policy initiatives has been to decrease collegiality, especially in relation to administrative tasks. Trowler, in his qualitative study of the attitudes of academics in a new university to change in higher education, found that many academics had developed 'coping strategies' to deal with their new environment, which often had negative consequences for students and colleagues; many of these strategies involved the non-performance of administrative tasks and were similar to the strategies described above by the legal academics I interviewed. Examples given by Trowler ranged from 'working to rule', avoiding or not attending meetings or making oneself deliberately unapproachable to avoid the increasing numbers of students, to putting most administration-related correspondence into the waste bin (Trowler, 1998: 122–23). It was the view of many of my respondents that such strategies had been in use for a long time in law schools, although some felt that their use may have intensified more recently. The culture of the law school, in this respect, appears little different from the predominant culture of the university.

Women and Administration

Nearly one-fifth of respondents said that administrative burdens fell unfairly on women. Those who commented on this were men and women at all levels of seniority, mostly (though not exclusively) in new universities:

> I think admin is concentrated in the hands of a capable few, who are mainly women, and not professors. I think women, because they *have* to multi-task, they *can* multi-task. Some men can, too, but women are better at that kind of thing than men are . . . I think men *won't* do it . . . I'm trying to think of any men in this department who have major admin responsibilities—apart from the dean and the head of department I don't think we have any. But all the professors are male. I think sometimes men prove their incompetence. They're given a job to do, and either deliberately or because they're not competent, they make a bad job of it, and so I suppose a good manager has no choice but to put the work where he knows it will be done competently.
> (lecturer, experienced, female, new university)

> . . . I think it would be fair to say there is perhaps a disparity between men and women when it comes to administrative responsibilities. I think it is more of the case here that women are seen as a safe pair of hands, that can do things properly, and that some men by being incompetent in past years have ended up not doing an awful lot, simply on the basis that they can't be trusted, or they won't do it as well as it ought to be done. I haven't spoken to that many female members of staff about it, but I feel it's a fair point. The bigger positions that require more effort and more input seem to be things that female members of staff are involved with.
> (lecturer, early career, male, new university)

> The heavy-duty admin work goes to women, very few men do a lot of admin. It's not very healthy, for example on open days. Women just seem to shrug and say that's how it is. The party line is 'It's very important.' But the reality is 'There but for the Grace of God go I.' It's something people don't want to get involved in.
> (lecturer, mid-career, new university)

> It's predominantly been seen as the regime of women. The heavy admin jobs have nearly all been done by women, except at the very top . . .
> (lecturer, experienced, female, old university)

Many of these respondents pointed out that the women involved in a lot of administration did not do research, which was then used as a justification for giving them more administration—but this merely perpetuated a vicious circle, which their overwhelming administrative burdens gave little indication that they would be able to break, despite their desire to do so. As one (male) respondent commented, the result of this inequality of burden was that '. . . as a result, the men tend to have more time and more energy to spend on research', and another commented:

... it's the same old problem with people doing that kind of job that are good, really good, and really committed and I suspect that other things of theirs go by the board ...
(principal lecturer, experienced, male, new university)

Some men were happy to accept the idea that the women who did so much administration *chose* to do it—(even when the women themselves, holders of first class undergraduate degrees and postgraduate qualifications, said that this was not the case).

The analysis of the issues here needs to be subtle. As one respondent put it:

Probably on paper it would look as though administration was evenly spread between men and women. But in effect, it isn't. The reason why is that it's done differently. There are some women who are enormously pragmatic in their approach to administration—just like a man, in fact, and there are some women who you would agree put *too* much into it, they're *too* concerned about the students, give them too much time. But that said, it is just so obvious that the men in general are much more prepared to fudge, skate over, cobble together, put forward proposals without adequate evidence. The end result is, the women who have important admin positions work doubly hard, doing our job to our own satisfaction, plus picking up the bits that others don't do.
(principal lecturer, experienced, female, new university)

There is considerable evidence in the literature that female academics tend to have more 'caretaking' commitments than their male colleagues, spending more time advising and counselling students, for instance, and that this hinders their career progression (Acker and Feuerverger, 1996; Park, 1996; Chrisler, 1998). Caplan, in her '*Woman's guide to surviving the academic world*' refers to the myth that 'they' really want you to do teaching, research and administration in equal amounts, and that, when it come to promotion, they will count all three as equally valuable.' She cites research evidence showing that although the 'publish or perish' formula in academia is legendary, women are more inclined than men to take seriously the stated tripartite duties of teaching, research and administration (Caplan, 1993: 53–54). There is also evidence from studies of female academics that women find it particularly difficult to avoid getting overburdened with administrative responsibilities. Writing on academic careers frequently comments on this phenomenon, and urges female academics to 'learn to say no.' Park is very critical of this strategy, arguing that one of the problems which female academics face is that they are given more 'opportunities' to carry out administrative tasks; advising them to 'say no' assumes that they can refuse without suffering any detriment. Given all the evidence about women's place in the hierarchy of academia (mostly in the lower grades), she argues that women cannot necessarily refuse to undertake administrative tasks without upsetting the 'gatekeepers' who may later play a role in their career progression (Parks, 1996: 56). Some of my respondents appeared to exemplify precisely the situation which Parks outlines.

In relation to university law schools in particular, Margaret Thornton has argued, on the basis of her research on Australian women lawyers, that women academics have gained only a qualified acceptance into the legal academy. 'We see an institutional tolerance of the docile woman who faithfully serves the corporate ethos in a variation of the traditional handmaiden role' (Thornton, 1998: 112). Thornton goes on to argue that in order to ensure their acceptance by the legal academy, women must slot themselves into '. . . one of the limited subject positions that reify the sexual regime. Such positions are characterised by conventional notions of the feminine, in that they emphasise appearance, sexuality, deference, docility, diligence, care and self-sacrifice' (Thornton, 1998: 112). These roles would typically include many pastoral and administrative duties (what Thornton terms 'the institutional caring and housekeeping roles'), which, she argues, are undertaken disproportionately by women, while men continue with their research-oriented careers. It would appear that this may well be a problem in some of the law schools in which my respondents worked, although in others there seemed to be a genuine sharing of burdens (not among everyone, but among 'good citizens' who were both men and women).

Good Citizens

It is clearly part of the culture in law schools that administration is carried out by 'good citizens'. It was commonly acknowledged by respondents that such people are generous and public-spirited, getting no reward for such behaviour in terms of promotion, or often even thanks. Administration is, as Henkel comments in her analysis of academic identity '. . . the normally unemphasised third component of academic work . . . not in the past seen as core to academic professional lives' (Henkel, 2000: 239). The decision to be a 'good citizen' may thus have profound consequences for professional identity. The balance which an individual achieves between the tripartite roles which traditionally go to make up the academic job has discernible career implications, widening or narrowing professional mobility and affecting the direction of professional development (Becher and Kogan, 1992: 110). The amount of altruism involved in a decision to take the idea of being a 'good citizen' seriously was discussed at length by one of the respondents, recently appointed to her first academic job. In her response, she not only discusses altruism, but points out the tensions inherent in a job which has apparently three components, but where career progression is largely dependent upon performance in one area:

> When I had my first job interview and they asked me about administration, I didn't know what they meant by administration. Now I see it, it's a demand for people to think more communally, and to think about the students. I think the people who do more admin, some of them, are the most generous people, the more communally-minded, the sort of people who think about other people, who just can't bear for some job to be shoddily done—they say 'I'll do it'—or they're concerned about the department, whether it runs well, or whether it ranks highly, and whether we're getting enough of this grade or that. I think the big tasks are taken on by people who believe

Administration, 'Networking' and Impact of Higher Education Policy 149

in the department, and have a feeling of loyalty to it. So in a way I think it's people like that, who will ultimately err on the side of being generous and unselfish.

I suppose it's a difficult job, the academic job, in a way, because you've got your private research, which generates your promotion, and how you get on, and your *personal* academic development, and then on the other hand you have these communal aspirations, and I find in general people like to moan about these communal aspects, rather than thinking of them as continual with the rest of their job . . .
(lecturer, early career, female, old university)

It was clear that personal decisions played a big part in how administration was carried out:

. . . when you're given an administrative task, you're deciding whether you will actually put any time into it or not . . .
(professor, experienced, male, old university)

. . . From the people I've seen that have been promoted, very few seem to be all-rounders, who devote equal amounts of time, energy and skill to all three aspects of the job. They're people who have generally committed themselves to the research aspects, and have not devoted so much time and energy to the teaching or admin side of it. It irritates me, because I think other people then have to pick up the load, which scuppers their own chance of building a good academic career. I mean, I work hard at all aspects of the job, and try to do them as well as I possibly can. But whether that's an aspect of my personality—I would worry if I didn't do them all as well as I could—or whether I just sort of lack the ambition or whatever to do it—I think I don't like that, the way some people just seem to be able to avoid doing some of these unpleasant tasks, which somebody has to do. I'm just probably miserable, because I've had so much admin, over the past few years. I'm finding it harder, now, to get everything done . . . On the other hand, I sometimes feel quite proud—you know, if I can do *all* aspects of the job, and none of them have suffered, that's an achievement in itself, really (I hope). I ought perhaps to be more proud of myself, instead of beating myself about things I think I should be doing more of.
(lecturer, early career, female, old university)

Gender issues are important here, as we have already seen; there is certainly an element, as Celia Wells has noted in her work on gender in law schools, of women being overloaded with administration, while '. . . the "absent-minded" male intellectual is excused from the mundane work of administration' (Wells, 2001: 124). However, it was far from true that the respondents as a whole characterised all good citizens as female. It appears that there is a small group of people, both male and female, who act in this way. Naturally, such different working practices can lead to resentment:

. . . Some people are spectacular, from early on in their career, at avoiding administration. They avoid students, in terms of the pastoral function, or doing anything too detailed with the students, or too time-consuming, in order that they can concentrate on their research and get promotion. So this is a highly invidious system, where colleagues who can perform in all three areas quite successfully are being given the short straw careerwise, they really are, because they're being held back by the amount of

work that effectively other colleagues are giving them—because that's what's happening, it's as direct as that, because we (who do admin) all know that we've picked up the tab for other colleagues who go the readership, chair route—we've all picked up their work, we've seen it happen . . .
(senior lecturer, mid-career, male, old university)

. . . there is the usual institutional problem that people who are bad at admin tend to have that work taken away from them and are not given anything in place of that work. People who prove that they can competently perform and function tend to get asked to do more of the same . . .
(reader, mid-career, male, new university)

. . . there is a sort of isolation of people—you don't recognise them for teaching or admin duties, even though you're supposed to be doing those two anyway, and you only recognise them for research, but if the time is not there for research, because they've been doing the other two components, then they're being left out or told off—and that leads to bitterness.
(lecturer, early career, female, old university)

I resent it if [people who don't do their fair share of admin] advance up the career ladder. Because it seems to me it's been done at the expense of other people . . .
(senior lecturer, experienced, male, old university)

In his discussion of the liberal law school, Bradney has pointed out the absence of very much discussion or analysis of administration as part of academic life (Bradney, 2003: 133). He argues that, despite this, administration is an important aspect of the legal academy, because of its intimate connection with the concept of collegiality, the practice of participation by academics in the management of all university activities (Bradney, 2003, ch 6). While the degree of participation by legal academics in the governance and policy-making structures of their universities will vary, and historically the notion of collegiality is one which has been particularly applicable in old universities, it would be too simplistic to say that collegiality is a notion which *only* applies in old universities, as the responses above indicate. Analysing the place of administration in American higher education, Kennedy notes that academics are asking themselves with increasing frequency whether their level of participation in university governance is worth it. His reply is widely applicable:

> The past two decades have been marked by an increasing attenuation of institutional loyalty on the part of the professoriate: it is said, with some justification, that many of the most distinguished research scholars owe their primary allegiance to the invisible academy of their discipline rather than to their university. To the extent that is true, it seems likely that it can only be reversed by the sense of shared responsibility and common purpose that comes from meaningful participation in the institution's future. Surely that is a central part of academic duty . . .
> (Kennedy, 1997: 146)

OUTSIDE CONCERNS

In line with Valimaa's observation that interaction with 'significant others' is an important key to academic culture / identity, I tried to ascertain how much interaction legal academics had with academics in other institutions. Nearly all the respondents had some contact with legal academics in other UK universities. In a few cases, this extended to colleagues in universities outside the UK These personal contacts were usually between experts working in similar fields, making contacts within specialisms a significant part of legal academic culture, as it is in other disciplines (Becher and Trowler, 2001: 67). Only a few people said they had contacts with academics working in disciplines other than law; contacts with other academics from the disciplines of criminology, sociology, social policy, history and philosophy were mentioned. But in the main, interdisciplinary contacts did not appear to form a significant part of the culture of academic law.

The most common form of contact with academics in other universities was through conferences, although other contacts were made as a result of having worked in a number of different institutions, through writing or editorial work, or acting as an external examiner. Conferences in the abstract were generally viewed in positive terms, although over a third of respondents, in both old and new university law schools, did not actually attend them. In old university law schools, however, there were few people who had *never* attended an academic conference; the majority of these respondents had, for various reasons, stopped attending. On the other hand, the respondents working in new university law schools who did not attend conferences had never done so.

Respondents who attended conferences gave three main reasons for doing so. The reason most often given was that a conference enables one to find out what's going on in one's field, exchange ideas with other experts and meet people with similar academic interests. This sort of contact with other specialists was important:

> They are a place where, apart from gossiping about the sex lives of your colleagues, you're going to find research and ideas being talked about. Not necessarily talked about in a new way—sometimes they are, sometimes they're not, but they're being talked about, so you know what people are thinking about before they publish those ideas . . .
> (professor, experienced, male, old university)

> I enjoy conferences, because I enjoy learning—even though sometimes you go to conferences and you don't hear anything new, and that's a bit disappointing. Nevertheless, it motivates you if you hear good speakers, and it keeps you up-to-date and makes you think about other things you might not actually have thought of, and it makes you meet people from other institutions, and also people that you've heard of, and you can discuss things.
> (lecturer, early career, female, old university)

Two other reasons for attending conferences were to maintain one's own profile in the field (mainly by giving papers) and to meet people from other institutions, in order to find out more about life in the legal academy as a whole:

> It's partly a consequence of wanting to meet people elsewhere, and partly because there's something interesting that's being discussed. I think it's just useful to have a perspective on your own institution and your own circumstances, to realise what's going on in the world. I think in the long run it's advantageous to know people in other institutions. If you're not going to stay in one place forever, you need to know what's going on elsewhere.
> (lecturer, early career, male, old university)

> Conferences are quite important, in terms of presenting—I try to do a couple a year.
> (lecturer, early career, male, old university)

> Yes, they're very important—for meeting with different ranges of people—it broadens one's range of contacts, it's important professionally, and also it sustains friendships which exist at a distance.
> (senior lecturer, mid-career, male, old university)

> I do go to conferences—partly because if things are not too happy in one's own institution, you might decide if you went somewhere else it would be much better, and if you talk to people in fact perhaps it's a bit the same everywhere—it's just the problems are more obvious in one institution than another.
> (lecturer, early career, female, old university)

The main reasons given by respondents in new universities for not attending conferences was that they were too busy doing teaching or admin-related tasks.

> I don't go because of time, really. I'd like to go to the SLSA, but—we've got budgets, as well, so if the conference is far away I'd expect the budget not to run to it, and also there are other things I find myself pushed into, more obviously related to what I'm teaching, As far as I know, the majority of people here don't know what fun it is [to go to an academic conference], which is very sad.
> (lecturer, mid-career, male, new university)

In old universities, the reasons for no longer attending conferences were very varied, ranging from a dislike of large groups of people to the difficulty of getting funding, but there were two reasons given by several people. Firstly, that conferences were not interesting:

> ... it's partly that quite a lot of the conferences I have been to are reassuring, in the sense that you come away disappointed—there don't seem to be new ideas floating around, and sometimes you hear recycled material that if you've been keeping up with the literature you already know about.
> (professor, experienced, male, old university)

The other reason which several respondents identified was a dislike of the social aspects of conferences, such as not liking large groups of people, or the 'networking' aspects of conferences:

> I don't like conferences—I went to one and ended up talking to all the people I already knew. It's alright if you go with someone else, but I don't like big crowds of people.

> The other thing about academics is, you meet a large number of academics who don't talk. I'm always struck by the level of bloopers. I used to think 'My God, people in our department aren't that weird—where do they all come from?' . . .
> (lecturer, early career, female, old university)

> I find them slightly annoying, to be honest. Because everybody has to put themselves in positions where they end up chatting to people who they think it's important to chat to, and I just find the whole thing very annoying.
> (lecturer, early career, male, old university)

Overall, the attitudes of legal academics to conferences reflect the ambiguities which commonly surround the academic conference. On the one hand, conferences can be affirmative experiences, providing intellectual stimulation and the opportunity to meet others with similar interests, a forum in which to showcase one's own work, receive (constructive) criticism and consider the work of others, as well as enabling one to exchange gossip, make contacts, examine the latest books and discuss potential projects with potential collaborators. Conferences are often seen as important in developing a reputation in a particular field (Blaxter et al, 1998: 66–67). On the other hand, they can be intensely threatening experiences '. . . at which speakers can feel on trial, their whole career and identity at stake' (Stanley, 1995: 172). There is some evidence that conferences in academic law may be particularly threatening in this way, since Becher and Trowler's research shows that gossip is a particular feature of the discipline of law (along with anthropology and sociology). '. . . it takes the form of rumour, and the dissection of personalities rather than the more serious-minded shop-talk indulged in by serious-minded scientists' (Becher and Trowler, 2001: 109).

NETWORKING

Trying to explore further Valimaa's idea of 'significant others', I also asked respondents whether they thought they had a good network of academic contacts, and whether this was important to them. Three-quarters of the respondents said they had a network of academic contacts; these respondents were situated in both old and new universities, and at all levels of experience, without differentiation in gender terms. All except one of the respondents who said they had a network said it was important to them. Respondents talked about networks in entirely personal terms; no one mentioned the kind of formal groups which commonly exist in the hard sciences (Becher and Trowler, 1998: 93).

The main reason for finding a network of academic contacts useful was research-related; several people in old universities mentioned in particular how helpful it was to exchange drafts of articles with other academics (not necessarily specialists in the field). Academics in new universities also mentioned that their network was important for stimulating ideas about teaching. These contacts belong to what Becher and Trowler term the 'inner circle' of professional acquaintances—critical friends to whom one sends drafts of papers for comment, the kind of people to whom one could go to for assistance over a knotty problem, and whom one would expect to help in one's turn (Becher and Trowler, 1998: 92):

> Yes, it's particularly important because I'm an organiser of things, so you need to know people. And partly because some of my work is comparative—so I can contact people I know in other countries and ask them 'Who do you know that I could ask about this?' For comparative work, it's not essential, but, you know, it's very helpful.
> (senior lecturer, mid-career, male, old university)

> Yes, because you can learn so much from others, and you can give as well. It's always good to talk to other people teaching law . . .
> (lecturer, experienced, female, new university)

> It's good to know a group of supportive people, who know what you're talking about when you speak to them—and it's also good to have people to bounce ideas off, and shamelessly ask to read drafts of papers etc.
> (lecturer, early career, male, old university)

> Yes, it's very important to me, because I depend enormously on people's feedback and exchange with people about their work and my work. I would say all my research is a dialogue . . . all my work comes out of exchange. I also enjoy it on a personal level.
> (professor, experienced, female, old university)

> . . . For whatever reason, people come [to this law school], and there is a disinclination to move—because of family ties, partners, whatever. One way round this is to network and go into other law schools and meet people from somewhere else, and find out what problems they experience, and how they tackle them, how they teach things.
> (professor, experienced, male, new university)

The other common reason for regarding the possession of a network important was for personal support. Respondents talked of seeking advice, the importance of having supportive people to turn to, sharing problems and companionship:

> Yes—and I find it quite useful. It's good to have a support network when times aren't that great, and to see how things are working at other places. You can learn things—about job opportunities, about how other people are being treated, how other departments are approaching things—it just gives you a view on what's happening.
> (lecturer, early career, male, old university)

> Well, there's a pint of beer at one level, gives me an excuse to go back to [my old university], also you can share problems . . . so it's both social and academic . . .
> (lecturer, early career, male, new university)

> I'd say I've got a reasonable network of academic contacts—certainly of fairly senior people outside my institution, so if there's a particular question I want to talk about, or some advice that I need, yes.
> (lecturer, early career, male, old university)

The use of networks for personal support may be particularly helpful in overcoming the 'politics' of legal academia—the academic who finds her course

Administration, 'Networking' and Impact of Higher Education Policy 155

endangered by a critical head of department, her research disparaged by an unsympathetic appraiser or her faculty the subject of an unfavourable research rating can regain a sense of self-worth through interaction with others who take a different view (Bradney and Cownie, 1996: 23). There is also evidence that these kinds of informal interactions with other academics may be particularly important for women academics, since research suggests that it is often a mentor or other person who is influential in encouraging women to advance their career (Aisenberg and Harrington, 1988: 50).

Not Having a Network

Those who did not regard themselves as having an academic network differed sharply about how they felt about this. Half of the people who did not have a network were happy about that. The response of the next respondent brings out some of the implications of the emphasis upon gossip which Becher and Trowler noted as a particular feature of the culture of academic law (Becher and Trowler, 2001: 109):

> It's a peculiarity of academia, that you can't get on without knowing people, but what's the point of a network, if you can't trust most of them not to bitch about you behind your back anyway? Obviously, that's not true if they're friends, but a network—I know too many people who say 'Oh, so-and-so's keeping an eye out for me.' And you know so-and-so is not actually keeping an eye out for them, but is saying horrible things about them. So it's a funny thing, networking, and I think networking is another sort of ambition thing, it's the people who want to get to the very top of the ladder and need to climb on heads to get there . . .
> (lecturer, early career, female, old university)

> I'm not a networker—but this should be put in context. I'm not a sociable person, and I don't socialise with my colleagues here, therefore I'm not in the way of socialising with colleagues from other institutions. I think it's very bad—I mean, I don't value that in myself—I just know that that happens to be me.
> (reader, experienced, male, old university)

The other half of the group who did not have a network said it was a matter of concern to them. Their comments, taken with those of the 'networkers', above, suggest that within the culture of academic law, networking is seen to be desirable, but not necessary:

> I don't know, it's the sort of thing I worry about—'Should I be out there, networking?' I don't know. Sometimes it has been a disadvantage, like I've been trying to put together an AHRB application, and I had to think for ages about who my external referees were going to be. I do sometimes worry that I'm not out there enough, that it's something I ought to be doing—getting myself into the academic community.
> (lecturer, early career, female, old university)

> . . . I'm not very good at meeting new people, and therefore at conferences I'm the sort of person who would press myself against a wall, so I don't know that I am going to

get a lot out of it, really. That makes me reluctant to go. Though I wish I could, because when I have been exposed to people from other departments I have found it to be quite an enjoyable experience, and quite nice, and you see they are real people, with real lives, and are perfectly normal . . .
(lecturer, early career, male, new university)

Professional Organisations

Another potential source of 'significant others' is the professional organisation. Respondents mentioned three main organisations—the SPTL (now the Society of Legal Scholars, though none of the respondents used the new name), whose membership was at one time largely restricted to academic lawyers working in old universities; the Socio-Legal Studies Association (SLSA), founded in 1990 to cater for the interests of legal academics adopting a less traditional approach to the study of law, and the Association of Law Teachers (ALT), whose membership was formerly largely restricted to academic lawyers working in polytechnics. A small number of respondents also mentioned other organisations to which they belonged; these generally focused on one particular area of law.

All the respondents were members of at least one of the three main professional organisations for academic lawyers. About a fifth were members of more than one organisation, and about the same number said that they had played an active part in an organisation, such as sitting on the executive committee or occasionally organising conferences at some time in their career. Most respondents appeared to regard membership *per se* as important—several people said that they valued the information they obtained from newsletters and email networks, several others mentioned the benefits of appearing in the membership directory of the organisation; another, slightly larger, group commented that holding the annual conference was an important function of the organisation, as far as they were concerned. But on the whole, academic lawyers are passive members of their professional organisations.

The Legal Profession

The legal profession was not an important source of identity for academic lawyers. Only about a quarter of the respondents had some contact with members of the legal profession, but much of that contact was minimal, such as sometimes teaching on continuing education courses for practitioners, or providing the occasional expert opinion. A few legal academics wrote practitioner texts, sometimes co-authoring them with members of the legal profession. Consultancy, giving expert opinions about an area of law, was the most common reason for having contact with the legal profession. It was noticeable that twice as many experienced academics engaged in some kind of work with legal practitioners as compared with mid-career or early-career academics. Equally, interaction with practitioners was something that far more men than women engaged in.

The small amount of contact with the legal profession provides further evidence that law as a discipline is becoming more academic in its orientation. It appears that for younger academics, interaction with the profession is not a particularly important part of their professional identity. Evidence about research in academic law, which I discussed earlier, also points to the fact that writing for practitioners is not an activity which is particularly highly valued within the culture of academic law. As far as the gender difference in interaction with the profession is concerned, given that there is considerable evidence of discrimination against women within the legal profession (Spencer and Podmore, 1987; Holland and Spencer, 1992; Hagan and Kay, 1995; Sommerlad and Sanderson, 1998) it may be that women legal academics do not choose to engage with a milieu where they feel that it is likely they will not be treated with respect.

In order to explore these issues further, I asked those who interacted with the profession how they thought legal academics were regarded by practising lawyers. A minority of respondents thought the relationship was positive, although even they acknowledged that in general there is a big gulf between academia and practice:

> They seem to tap my brains quite a lot. I think with a certain amount of respect. Perhaps I just know the right people. I think if you deal with cutting-edge things [such as my area of law], quite difficult legal issues can walk through the door, and the divide between academia and practice isn't as great as it is in other areas . . .
> (principal lecturer, experienced, male, new university)

> I think a lot of them can't understand why we put up with it. They respect us, but they think it's very odd.
> (professor, experienced, male, new university)

> . . . I think academics are very highly regarded by the better practitioners—but others just say 'In practice it works like this.'
> (senior lecturer, experienced, male, old university)

> They regard me as less head in the clouds than most academics, because I'm writing with them. I think the fact that I was a practitioner before I became an academic gives me acceptability with practitioners, although I have to say my experience of most practitioners is they'll judge people as they find them, and judge them by the way in which they work. Some academics are very good, others are not.
> (reader, experienced, male, old university)

However, most academics who had experience of working with practising lawyers thought that the profession regarded academics with some suspicion, and in some cases, with outright hostility:

> Occasionally I'm asked to act as an expert witness, which I decline to do, or to give written advice on a particular problem, which I do. But my experience of the profession is that they're very anxious to get your opinion, and very reluctant to pay for it. I

don't really know how to pitch my fee demand. In fact, I think there are some members of the profession who expect to get advice free. I can give you a specific illustration. There was a graduate from this department, who had a [legal] problem, wrote quite a lengthy letter, said would I be prepared to give an opinion? I wrote back and said yes, but I would demand a fee, gave him some idea of what the fee was, did he want to proceed on that basis—and that was the last I heard of it. I did an opinion for a local firm, and bearing in mind that I did all the research and typed it up myself, I charged £100—and I had to threaten legal proceedings to get it—and the opinion amounted to some four or five typewritten pages.
(professor, experienced, male, old university)

I think perhaps the lower ranks of the profession don't have as much respect for academics as perhaps judges do, who are citing articles in their judgments. It very much depends—I mean, I find that some of the younger solicitors, perhaps fairly recently graduated themselves, I haven't had any difficulties there. Some of the slightly more senior people that I've come across aren't—some are quite condescending, especially if you trespass onto their patch. I remember a few years ago someone saying to me 'How can you teach it if you don't know what's happened? You're not in touch with the law.'
(lecturer, early career, male, old university)

I think we get a lot of disdain in some cases. Others want to use academics for training and stuff.
(senior lecturer, mid-career, male, old university)

I suppose people's perception, particularly if they're in practical areas, tends to be that academics aren't very practical people—probably the popular perception of academics is that they have airy-fairy ideas, and couldn't change a plug to save their lives—but I probably don't fit that description myself.
(senior lecturer, experienced, male, old university)

The fact that the relationship between academics and practitioners is not an easy one is unsurprising, given the long-running division between legal academia and legal practice (see for example Sugarman, 1983, 1986; Twining, 1994). This was well summed-up by one of the respondents, who had extensive experience of interacting with the legal profession:

I think the difficulty for academics when dealing with practitioners is that with the exception, perhaps, of very well-known academics, and particularly people who write or contribute to well-known practitioner works, I don't really think practitioners have much understanding of what we do or really much interest in what we do. I think we're very peripheral to their concerns. They are perhaps marginally interested in us as the feed for their new talent into their firms or chambers, and as writers of references, and that sort of thing, but I don't really think they have any clear picture of academia. For example, I don't even think they understand the pecking-order in academia.
(lecturer, experienced, male, old university)

This picture of two very different worlds may go some way to changing the views of those outside the legal academy who still persist in their view that academic law is an exclusively applied subject.

THE CHANGING WORLD

Another 'significant other' which affects the culture of legal academia and the professional identities of those working within it is the government. The extent of the changes which have taken place in higher education over the last few decades has been a recurring topic in the literature (Salter and Tapper, 1994; Martin, 1999; Taylor, 1999, Kogan and Hanney, 2000). One of the most obvious of this has been the move from an elite to a mass system, resulting in vastly increased student numbers (Kogan and Hanney, 2000: 67). As far as law schools are concerned, Harris and Jones' 1995/6 survey shows that law schools have not been immune from the general trend (Harris and Jones, 1997). Coupled with the increasing numbers has been a significant decrease in resources; in its *First Report on Legal Education and Training* the (now defunct) Lord Chancellor's Advisory Committee on Legal Education and Conduct commented 'It would not be an exaggeration to say that many universities, including law schools, are facing their most severe financial crisis since 1945' (ACLEC, 1996: para 3.32).

The changes experienced by law schools, along with the rest of the higher education sector, have, however, gone much further than student numbers and units of resource. Since the beginning of the 1980s higher education has been subject to a number of sweeping policy changes. The sector has experienced the abolition of the binary divide, the establishment of the Higher Education Funding Councils, and the increasing influence of ideas of 'management', with the Jarrett Report recommending that vice chancellors should assume the role of chief executives, to whom deans and heads of department should report as line managers (CVCP, 1985, recommendation 5.5(d): 36). Universities, like other public bodies, also came under increasing pressure to incorporate the values of the market into their organisations, and to reduce their dependence on the state (Kogan and Hanney, 2000). The strategies used by the Government to drive such policies forward, which included emphasising the efficient and responsible use of resources, the use of performance indicators and an emphasis on public accountability became known as 'new public management (Minogue et al, 2000). The cumulative effect of these developments was to bring about a major change in the relationship between universities and the state. The state, as paymaster, exerted its power, and by the mid-1990s had established a framework of legal regulation, incentives, rewards and sanctions, within which universities had to operate (Henkel, 2000: 47). As far as individual academics were concerned, these policy initiatives resulted in the introduction of research assessment, teaching quality assessment, and an increasing emphasis on notions of audit and accountability.

In order to explore the ways in which these changes have impacted upon the culture of law schools and the identities of their inhabitants, I asked all the respondents who had been in academic life more than two years whether academic life had changed since they came into it, and if so, to talk about those changes. All of them agreed that it had changed. Across the board, they pointed to four indicators which they regarded as providing evidence of change: increased numbers of students, an increasing emphasis on research and publication, the increasing pressures of academic life and increasing amounts of bureaucracy. These changes were indicated by both men and women, at all levels of experience.

Although respondents in both sectors pointed to all four types of change I have enumerated, there was a difference in emphasis between respondents working in old universities and those working in new universities. Respondents working in old universities placed most emphasis on the increased pressure to research and publish, particularly the pressure generated by the RAE. They also tended to contrast the increased pressures experienced by those working in contemporary law schools as compared with the situation in the past. Respondents working in new universities, however, placed most emphasis on the increasing numbers of students and the types of demands made by a diverse student body, as well as the increasingly bureaucratic nature of academic life and the increased presence of audit and other monitoring mechanisms. These differences appear likely to result from a difference in culture between old and new universities, in part arising from their different historical origins (Fulton, 1996).

Increased Pressures in the Contemporary Law School

For some respondents, the opportunity to talk about changes in academic life brought forth memories of a more relaxed era, when notions of audit and accountability appeared to be alien to the culture of law schools:

> It's certainly changed. When I joined, it certainly was in every sense of the word still very much a gentleman's profession. There was highly selective admission in terms of the achievements of students, there were no external audits or assessments, there was a gentility about the place which was at the same time attractive and also held the danger that there was a tendency for some people to see it as a gentleman's profession in the sense that you didn't have to work very hard. Now, it's changed out of all recognition . . . It is no longer a gentleman's profession, it's actually jolly hard work — and there doesn't seem to be a part of the year when there's any let-up. I know we have vacations—but vacations aren't what they were in 1973!
> (professor, experienced, male, old university)

> Has it changed? God, yes! When I first started in academic life, I would say that there was a sort of relaxed gentility about it all. I referred to it occasionally at that time as being the last bastion of English amateurism—nobody taught us how to teach, we weren't expected to go through personal appraisals, if you didn't want to do research nobody bothered about it. There were no teaching assessments—if the students thought you were a good teacher, all well and good; if they didn't, well, nobody seemed to be particularly bothered about it. It was all pretty laissez-faire. From that position, we have now entered something which I consider to be *excessively* regulated, *incredibly* bureaucratic, *terribly* frustrating . . .
> (professor, mid-career, male, old university)

Administration, 'Networking' and Impact of Higher Education Policy 161

> . . . Life in the new universities was pretty cushy in those days. We didn't do a lot of teaching, administration was much simpler. We had much more control over how we ran things. We didn't have email, we didn't have voicemail, just answerphones. Numbers were about half what they are now, in terms of students, and really, you never did anything in those months over the summer, and there was no pressure to publish, none at all . . .
> (principal lecturer, experienced, female, new university)

> . . . I think now, we've changed, we put a lot of pressure on people. There was probation, but no one ever seemed to fail probation; you just sailed along, ploughing one's own furrow. And quite apart from that, there were not the pressures in terms of administration, red-tape and so on. Vacations were vacations—I'm not saying one went away for the whole period, but nothing ever happened in vacations. Nowadays, we have meetings in vacations, and if you take a holiday, invariably you miss something. I used to have a coffee break and a tea break, I used to spend about an hour and a half a day on all these various breaks I was having. Now, that's all gone—I do take time for lunch—it's not the sort of lunch I used to have, but I do take time for a proper break. The demands are much, much greater . . .
> (professor, experienced, male, new university)

> . . . I think overall, there's been an increasing pressure to achieve specified goals, and I think there's little coherence to how those goals are expressed, and the particular time at which those goals are imposed. It seems to me there are a number of different organisations basically imposing different goals, and we lurch from trying to satisfy one or the other . . .
> (lecturer, early career, male, old university)

Recent policy changes in higher education appear to have led to profound changes in the culture of university law schools, which are reflected in the comments made by these respondents. It is equally clear that such changes have affected the construction of professional identities in the law school: no longer is it acceptable for an academic lawyer to behave as if they are a member of a 'gentleman's profession'.

Student Pressures

The phenomenon of increasing student numbers is one which has been commented on extensively in the literature (see, eg, Kogan and Hanney, 2000: 51; Martin, 1999: 8). In terms of law schools, Harris and Jones' survey recorded a 50 per cent increase in the number of full-time law students since the similar Wilson survey reported in 1993, 'This figure, though dramatic, is not out of line with the general increase in students in higher education over this period' (Harris and Jones, 1997: 67). Respondents in my study pointed to a number of different ways in which they think greatly increased numbers of students have changed the culture of academic law:

> It's changed enormously. The whole slant has changed. As much as anything, it's the sheer practicalities of it—the numbers of students, the reduction in the number of

staff, therefore the increased teaching loads, the removal of any pressure to publish or do research. We are seen in this institution very much as teachers, and therefore it's the ability to teach as many people as possible, in as short a period of time as possible. That *was* never the case when I first came here . . .
(principal lecturer, experienced, female, new university)

. . . I think the biggest change is incremental—the sheer numbers of students we teach . . . essentially we're expected to do the same job with no increase in resources, and I actually get the sense now that it's gone as far as it can do now, in higher education, and it's about to burst at the seams if we take it any further. I certainly do think that we are increasingly short-changing our students, we're not teaching them enough. I don't believe in spoon-feeding them, but I do believe that, you know, education is about the engagement of minds. Half-an-hour's contact time every two weeks or whatever—it's risible, it really is.
(senior lecturer, mid-career, male, old university)

. . . I think students have definitely become more demanding . . . People have mentioned to me as a possible rationale that it's now that students are paying fees, that they are expecting more in return—so they will say to you 'I pay my fees, you know, I'm entitled to this'—but I think it started before . . . but fees give students a bit more of an excuse to be more demanding, they use that often, they refer to it, they say 'I've paid my fees' or whatever, so they do use it, but I think that's part of a bigger picture of students being more tuned in to their rights, their entitlements, and being more demanding. So that's one definite change . . .
(lecturer, mid-career, female, new university)

I think the quality of students that we have, it's a very difficult point, but the students we have now are far less able than the ones I've taught in the past. You have to work a lot harder, they need far more support, there's not the autonomy of learning—which to me is an anathema, because to me university life is about being autonomous in your learning . . .
(principal lecturer, mid-career, female, new university)

Well, I think it has got less pleasant. The sheer numbers with whom one is involved have grown to such an extent that it is very difficult now to relate to students as individuals. You have to make a real effort, and even then you can only get to know a few of them . . .
(professor, experienced, male, new university)

Evidence gathered by the Law Society's cohort study of law students suggests that, as a whole, law students continue to be drawn from predominantly middle-class backgrounds, though the extent to which this is the case varies as between old and new universities (Halpern, 1994: 21–22). Nevertheless, the challenges faced by legal academics in dealing with not only increasing numbers of students, but a greater variety of types of student, with different backgrounds and different educational experiences before they arrive at university, are similar to those being felt across the academy. Martin, in her study of *Changing Academic Work* notes that:

> Teaching more students and teaching students who are aware of their right to satisfactory service means that the focus of teaching has shifted away from the needs of the

teacher to those of the student—in theory at least. So at the same time as the contemporary university teacher has to attend to the needs of more and more varied students ... they are also being asked to attend to more flexible ways of teaching ... They are being encouraged to explore the resources available in multi-media packages and through a range of websites ... And, while they are trying out these new ways of teaching new courses with these new students, they are also attending to demands for accountability ...
(Martin, 1999: 11)

The responses of the law teachers I talked to suggest that the advent of mass higher education in law schools has profound consequences for the culture of academic law and the professional identities of academic lawyers. Together with the rest of the university, law schools, and those who teach in them, are having to come to terms with a move from elite to mass higher education which puts considerable pressure on individuals, as well as on the system as a whole.

Bureaucracy, Audit and Accountability

The attitudes of the respondents in my study towards the increasing amounts of bureaucracy and 'audit' now found in academic life reflect the feelings of academics across the academy. Morley argues that 'the two major accounting systems in higher education in Britain today are creating a pincer movement of fear and alienation [which] ... could have detrimental long-term effects on academia.' Like many academics, she is not opposed to accountability *per se*, but she goes on to comment that '... the increased regulation, surveillance and bureaucracy associated with quality assurance are being experienced as rituals of power and domination by UK academics' (Morley, 2002: 128). Henkel notes that as a result of recent policy changes affecting higher education, academics in her study felt that academic work and academic relations are increasingly bureaucratic. They perceive a shift in their relationships with administrators, so that now they spend significant time meeting administrative needs, rather than the reverse (Henkel, 2000: 253). The international survey of the academic profession carried out on behalf of the Carnegie Foundation found that the majority of British academics regarded academic administrators as autocratic (Altbach and Lewis, 1996: 30). These types of issue were reflected by my respondents, in their consideration of the changes they have experienced during the course of their professional lives:

> ... everything seems to be more driven—if it's not one RAE round, it's the next RAE round. If it's not your concern with intakes of students of the right quality, it's your concern that too many of them don't fail. It's the external measure in the league table, be it RAE, or be it other indicators. I would be the last person to say, to be honest, that universities should be in such a privileged position that they should be free from all external constraints, but (this is a familiar refrain, isn't it?): It's the quantity of it at the moment. You get to this stage in a long term, and most colleagues look haggard. I

mean not haggard simply because of the amount of teaching, it's all the other stuff. That's changed beyond recognition . . .
(principal lecturer, experienced, male, new university)

I think it was more free and easy when I first came into it. The central managerial structure is more apparent. There wasn't the same pressure, in the past, to perform, or tests imposed upon you. Consequently, people are looking back to a golden age, or what they perceive as a golden age. I'm not so sure it was that free and easy—I think if you were ambitious, there was still a certain amount of pressure—but it was self-imposed.
(lecturer, experienced, female, old university)

. . . There's an increased amount of bureaucracy and administration. There is an increase in paper, email is just a blight—there are email messages by the dozen. We are now accountable to external bodies—now I don't necessarily have a problem with being accountable to external bodies, but I suppose I don't—it's not in my nature to jump when I'm told to jump by external bodies, and I find that's what we do these days, whereas I hate to say it, but when I came into academia, you didn't. So that has changed immensely . . .
(principal lecturer, mid-career, female, new university)

. . . there's a feeling that you constantly have to watch your back, constantly have to record conversations with students and make sure you have a piece of paper for this, and a piece of paper for that. We're forever having a look at the syllabus, or it's 'Let's change the structure of the year.' Rather than just getting on and doing the job of educating people.
(senior lecturer, experienced, male, old university)

. . . I think a lot of the changes which have been made are meaningless, in an irritating kind of 'rearranging the deckchairs' kind of way—ie semesterisation, modularisation and so forth, and filling in endless forms to carry on doing more or less what you were doing before.
(principal lecturer, mid-career, male, new university)

The RAE is not the only aspect of audit which has come in for criticism. Commentators on legal education have been particularly critical of the assessment of teaching quality. Brownsword, himself an assessor, has written an extended critique of the whole process (Brownsword, 1994: 530) while Mike Allen, one of the first cohort of law assessors, resigned before conducting any assessments and published an open letter enumerating the failures, as he saw them, of the system which he found when he began his training (Allen, 1993: 25). Bradney has argued that the teaching quality assessment exercise in law taught the academic community little about the concept of quality in teaching, not only because of procedural problems with the exercise itself, but because the exercise was not accompanied by any serious debate about the nature and purpose of university teaching (Bradney, 1996).

CONCLUSION

Internally, academic law is a communicative culture, in the sense that the majority of its inhabitants have what they regard as good networks of academic contacts, which they value. They also meet each other regularly at conferences. However, contact with academics working in other disciplines, and with members of the legal profession is important only to a minority of academic lawyers.

To some extent, the various levels of the culture explored in this chapter provide something of a balance to the positive attitudes of legal academics to their job, and the satisfaction they experience in doing it. Here, they acknowledge the negative aspects of administration, including the tendency for 'good citizens' and women to shoulder excessive burdens, which adversely affect their career progression.

There is evidence here that the changes in higher education which have affected the academy as a whole have impinged on academic lawyers too, though the experience in this regard of those working in old and new universities was somewhat different, with the former being more concerned about pressures to publish, and the latter about the demands made by an increasingly large and diverse student body, in the context of a growing amount of bureaucracy and audit. It is these more negative aspects of the law school culture which have caused commentators such as Collier (Collier, 2002: 30) to argue that we are currently witnessing the 'proletarianisation' of legal academics—Halsey's famous 'decline of donnish dominion' (Halsey, 1992). This is a subject to which I will return in the final chapter. At this stage, it is enough to note that the increase in surveillance, of various kinds, now experienced by legal academics has undoubtedly affected both the culture of academic law, and the professional identities of legal academics.

8

Identity Matters

INTRODUCTION

ALTHOUGH SOME WRITERS on higher education have argued that the personal characteristics of members of the academic profession are unimportant (Clark, 1987: 107), I have argued throughout this book that it is the interplay between discipline and individual practice, between culture and identity, that is crucial for a proper understanding of the lived experience of being an academic lawyer. In this chapter, the emphasis is apparently firmly on identity—gender, race, class, sexual orientation and the way we dress are personal matters. However, it would be inaccurate to say that these things are unaffected by the culture in which they exist. 'Identity' is about the ways in which individuals are distinguished in their *social* relations with others. As Jenkins argues, identity includes not only our understanding of who we are, but of who other people are, as well as their understanding of themselves and others (Jenkins, 1996: 4–5). In exploring the professional identities of academic lawyers, what is revealed is not just a wealth of information about how individuals see themselves as academic lawyers, but how they are seen by others. In turn, these professional identities are moderated by the culture in which they operate, and have effects upon that culture, helping to establish 'the way things are done' (Billington et al, 1991: 4). It is here that we see again the utility of Bourdieu's concept of habitus, as a way of understanding individuals as a complex amalgam of their past and present, an amalgam that is always in the process of completion and therefore open to change (Tett, 2000: 185).

Although for the purposes of analysis, the various aspects of identity discussed in this chapter are organised under separate headings, it is important to acknowledge that these social categories all interact and/or compete with one another in Giddens' 'project of the self' (Giddens, 1991):

> Gender, ethnicity, 'race' and class may be seen as cross-cutting and mutually interacting discourses, practices and intersubjectivities that coalesce and articulate at particular conjectures to produce different and stratified social outcomes.
> (Anthias, 1996, quoted in Archer et al, 2001)

GENDER

There has recently been a flurry of writing about women legal academics in the UK (Cownie, 1998, 2000b; McGlynn, 1998; Wells, 2000, 2001, 2001a, 2002). Richard Collier has also written extensively about gender and the law school, analysing in particular the relationship between law, legal academic careers and masculinity (1991, 1998, 1998a, 2002). There is a great deal of writing about women in the legal academy in the United States—in 1999 the Association of American Law Schools ran a workshop for women in legal education entitled 'Getting Unstuck—Without Coming Unglued' for which Robbins and Okonska compiled a 35-page bibliography, the majority of which is composed of material specifically relating to the legal academy (Robbins and Okonska, 1999). There is similar work in other jurisdictions, Canada and Australia in particular (see McIntyre, 1995; Thornton, 1996). There is copious evidence from that work, and from writing about women academics in general (of which there is also an increasing amount), that women in the academy (in the UK, as elsewhere) do not fare any better than women in other professions when it comes to equality of treatment in the workplace (see, eg, Acker, 1994; Davies et al, 1994; Brooks, 1997).

In the current study, I did not want merely to re-investigate the position of women in the law school, but to explore instead the extent to which awareness of these issues have permeated the culture of legal academia. The first question I asked about gender was 'Do you think that being a legal academic is different for women, as compared with men?' It is a feature of this study that, in examining issues relating to gender, I interviewed men as well as women. In her study of gender and merchant banking, *Capital Culture*, McDowell notes that the comparative experiences of men and women in the same occupations are not well established, because many explorations of gender issues at work have focused exclusively on women (McDowell, 1997: 85). In attempting to uncover the lived experience of legal academics as a whole, I regarded it as a particular contribution of this study that I could collect responses from both men and women about these issues.

Overall, two-thirds of the respondents agreed that women's experience of working in law schools is different from men's. The extent of agreement was slightly greater in old universities than new, but there was little difference between the sexes, or between people at different stages of their careers. Just under a fifth of the respondents were uncertain about the answer to this question—generally because they did not see any difference in their department, but were aware of a different picture in legal academia as a whole; there were more women than men in this group. Less than a fifth of the respondents said that they did not believe the experience of legal academia was different for men and women; this group contained significantly more men. Overall, then, there appeared to be quite a high level of awareness that the culture of academic law affects men and women differently.

Identity Matters 169

The small minority who thought that being a legal academic was no different for women than men (most of them male) seemed to be almost completely unaware of the sorts of issues raised by the other respondents:

> I don't see why it should be [different for women]. I don't see that it is.
> (professor, mid-career, male, old university)
>
> It doesn't make any difference—I don't feel that any of my colleagues are treated differently because they're a woman.
> (lecturer, early career, male, old university)
>
> No, I don't think there's a difference. Probably when I came here there was probably discrimination against women in terms of appointments and promotions. But there certainly isn't any more. It is absolutely a level playing field.
> (lecturer, mid-career, male, new university)

However, in general, the very broad range of responses, pointing to many different aspects of differential treatment of men and women in contemporary law schools, reflects the large number of concerns which have been raised by academic writers on the subject. Reasons for believing that male and female legal academics have a different experience in their working lives varied. Two of the main reasons given were the disadvantages resulting to women as a result of child-bearing and child-care, and the very obvious lack of women holding senior posts in law schools. The evidence that domestic responsibilities impact upon career development is well-documented (see, eg, Williams 2000; Hakim, 2000). This is reflected in the responses offered by the respondents:

> Obviously having children and the career break—you can probably lop two years off a woman's progression for one child, and probably an increasing number of years for every subsequent child—which is obviously a disadvantage . . .
> (professor, mid-career, male, new university)
>
> . . . It's still the case that the woman is expected to look after children, and it doesn't seem to be any different in academia than anywhere else. So I think that is certainly true, which I think makes it harder for some women to come through, and get to the rank of professor. I think you've got to be more hardworking , and have more ambition, than the equivalent male . . .
> (lecturer, early career, male, old university)

There is also considerable evidence which suggests that all women in heterosexual relationships are disadvantaged by domestic burdens, and that this is the case, even in dual-career households where both partners have jobs of equal status (Laurie and Gershuny, 2000):

> I suppose it comes down to what I regard as a basic difference between men and women, anyway, and that's that—there's always kind of—I never feel I can devote 100 per cent of my energies to this job at any particular time. There's always other things that I've got to think about as well, that I can't just forget about, and completely dissociate myself from. You know, there's always a bit of me that's thinking 'What are we going to have for dinner tonight? Have I picked my son up? We've got to go to the dentist.' I always kind of feel those pressures on me—and I don't think

men do. I kind of get the impression that, you know, they can devote all their energies to this job.
(lecturer, early career, female, old university)

Writers on the position of women in law schools have repeatedly called attention to the relatively small number of women holding senior positions in university law schools. Clare McGlynn's empirical study found that in 1997 only 14 per cent of law professors were female (40 per cent of other senior staff and 46 per cent of lecturers were women) confirming the evidence from other sources, such as the Higher Education Statistics Agency which convey a similar picture for academia as a whole (McGlynn, 1998: 41). McGlynn's global figures mask considerable differences between old and new universities. Elsewhere, she points out that in general there is a greater representation of women at all grades in new universities (McGlynn, 1999: 82). Wells, discussing her study of women law professors, notes how her interviewees were particularly likely to relate 'gender stories' when the subject of promotion was mentioned (Wells, 2002: 20). Difficulty in obtaining a chair was the other main factor referred to by the respondents in my survey:

It's tougher to get to the top . . . I think it isn't easy for a woman to make it in academic life. There are still a whole load of cultural assumptions that are made. I don't think people are deliberately discriminatory, it's just the way the system works. Professors are men . . .
(professor, experienced, male, new university)

. . . I think the role model thing matters, I really do. I think it's a big problem for younger women if there aren't any senior women around. That's not to say senior women are always nice and cuddly and supportive to younger women, because unfortunately they're not. But I do think it matters . . .
(professor, experienced, female, old university)

It must be [different for women], simply because, in my experience, you're always in the minority if you're an academic lawyer. So that must be a difference. And there are even fewer women in any senior positions, so I guess if I was a member of a group who was in a minority, and there were even fewer of my group in senior positions, then I'd perceive that as a disadvantage for me—there'd be fewer role models, if nothing else.
(lecturer, early career, male, old university)

. . . I know very few women professors. I have only worked in departments which had one female professor, and they're both people who have done an awful lot of research, they've published widely, but I've seen men be promoted to professor almost by serving time and doing reasonably well—in some departments, not all. That's not to devalue the male professors that are out there, because many of them are extremely competent. But I'm not sure that the same rules apply . . .
(lecturer, early career, female, new university)

There were a wide range of other factors which respondents regarded as resulting in differential experiences for men and women working in law schools. These included the tendency for women to be overloaded with administration (a central characteristic of Thornton's 'dutiful daughters' (Thornton, 1996), and the effects of masculinity—ways in which women's behaviour, when different from stereotypically male behaviour, appears to disadvantage them in the workplace (a phenomenon which Acker terms the 'male-as-norm bias' (Acker, 1994: 131).

> ... We have a lot of women in this department, but disproportionately I guess they are the ones who get the dogsbody jobs. I am sure they have their own networks and I am sure they find ways of supporting each other against the encircling dominance of a certain style of male culture, but I wouldn't like to speak for them ... I think, to be blunt, they are being horribly ripped off by the institution.
> (principal lecturer, mid-career, male, new university)

> ... I would say though that on average my female colleagues are very good at the communicative bits of the job, the emotional housework sort of bits. A greater proportion of them take that seriously. It's a bit of a burden to them really, although they all believe in it ...
> (professor, experienced, female, old university)

> I could make some sort of crude generalisation. For example, my comment about having to be selfish to become a professor. I think quite a lot of women would feel uncomfortable about being as selfish as some men are prepared to be in order to achieve that—but that's probably a gross generalisation—obviously, some men are not that selfish, and some women are prepared to be just that selfish—but it's a stereotypically masculine way of operating ...
> (professor, mid-career, male, new university)

> It's partly a matter of confidence, in my experience. I find able women more often consult me about what to do next, and I'm thinking 'You know, actually, you don't need to do this.' Whereas men are more likely to go off and do it, and piss me off! ...
> (professor, mid-career, male, new university)

> ... I think the pressures to produce research, for example, and just the ways that people in academia seek to bolster themselves by putting other people down is actually, I think, psychologically more difficult for most of my female colleagues to cope with. It's not true for all, but I do think that in general the job is done in a male way.
> (lecturer, early career, male, old university)

The 'credibility gap' was mentioned by several respondents. These interviewees were drawing attention to the way in which, if women do things differently from the hegemonic male, their achievements may not be acknowledged or rewarded (this is, of course, also a problem for gay men). An engagement with masculinity has been seen as crucial to the feminist critique of law for some time (Naffine, 1990). Feminist legal scholars have also drawn attention to the congruence of law and masculinity (O'Donovan, 1985; Smart, 1995; Thornton, 1996). This is a particular problem in the context of the academy, with its attachment to the notion of rationality, a quality also stereotypically associated with men (Lloyd, 1984). Wells argues that the association of law and the academy with ideas of rationality, neutrality and objectivity means that being a *legal* academic may prove a 'double jeopardy' for women (Wells, 2001: 119). Collier's interest in 'the social dynamics whereby discrimination is reproduced and legitimated on a daily basis in the field of law' (1998: 23) leads him to interrogate the ways in which practices have been historically constituted by reference to a 'masculinist' vision of 'professional' work, and what implications stem from this for both men and women in the legal academy (Collier, 1998: 25). Collier too associates the gendering of cultural, symbolic and economic capital in the legal field with the invocation of rationality, objectivity and authority as key masculine qualities, and argues that it is the hegemony of this particular form of (heterosexual) masculinity that makes it so hard for those other than the stereotypical white heterosexual male to take their rightful place in the law school:

> ... it's the general problems of work-family divide, of out-and-out discrimination, which undoubtedly still affects women. And the construction of their commitment levels. If women do things at all differently, then that may be downgraded, or devalued. So I think it's those sort of typical problems that they face.
>
> A lot of it is also that there's a high level of informality about things, which it has taken me a long time to realise—that actually, for instance, the level of pay they quote is often actually up for negotiation, and that those who shout loudest and push hardest get more. And on the whole, men are better at that than women, more competent at it, and better at feeling they're worth it, and I think that contributes to the pay gap.
> (lecturer, early career, female, old university)

> ... I think there is a perception that many women become academics because of its flexibility, because it suits them if they have a family...so I think there is a perception that a lot of younger women do it or go into it for its convenience, and that is a potentially damaging stereotype, because it helps them imagine that women are less ambitious, less flexible, less likely to be there all hours, whereas for men its more likely to be perceived as a career choice and that, you know, there are other things they could be doing, and therefore the fact that they're doing this must mean they're incredibly committed to being an academic. I'm sure for some women it is an excellent choice, but I also know that for some male colleagues its partly to do with family commitments...
> (lecturer, mid-career, female, new university)

> There is certainly a male/female distinction, and a general tendency for women to be seen as not capable of doing the job, or not as important, or whatever ... I think women definitely have to work that extra bit.
> (lecturer, early career, male, old university)

One respondent gave a response which could clearly have been informed by the work of Carol Gilligan, especially her famous analysis of the different masculine and feminine 'voices' she identified in her work on moral reasoning (Gilligan 1982):

> The thing about administration is, it tends to end up at the point of least resistance, which can often be female—I think it goes back to a stronger propensity on the part of women to be social. Administration involves communicating with people, which women find natural, whereas there are some men I'm aware of who are perfectly happy coming in, doing whatever it is they have to do and buggering off. And I think

women actually find that quite difficult, you know, they want to communicate, want to make contact with their fellows.
(professor, mid-career, male, new university)

Some respondents saw it as an issue of patriarchy:

I went into academia thinking there would be very few differences [between men and women working there] really, because, you know, academia is meant to be more politically correct, and slightly more enlightened, and more left-wing. So my view was there'd actually be less discrimination or prejudice against women. And actually, I think I've changed my view on that. I sort of oscillate a little—I don't think it's just a gender divide, I think it's also an age divide, and that's why I think young male academics also have quite a difficult time of it—because it's about patriarchy. And I think it *is* patriarchal, as opposed to just hierarchical. I think there's an added disadvantage, in some ways, in being taken seriously as a young female, but I think it's still difficult for young male academics . . .
(lecturer, early career, female, new university)

. . . What makes it harder for women is—how can I put this? I think senior male colleagues wouldn't do this consciously, but they adopt a sort of father-figure attitude to these women, which isn't helpful. Two things happen. They shower them with advice, based on their experiences, which will necessarily be different, or they can suffer rejection from these women, and they get alienated. So I've seen several cases, where very nice junior women colleagues have a problematic relationship with senior male colleagues. And it is because of gender, and it plays very badly against women. Conversely, some of the female professors mother some of the junior male colleagues—who are often quite happy about it.
(reader, mid-career, male, old university)

The 'masculinity' of legal academia was also mentioned by several respondents:

I think there's the usual problem about credibility gaps—that women have much greater difficulty establishing credibility—if there is anything particular about law, it's that law, like, I imagine, the natural sciences, has been perceived as a rather masculine subject in the past. It's not a soft subject—it's not sociology or something, and therefore women have got to establish their credibility within it . . .
(lecturer, early career, female, old university)

. . . I think academia still is a man's world, even though there are a lot of female academics, and a lot of them holding high office. But that whole thing about in order to succeed, you've got to succeed on men's terms, and there is a lot about the problems that women are 'emotional' and that women are irrational and subjective . . .
(lecturer, mid-career, female, new university)

It's very difficult to put my finger on—but I do imagine there's a difference in the perception of women. It's complicated. Students perceive them as different, too. It comes across that there are subjects that are perceived as male and female subjects—in X [legal subject], the whole team is male, and team meetings are very much shaped by that fact—swearing is ok, the atmosphere is shaped by it being all-male. Things away from the core can tend to be seen as female.
(senior lecturer, mid-career, male, old university)

174 Identity Matters

In his analysis of the legal academy, Collier has pointed to the power of hegemonic masculinity to disqualify that which is not part of its method (subjectivity, alternative accounts of 'reality', the transgression of the heterosexual imperative), thus excluding that which might challenge masculinism as a pervasive ideological support of male power; '. . . that is, the naturalisation of sexual difference, the sanctioning of the political and dominant role of men and the institutional enforcement of hegemonic heterosexuality . . .' (Collier, 1991: 432). In the context of the present study, it is Collier's next argument which is particularly pertinent, since he identifies masculinity not as a fixed entity, but as something continually 'in process':

> Hegemonic masculinity must be constantly produced and reproduced, and the gender regime at any historical moment is always dynamic. This is as true of a specific institutional setting (for example, a law school) as in society generally. This is a matter of locating the politics of masculinity as not simply at the level of the personal (be it as a matter of choice, conditioning, human nature and so forth) but as embedded in the gender regime of specific institutions, as part of politics and the organisational sexuality of organisations . . .
> (Collier, 1991: 432)

Collier's insights reinforce the theoretical model I have adopted; not only in emphasising, as I have, the fluidity of identity, but in pointing to the interplay of identity (personal choice, human nature) and culture (the gender regime of institutions), the relationship which is at the heart of my analysis.

There appears to be consensus among commentators writing about the legal academy that there is no *single* cause of this phenomenon; as I have said before, this is a matter of great complexity (Cownie, 2000b). McGlynn points to a number of features which might make it difficult for women to play an equal role in the legal academy. These include the reception of feminist scholarship, the small number of female role models and the role of male gatekeepers. She explicitly relates her work to the culture of the law school:

> These issues are important—not just because of discrimination, but because women also play an essential role in determining the culture of the law school and, therefore, the learning environment of law students. An ethos which marginalises women academics and/or feminist legal scholarship, and in which authority, men and masculinity are inextricably entwined, becomes embedded in students' learning of the law and legal culture.
> (McGlynn, 1998: 57)

Noting that the three major theoretical explanations for women's differential position in organisations are structure, agency and culture, Celia Wells canvasses a number of ways in which these factors might explain the position of women in the legal academy (2001). Gender, she writes, is often 'submerged—there but not there' within the culture of the law school (Wells, 2001: 136). One of the ways in which she seeks to deconstruct the position of women in law schools is by turning her attention to the intersection of gender, management and university organisational structures. 'Management, like law, is an occupation that is historically and culturally associated with men' (Wells, 2001: 127). This is a theme also taken up by Richard Collier, who has focused on the way in which changes in higher education, in particular increased 'managerialism' and external assessment (which he associates with the rise of 'entrepreneurial masculinism') have resulted in the 'remasculinisation' of the legal academy (Collier, 2002: 20). One of the most interesting points he makes, in the context of the present study, is the importance of *conceptualising* the way in which the masculine subject is understood, because:

> Developing any meaningful agenda of change around a question of 'women and law school' also involves addressing men as social subjects—and culturally masculine practices—in ways which are grounded in social relationships, not in abstract notions of gender ideals which would, so often, appear to 'float free' from what men actually do.
> (Collier, 2002: 27).

The strength of the present study is to give a rich picture of the ways in which the men and women who work in the legal academy perceive the ways in which women, in particular, are treated differently in their working environment, thus revealing how the culture of academic law affects the professional identities of a large proportion of its members. 'Compliance with gendered expectations of appropriate behaviour is not only central to an acceptable identity, but reaffirms institutional relationships . . . thus the constraints on gender identities can be seen in the expectations and rewards that accompany differing forms of their expression' (Letherby and Shiels, 2001: 131). The relationship between culture and identity, here as elsewhere in the law school, is complex. My enquiry has uncovered widespread acknowledgement, on the part of both male and female academics, that the lived experience of legal academics differs for men and women. It is not the case that this is a 'problem' only perceived by women. However, even widespread acknowledgement of a problem does not guarantee its speedy solution, especially in the light of my finding in chapter 4 of this study that awareness of gender issues in the legal academy may be somewhat superficial. As I have pointed out before, our state of knowledge about the position of women (and men) in the law school is one of considerable ignorance (Cownie, 1998). The work of scholars such as those I have just discussed, and this present study, addresses some of the gaps in our knowledge, but there is still much to be done.

CLASS

Class is an important aspect of identity (Jenkins, 1996: 85), and in *Homo Academicus* Bourdieu famously drew attention to the influence of social capital in academic life (Bourdieu, 1988). In his analysis of *The Decline of Donnish*

Dominion, Halsey (1989) found that class origin had a predictive value in identifying those that are promoted into the professoriate, with professors being significantly more likely to have sprung from the middle classes (Halsey, 1992: 204). Harrison begins his article on class bias in law school appointments in the US with the following story:

> I telephoned an old friend the other day at another law school. 'What's up?' I asked.
> 'Faculty retreat' he replied.
> 'Sorry to hear it. Any topic, or just a weekend of touchy-feely?'
> 'Serious business.' he said 'The theme is "Recruiting for Diversity". One session on race, one on gender.'
> 'What about class—you know, poor and working-class candidates?'
> 'Are you kidding?' he responded 'Too important'.
> (Harrison, 1991: 119)

Harrison argues that class-based differences relating to fundamental matters such as one's conception of justice have great potential for different perspectives in research and approaches to teaching; some of the points he makes are reflected in the responses discussed below.

Stereotypically, academia has a very middle-class image. The pages of academic novels, from *Lucky Jim* to *Changing Places* are littered with images of the middle-class milieu of the academic life. Both Wells and Collier, writing about legal academics, make similar comments about the '(very) middle class nature of the legal academy' (Wells, 2001: 136; Collier 2002: 28). When I asked how they would regard themselves now, as legal academics, in terms of class, all the respondents agreed that this is a middle class job.

In this section of the study, I was interested to find out the effect of class background upon the professional identities of academic lawyers. Class is a contested concept in the literature, with major debates taking place (between, for example, supporters of Wright's neo-Marxist theory of class and those of Goldthorpe's neo-Weberian theory of class (Edgell, 1993)and between those who argue for 'the death of class' (Pakulski and Waters, 1996) and those who still regard it as a useful concept (Crompton, 1998). Most studies of class define it in occupational terms, and define class location as determined by the occupation of the male 'head' of the household (Edgell, 1993: 39). While this approach has been subjected to a range of criticism (notably from feminist scholars), occupational class schemes are so widely used that they are arguably the most familiar to non-specialists, which was a particularly important consideration for the present study.

In order to obtain a very basic indication of the class background of my respondents, I asked them to describe their background, thinking about the schools they had attended, their parents' employment, the houses they had been brought up in and so on. I used father's occupation to analyse the class background of the respondent, based on the Registrar General's original classification scheme (Census, 1992, para. 7.51). This conceptualises the boundary of working class and middle class as a manual/non-manual divide, which is how the respondents also characterised that boundary. The disadvantage of this system is, of course, that the category of 'middle class' is so broad that it gives rise to apparently endless debates about whether it is appropriate to talk of 'the middle class' as a singular entity, or whether it would be more appropriate to talk of 'the middle classes' (Roberts et al, 1977; Giddens, 1991). This difficulty was reflected in the decisions of a significant number of respondents to classify their background as 'lower middle class'. This appeared to refer to occupations falling within the Registrar General's class 3 (skilled non-manual); I have therefore adopted this in my discussion. This results in a classificatory scheme which is composed of 'middle class' (professional, managerial and technical); 'lower middle class' (skilled non-manual) and 'working class' (skilled manual, semi-skilled manual and unskilled manual).

In old universities, about half of the respondents came from middle class backgrounds, and about a quarter from working class and lower middle class backgrounds respectively. In new universities, about half of the respondents came from lower middle class backgrounds, and about a quarter from middle class and working class backgrounds respectively. These results are quite similar to those obtained by Halsey in his large-scale survey of academia (Halsey, 1992: 204). It would appear from this data that although legal academics unquestionably perceive their current status as inherently middle class, they do not all come to that position with the same 'cultural capital'. They are also drawn from a slightly wider class background than the students they teach; according to the Law Society's longitudinal study, only about 18 per cent of law students' parents were engaged in working class occupations (Halpern, 1994: 21).

Only 10 per cent of respondents had attended private schools for any stage of their education. The vast majority of respondents (80 per cent) came from a family where neither parent had been to university. Only two people had fathers who had themselves worked in universities, and no one had a mother who had been an academic. Several respondents (mostly working in old universities) drew attention to the consequences that this lack of experience of higher education could have, in terms of 'cultural capital':

> ... Once I got to grammar school, the whole thing became a deep mystery for my parents. Nobody on either side of the family had stayed on at school beyond the usual leaving age, and no one had been within a sniff of a university. They had no concept of what I was doing or why. They were very pleased, and proud, but had not the faintest idea, really ...
> (lecturer, experienced, male, old university)
>
> ... It was a disadvantage in some ways. My parents didn't know anything about universities, so I had to do all the investigation myself. The school was used to it, but didn't know anything particularly about law. I feel ambivalent about the particular university I went to, although I did very well there ...
> (professor, mid-career, male, old university)
>
> I think if I look at my peers, I do find that the fact that they were from a 'better' background allowed them to perform better at university and probably accelerated their

> career. If you have that background, you know where you are going, you get better advice, of course; you just get a lot more advantages...
> (lecturer, early career, male, old university)

> ... I think the biggest jolt was from school to university. I went to my local university; it was a sort of half-and-half existence, and I was subject to all sorts of pressures... I think it's the lack of confidence that's the problem. I don't think any university did anything to address it—it wasn't even acknowledged. People might be kind, and be trying to help, but they don't know what the problems are, or how you feel—it's not just money worries, it's about culture, really, without being too extreme about it...
> (lecturer, experienced, female, old university)

The next question I asked was 'How, if at all, has your background affected you as a legal academic?' The vast majority of respondents did not think their class background had significantly affected them. However, nearly half this group (about a third of the total) qualified their answer, by saying that although in general they felt their social background was unimportant, it had affected them in terms of its influence on their research interests, or in giving them a particularly keen sense of the importance of education. This group had no particular features, in terms of institution, gender or experience, but in terms of class background contained almost noone with a middle class background.

Research, as we have seen, is a central part of the professional identity of the majority of legal academics. For a significant number of respondents, class background had affected their research, in that personal experience of less privileged circumstances had led several people to take a particular interest in subjects such as welfare law, criminal law or labour law:

> It's shaped the work I'm interested in—which is labour law—you don't need to be a psychologist to see that it's linked with the environment I grew up in, the values I acquired, and how I look at the world...
> (lecturer, early career, male, old university)

> Because I had knowledge of a working-class background, I'm much more aware of the poverty level, even in subjects I teach. I have an awareness of a different point of view. Also, I'm interested in working-class movements—that's to do with my background. It does have an influence...
> (lecturer, mid-career, male, new university)

Personal or family experience of the importance of education in facilitating social mobility was also an important factor in the construction of the professional identity of these respondents. These are academic, as opposed to practising, lawyers—and that is significant:

> ... it was incredibly important for my parents that you used education to get a good job. I think because both my father and my mother's father came from very poor backgrounds—so education was instrumental... when I was at Oxbridge, I resented the cosiness and complacency of other people—they were nice, but I thought they were homogenous, they lacked any kind of ambition, in my view, to do anything other than enrich themselves and be comfortable...
> (reader, mid-career, male, old university)

The fact that my father was deprived of education (he passed the 11+ but they couldn't afford to send him to grammar school) had a tremendous effect on me in terms of my commitment to education . . .
(professor, experienced, male, new university)

About a fifth of the respondents felt their backgrounds had been a disadvantage in the context of their job; most of these people (who came from a range of social backgrounds) were working in old universities:

> It certainly hasn't made it easier. Some of the recruitment procedures are very much kind of informal—and interviews are shaped by the expectations of those conducting them—they expect people to speak eloquently and so on. I know when I started as an academic, people who didn't know my work they saw me as not coherent and so on. So it certainly hasn't helped in any way.
> (senior lecturer, mid-career, male, old university)

> I still approach things differently, in some ways. I tend to be much more straightforward in negotiation with people—I have to tone down what may otherwise appear to be abrasive. I have to adjust to the middle class mores, the middle class ways of doing things. I've got a friend from the same background as me. She's doing a PhD and we email each other. She thinks middle class people are sly, because they don't say what they want, they don't ask outright.
> (lecturer, experienced, female, old university)

> . . . Perhaps there's still an element of the old-boy network, and I notice it at conferences. Also, there's a classical style to the law, Latin expressions and judgments delivered by judges who use examples derived from the Classics . . . I also notice, in terms of appointments, if someone has a PhD from Cambridge, they are more highly regarded 'So-and-so at X college has written this reference; it's the best reference I have ever seen.'
> (lecturer, early career, male, old university)

> . . . It's probably why I've always worked in a new university. It's to do with what you regard as an environment sympathetic to your background . . .
> (professor, mid-career, male, new university)

Conversely, a similar number of respondents (who all came from middle class backgrounds) felt that their background had made working as a legal academic a relatively unproblematic choice of career:

> I guess if you come from a reasonably educated background, it gives you certain kinds of advantages. It's probably a matter of confidence. Certainly, going to university was something that was expected. There were twenty-eight people in my sixth form, and fifteen went to Oxbridge and the rest to other universities. Becoming an academic would be something that's more achievable if you come from that class background.
> (senior lecturer, mid-career, male, old university)

> Most of the students are from the same background as me, so it's no problem at all . . .
> (reader, experienced, male, old university)

> As an academic, yes—it's perhaps easier to deal with some of my peers . . .
> (lecturer, mid-career, female, new university)

180   Identity Matters

Despite all agreeing that being a legal academic was a middle-class occupation, about a fifth of the respondents did not feel that they wholly identified with the middle classes. This group was a mixture of people from working class and lower middle class backgrounds who still felt distanced from the middle class milieu of the legal academy:

> I think about it a lot. Some people say 'You're middle class', and I guess in some measure that would be true, but I still think of myself as a working class person in a middle class profession.
> (lecturer, early career, male, old university)

> I find it really difficult to put myself in a category, really. Within my working environment, it's middle class. But in my home life, it's more of a mix. I know I'm middle class in terms of career, but I feel different—I don't have the same background as my middle class friends so their families, and what they do when they go and visit them for the weekend and so on is very different. Their parents are well-educated, and mine are not, so it makes a difference. But not within my job.
> (lecturer, early career, female, new university)

> I feel in that kind of nebulous position that you find yourself in if you're from a working class background, but end up working in a profession, and in economic terms earning a middle class wage. I'm distanced from my own background, but I'm never fully a part of the middle class. I wouldn't say I was middle class. It would be impossible to feel entirely comfortable with that. In some ways, I'm cut off from a sense of belonging. I'm no longer part of the class from which I emerged, and I'm not, and have no desire to be, a member of the class in which I work. It has its downsides—but I find my sense of belonging elsewhere.
> (senior lecturer, mid-career, male, old university)

Taking the respondents as a whole, they perceived class background as having little or no effect upon their professional identity as an academic lawyer. Influences which were discussed were often relatively benign, such as the promotion of an interest in social welfare law or employment law. About as many people thought their social background had been an advantage as thought it had been a disadvantage. However, a significant number (about a fifth of the total) did not feel at ease in the inherently middle class atmosphere of the legal academy. This group reflected views similar to those expressed by Ryan and Sackrey in their study of working class academics in American universities, *Strangers in Paradise* (1984). Ryan and Sackrey, themselves having experienced the social mobility they were investigating, found themselves questioning whether the trip from working class boy to college professor had been 'worth the toll' (1984: 4). Their concerns centre on whether the 'social mobility game' makes losers of many of the winners, in that the new higher social status brings discomfort and unease:

> It became clear for us that to grow up working class, then to take on the full trappings of the life of college professor internalises the conflicts in the hierarchy of the class system within the individual upwardly mobile person.
> (Ryan and Sackrey, 1984: 5)

Anderson also discusses the tensions between her working class roots and her middle class status as lecturer. 'I still do not feel that I inhabit the academy in the same way as students and colleagues of middle class origins' (Anderson, 2001: 141). In order to enter the middle class academy, she found that she had to subjugate her Glaswegian working class accent and mode of expression; now, she has learned to 'play the game' and can 'pass' as middle class, outwardly adopting modes of behaviour that come from outside working class experience, but 'passing is not the same as belonging' (Anderson, 2001: 144).

Class is an important aspect of academic identity; it can affect attitudes and behaviour in respect of the 'core' academic activities of teaching and research. In considering the lived experience of legal academia it is thus a factor which is too important to be overlooked.

RACE, ETHNICITY AND LEGAL ACADEMICS

The structured inequalities found in the wider society also affect the culture of academic law, which, like other disciplines in the academy, is predominantly 'white' (Becher and Trowler, 2001: 153). A person's ethnic origins also affect the construction of their professional identity as 'academic'. Writing about minority ethnic women academics Housee notes:

> Identities within universities are constructed within conditions where white, middle class cultures are represented as the norm . . . within this context, our identities as black female lecturers are racialised and gendered in a way that can sometimes present us as passive and powerless and where other times our differences are privileged. (Housee, 2001: 82)

Although it is important to acknowledge the role of ethnicity in the construction of identity, it is equally relevant to bear in mind that, as with the other 'identity matters' discussed in this chapter, people are not defined merely by one aspect of their identity. As Henry argues, it is important to recognise that people from minority ethnic backgrounds '. . . occupy a variety of different identities simultaneously in terms of their ethnicities, sexuality, religious beliefs, physical abilities, socio-economic status and so on' (Henry, 1994: 44). There is always a danger that a person's racial characteristics come to dominate all other aspects of their identity; the reality, as Mirza notes, is that 'Black people in Britain do not live a one-dimensional life defined by the racism of others' (Mirza, 1995: 151).

I did not use race as a factor when selecting respondents to interview, and only one of the legal academics I interviewed came from a minority ethnic background. This is not particularly surprising. Although there is some evidence that concern about equal opportunities issues (including those relating to ethnic origin) has grown in recent years (Ramsden, 1996: 29), and universities are now subject to new obligations imposed by the Race Relations (Amendment) Act

2000 to promote racial equality, there are still very few academics from ethnic minority backgrounds working in English universities—according to figures published by the Higher Education Statistics Agency, around 5 per cent of all academic staff (HESA, 2002). There has been very little investigation of the experience of ethnic minority legal academics. Neither Leighton et al (1995) in their survey of law teachers, nor Harris and Jones (1997) in their survey of law schools, gathered data on the ethnic origins of legal academics; that fact in itself shows that there is a great deal to be found out in this area. Heward et al comment that when researching the life histories of professors, 'Vain attempts to locate senior academics in law and biology [the disciplines which were the subject of the investigation] suggested that only the very smallest numbers enter or succeed in the profession' (Heward et al, 1997: 208).

Heward et al's research compared the careers of successful white men, women and members of ethnic minority groups who became professors of law or biology in UK universities, and revealed the extent to which members of ethnic minority groups may be seen in stereotypical ways. Respondents talked, for example, of wanting to appoint staff from among such candidates, but the few applicants who had been considered 'were not of the right calibre' (Heward et al, 1997: 212). The informal processes of networking, invitations and recommendations by senior members of the profession were identified as especially problematic for minority ethnic academics (1997: 215). Given Becher and Trowler's comments about the unusually significant role played by personal contacts in obtaining promotion in academic law (Becher and Trowler, 2001: 79) this is arguably a particularly acute difficulty for minority ethnic academics working in the legal academy. It is something to which Goodrich and Mills draw attention in their analysis of 'the law of white spaces'; the ways in which the racial dynamics of the law school go unrecognised, ignored or denied (Goodrich and Mills, 2001: 16):

> The ideal type of the heroic white male intellectual is never expressly stated. Much more insidiously, the everyday rules of good behaviour, of belonging to the institution, of being a successful academic, lawyer, or whatever, are maintained as insider knowledge . . . Only someone schooled in the manner of the insider can know the rules in the manner of the insider. Although outsiders can learn the insider's way of knowing, their difference will always distinguish them, preventing any real penetration of the boundaries between the identical and the different, the similar and the outside.
> (Goodrich and Mills, 2001: 21)

Goodrich and Mills' main argument is that in relation to all aspects of the culture of academic law '. . . the most subtle aspect of racialized dynamics is that of the tacit assertion of the continuing superiority of the norm. Whiteness is itself the implicit criterion of knowledge, the rule of the institutional game' (2001: 22). They also draw attention to the ways in which the scholarly norms of academic law reflect a lack of consciousness of the dynamics of race (2001: 25). The curriculum of the legal academy certainly does not seem to have been subjected to examination from the perspective of 'race' of the kind which has been found in the discipline of sociology, for example, where, as Housee notes, curriculum development has a long history of intense debate informed by 'identity politics' (Housee, 2001: 84).

Further evidence that the lived experience of being a legal academic who comes from a minority ethnic background can be problematic comes from Montgomery's report of her disillusionment with the culture of a number of academic law departments in which she studied and worked. She is particularly critical of the way in which it is assumed that '. . . because academia is a space for intellectual thought, those within that space are incapable of discriminating on the basis of colour or "race" ' (Montgomery, 1997: 68). She also tells a story about going for an interview for an academic job; of the five candidates, three were black women; all were involved in the process of taking a higher education institution to an industrial tribunal (Montgomery, 1997: 70). This story has resonances with Goodrich and Mills' analysis of a case brought by a minority ethnic law lecturer, Asif Qureshi, against the University of Manchester and the dean of its law faculty, which resulted in a finding that the respondents were liable on the basis of discrimination and victimisation. It is a story of injustice and exclusion, familiar enough to any employment lawyer. But its location within the legal academy gives it a particular resonance. This is a case in which we are told, among other things, that eight academics (some of them members of the law department) apparently failed to notice that they were reading only the odd-numbered pages of Qureshi's CV (someone having forgotten to photocopy the even-numbered pages) (Goodrich and Mills, 2001: 34).

Given that there are so few minority ethnic legal academics, it is unsurprising that I only interviewed one such person. It was not the objective of this study to portray in particular the professional identities of members of minority ethic groups, but the existing literature suggests that this would be a fruitful site of further investigation.

SEXUAL ORIENTATION

I did not ask any of my respondents about their sexual orientation, having decided, as with ethnicity, that a general investigation of the academic discipline of law would not be the best way to explore the lived experience of sexuality as it affects the culture of academic law and the professional identities of legal academics. (In this context, as in other work on sexuality, it is important to acknowledge that it is not solely non- or counter-hegemonic sexuality which should be the subject of investigation; hegemonic (male) heterosexuality also demands attention (Bell and Valentine, 1995: 143).

There is, however, evidence from the literature that working as a lesbian, gay or bisexual academic may have particular resonances, both in terms of the culture of academia and the working out of professional identities within that culture, and this is likely to be a fruitful area for future research. Talburt's ethnographic case study of lesbian academics in the United States, for example, illustrates some of the ways in which qualitative examination of these issues could throw light on the ways in which professional and personal identities work out within the culture of the academy (2000, reviewed in Gunter, 2001). The lived experience of gay or lesbian academics in the UK does not appear to have attracted as much attention as other forms of minority experience. For instance, the recent collection on identity and difference in higher education edited by Anderson and Williams, which addresses differences arising out of class, race and gender, is silent on sexual orientation (Anderson and Williams, 2001). The second edition of Becher's *Academic Tribes and Territories* (Becher and Trowler, 2001) extends the scope of its analysis to include more aspects of academic life than the first edition, and contains a section on 'race, ethnicity and academic careers' and one on 'women's academic careers', but nothing on the effect of sexual orientation on academic careers. The lack of analysis in this area is a phenomenon also noted in the report of a pilot study carried out for the AUT on lesbian, gay and bisexual participants in UK universities, published recently (AUT, 2001), which comments that while the disadvantages faced by women and ethnic minorities in higher education are now well-established, the problems facing lesbian, gay, bisexual and transgendered individuals are less well known (AUT, 2001: 3). This study found evidence that there is a glass ceiling operating against the promotion of gay men, which is of a similar magnitude to that facing heterosexual women. Gay men and lesbians who were academics expressed relatively low levels of 'comfortableness' in their working environment, and high perceived levels of discrimination; lesbians faced the highest perceived levels of harassment. There was also clear evidence that many of these workers were not 'out' in the workplace, thus making them a 'hidden' aspect of the culture of academia (AUT, 2001).

Within the legal academy in the UK, there is a now a considerable body of work which discusses various aspects of sexuality and law; for example, Herman and Stychin, 1995; Moran, 1996; Stychin and Herman, 2000; as well as Skidmore's discussion of 'a legal perspective on the sexuality of organisations' (Skidmore, 2001). However, these interests do not appear to have spilled over, to the extent one might have wished, into analysis of the legal academy. Clearly an important part of the dominant 'masculine' culture of the law school (discussed above in relation to the position of women in the legal academy) is heterosexuality. At first sight, the law school, like other organisations, might appear to be an asexual space, but, as Burrell and Hearn note, on closer examination, it becomes all too obvious that this is a context within which specific sexual practices are performed (Burrell and Hearn, 1989: 18). The sexuality of organisations is the subject of an extensive literature within the social sciences, which would provide a rich source of ideas with which to examine the culture of the law school and the professional identities of legal academics (see, eg, Collinson and Hearn, 1996; Hearn and Parkin, 1987; Acker, 1990). A particularly noticeable theme in this literature is the emphasis upon the role of work and workplaces as active forces in the social construction of workers as embodied beings. 'Rather than seeing the workplace as a site which men and women as fixed and finished products enter to become labour power, the ways in which the workplace or organisation plays a key role in the constitution of subjects is becoming clear' (McDowell, 1997: 12).

Theoretically, I have argued that work is a 'performance', and here the emphasis is on that performance being undertaken by embodied, gendered and sexed individuals. It is a taken-for-granted assumption that workers will conform to a heterosexual image of masculinity and femininity; the dominance of those norms is not achieved solely through decree or power, but also by self-surveillance and self-correction (McDowell, 1995: 78). Examination of sexuality in the context of the lived experience of legal academics is, therefore, an aspect of the 'performativity' which, I have argued, lies at the heart of identity. Sexualities, like genders, can be conceptualised as '. . . performative constructions naturalised through repetition' (Bell and Valentine, 1995: 143.) One aspect of performativity, to which Bell and Valentine draw attention, and which appears to be an unexplored area of the professional identities of academic lawyers, is the notion of 'passing'. Given that performers of non-hegemonic sexualities often find it difficult to operate within the dominant heterosexual boundaries they experience at work, they adopt the mantle of an 'apparent' heterosexual identity; though in their 'private' life they may be 'out'. Consequently, they shuttle through different appearances, sometimes maintaining multiple identities in different spaces at the same time or in one space at different times (Bell and Valentine, 1995: 147). This is just one illustration of the way in which sexual identity may impact upon professional identity, and one of the areas which it would be interesting to explore in the future.

However, in general, the hegemonic masculine heterosexuality of the law school is rarely *expressly* problematised. In this area, the work of Richard Collier is pioneering in exploring in a number of different ways the hegemonic nature of male heterosexuality, and the ways in which that affects the culture of the law school, making it more difficult not only for women, but for any men (gay or straight) who do not fit in to that stereotype to establish their professional identity as 'academic lawyer' (Collier, 1998, 1998a, 2002). Among other things, Collier has drawn our attention to the need to unpack the nature of the 'masculinism' of the legal field by focusing on 'what men *do*'. 'Institutions do not merely reflect a dominant sexual ideology; they are, crucially, sites for the active *production* of gender divisions' (Collier, 1998: 25). Collier cautions against focusing too exclusively on women legal academics; there is a danger, in so doing, of missing the point:

> So long as the sexed specificity of men is *effaced* within debates around gender, power and the legal profession it remains likely that 'the problem of men' will continue to be turned on its head and, in a neat discursive twist, the 'masculinism' of 'law' becomes, like so many others, a 'women's problem' a question of 'women in law'.
> (Collier, 1998: 38)

186 Identity Matters

Collier's work, valuable as it is in drawing our attention to the importance of sexuality in the context of the law school, remains at the level of the theoretical. As yet there is little empirically-based evidence about the lived experience of this aspect of the culture or its effects upon the professional identities of legal academics. Ruthann Robson's discussion of her experiences teaching a course on 'sexuality and the law' at the City University of New York (Robson, 1998), is therefore particularly useful in giving some insights into the issues which may arise in the context of the legal academy. Identity is a key theme of Robson's analysis. 'Within the classroom dynamic, my lesbianism is submerged into the identity of professor' she writes. The effect of her sexual orientation upon her professional identity remains problematic, however: 'The lesbian students often experience this stance as betrayal, while the non-lesbian students seem to wait for me to put my professional imprint on a specific lesbian perspective that will both settle the disputes between lesbian students and serve to neutralise the "authority" of my comments' (Robson, 1998: 220). Robson's work is a welcome example of some of the effects of a gay, lesbian or bisexual sexual orientation upon professional identity. It serves as an indicator of the potential for future research on the construction of the professional identities of academic lawyers within a dominantly heterosexual culture, and one in which, as I have discussed above, law itself can be analysed as a masculine discourse. As Squirrel argues in relation to school teaching, it is important to encourage discussion about a range of issues which could also fruitfully be explored in relation to the legal academy, including curriculum development, enforced conformity, the role of heterosexual colleagues, and the pervasiveness of heterosexism and homophobia in education (Squirrell, 1989: 33). I would argue that it is not only important to encourage discussion: what we need is further qualitative empirical investigation into this aspect of the 'private life' of the law school, which would seek to uncover what Collier has described as '. . . the profound privileging of homosocial culture and practices' which permeates the law school (Collier, 1998: 44).

DRESSED FOR THE PART?

Theorising Dress

Research into everyday clothing practices is still in its infancy. Although there has been a great deal of research into clothing, dress and fashion, very little of it is focused on everyday lives, so the analysis of clothes as a lived experience is under-developed (Guy et al, 2001: 4). Yet the clothes we wear are an important part of our 'performance', in the world of work as elsewhere. Craik illustrates the utility of Bourdieu's concept of *habitus* in theorising our use of dress; our 'habitus' of clothing, she suggests, creates a 'face', which positively constructs an identity. We use the way we wear our bodies to present ourselves to our social environment (our culture) 'mapping out our codes of conduct through our fashion behaviour' (Craik, 1993: 5).

My interest in the clothed bodies of legal academics arises from a recognition that dress is a cultural artefact, but at the same time has an important role to play in the construction of identity '. . . clothes bear the indelible imprint of the individuals and societies which wear them. Dress as a social script or text tells us who we are, what we have been, and what we are becoming' (Keenan, 2001: 25). Conceptualising the body as 'the existential ground of culture and self' (Csordas, 1990) provides an example *par excellence* of the interplay between culture and identity which lies at the heart of my analysis. In this context, Entwistle's theory of dress as 'a situated bodily practice' has proved particularly useful:

> Dress lies at the margins of the body, and marks the boundary between self and other, individual and society. This boundary is intimate and personal, since our dress forms the visible envelope of the self and . . . serves as a visual metaphor for identity; it is also social, since our dress is structured by social forces and subject to social and moral pressures.
> (Entwistle, 2001: 37)

Dress can also readily be theorised as part of performance. Clothes form a significant part of what Goffmann termed 'front' (Goffmann, 1990: 32). For Goffmann, the body is both the property of the individual and the social world. It is the vehicle of identity, but this identity has to be 'managed', in terms of social situations which impose particular ways of being on the body. Thus, the individual feels a social or moral imperative to perform their identity in particular ways—and that includes ways of dressing (Entwistle, 2001: 47). I have already argued in chapter 6 that performance, most obviously in relation to the legal academic as lecturer, is an important part of professional identity for legal academics; several respondents referred to the performative aspects of legal academia when they were discussing dress:

> . . . I always dress very smartly for work—and that's the other aspect of clothing at work, for me, it's part of doing the performance. So particularly when I have to do my Monday morning lecture, part of how I get myself into the mood is to really dress up . . .
> (professor, experienced, female, old university)

> Certainly, in the lecture theatre, I do see it as a bit of a performance, in the sense that it's not just a question of going in and standing up at the front and delivering material. I mean, I go in there, and I try to engage my audience, try to get some rapport from the audience. I like to feel it's a bit of an occasion, so I like to dress as I see it in the way in which I would if I was going out socially, for example, on a semi-formal occasion. So just as I'd go to a dinner party normally in a shirt and tie, so I'd go to a lecture in a shirt and tie.
> (reader, experienced, male, old university)

The 'Dress Culture'

In order to find out the extent to which legal academics regard clothes as a significant part of their professional identities, I first asked the respondents 'How do you choose what to wear to come to work?' Respondents used three terms to describe the style of dress they wore to work: 'casual', 'smart-casual' and 'smart'. Casual clothes, for both sexes, were jeans or chinos, worn with sweatshirts, t-shirts or a casual shirt. Smart-casual for men referred to slightly less casual trousers, worn with a smart shirt, and possibly an unstructured jacket. Smart-casual for women generally meant smart, tailored trousers or a smart skirt and a top which was not a t-shirt or a sweatshirt. Smart clothes for men meant a suit and tie; for women, suits (including trouser suits) or tailored outfits.

Using these loose categories, I was able to discover that there were no significant differences in clothing choices between people with different amounts of experience, or between those working in old and new universities. The differences which were revealed related to gender. The largest group of respondents (nearly half) described themselves as dressing 'smart-casual'; this group contained slightly more women than men. Just over a quarter described themselves as dressing 'casually'; there were significantly more men than women in this group. Just under a quarter described themselves as dressing 'smartly'; this category contained significantly more women than men.

The culture as a whole is clearly one in which casual dressing is acceptable. The fact that one is not obliged to 'dress up' was a very appealing aspect of the job to many people:

> One of the things I like about being an academic is that you don't all have to dress the same, you don't have to wear a uniform . . .
> (lecturer, early career, female, old university)

> [I just wear] Whatever's in the wardrobe and doesn't need ironing. We have a *very* relaxed dress code. So, just anything that's comfortable, fairly acceptable in appearance, and neat. I will wear jeans, but I don't wear old jeans. Sometimes, I don't give a whole load of thought to it—but that's how it is; nobody puts any emphasis on it at all. There's no pressure on us at all. I think there's the usual thing—first few weeks of term, everybody puts on a nicer shirt, nicer pair of trousers, and the shirt's all pressed—then two weeks into term, it's back to normal.
> (lecturer, early career, male, old university)

The ubiquity of casual dress means that the cultural norms relating to dress found in legal academia are very different to those found in other professional jobs (such as the merchant bankers interviewed by McDowell, who always dressed in suits (McDowell, 1997)). Respondents who had worked in business themselves drew attention to this:

> . . . I don't really have special clothes for work. It's different, being an academic. In my previous jobs, I wore high heels—they don't really seem appropriate now.
> (lecturer, mid-career, female, new university)

> One of the things I like most about the job is that there is no dress code. And I know it sounds silly, but I actually came from a private sector job, where the uniform was a suit and tie, black leather shoes, well-polished, hair neatly cut. I don't choose what to wear to come to work any more; I simply put on the clothes that I would put on for any more formal social setting. I would deeply resent being given a dress code for work. I would see that as nonsensical . . .
> (reader, mid-career, male, new university)

In particular, respondents contrasted the norms relating to dress in academia with those found in the legal profession. This was particularly obvious in relation to legal academics teaching on any of the vocational courses offered by some law schools:

> . . . I just choose things which are comfortable. I could come in a pair of jeans if I wanted to, and no-one would complain. When I teach on professional courses, I wear a suit—that's expected—it creates a sort of aura of professionalism. Students expect it—they regard a suit as 'professional'. When they do video presentations, they turn up wearing suits—though they're not obliged to. There's this kind of aura of gravitas if you've got a suit on. But by and large, I wear what's comfortable, and don't worry too much about what it is . . .
> (lecturer, mid-career, male, new university)

> . . . There was never, I think, the feeling, starting an academic job, that you went out and bought a whole new load of clothes for starting work, in the way that if you went into practice you'd need to.
> (lecturer, early career, male, old university)

It is unsurprising that there were significantly more male 'casual dressers' than female. Quite apart from societal norms, casual dressing fits in with the dissociation of mind and body stereotypically found in images of 'the intellectual', springing from the Cartesian dualism which has such a long history (Csordas, 1994: 7). Looking at professors in particular, Green comments:

> In contemporary Western society, [acceptable levels of femininity] involves the ideal of a thin, white, heterosexual presence, and at least an efficiently managed body, hairstyle and persona. By contrast, male professors are granted the licence to fill out their academic roles with generous corporeality, including the booming voice and spreading torso which accompany many men into middle age. Women academics of the same age groups routinely struggle to conceal the weight gains that often accompany the menopause, lest they be exposed as fleshy matrons who threaten the masculine orthodoxy.
> (Green, 2001: 99)

Enhancing the Performance: Wearing Smart Clothes

Within the general culture of casual dress found in law schools, several respondents identified specific occasions which called for smarter clothes (usually a suit). These included any occasion on which one might be interacting with professional lawyers, 'open days', graduation days (even if not actually taking part in the ceremonies), and (generally for professors) going to university meetings. It is noticeable that the majority of these occasions involve 'outsiders'; they are occasions on which a 'professional' image is regarded as important, and where casual dress might be misinterpreted as disrespectful. This attitude to dress reinforces the idea of dress as part of 'performance'; these respondents 'dress up', in order to present a particular image of themselves and the law school. On these occasions, they look more like practising lawyers:

> I'd only dress differently if I'd got to go to London for a meeting, or if I'm delivering a course to outside people . . .
> (lecturer, early career, female, old university)

> If I am involved in one of the open days then I would dress more smartly. When you have potential students coming round and you want to create a reasonably favourable impression, and I don't want to seem disrespectful to them. Normally, I would wear something fairly casual, quite often jeans, to be honest . . . but I would put on a suit for an open day. Other than that, I would rarely wear a suit—indeed, I only own one suit.
> (lecturer, early career, male, new university)

Dressing more smartly when dealing with the public or representing the department at a meeting with representatives from other departments appears to be a general feature of the academy (Rucker et al, 1999: 67).

About a fifth of respondents habitually wore smart clothes to work in. In most of these cases, smart clothes were used to gain authority. 'Being taken seriously' was a particular matter of concern to younger academics, who did not wish to be confused with students, but, to the contrary, wished to establish their credibility as legal academics. This was a reason for dressing smartly:

> I think I tend to dress relatively smartly to come to work. I think that is partly because I'm young, and I have had one or two occasions, when I first started teaching, walking into the classroom on the first day of term and all the students thinking that I was one of them. I want to make a conscious effort to look different from the students, particularly when there are mature students in the group. I think the more professional you look the more it will help . . .
> (lecturer, early career, female, new university)

> Well, I suppose at the outset I decided to dress smartly, because when I first started here I looked very young, and I was concerned that I might have been mistaken for a student—and the last thing I wanted was someone shoving me on a library tour—and also, I was worried that I actually wouldn't be taken seriously by the students. And the crazy thing is, I actually had it confirmed on a social occasion run by the student law society. I got talking to some students, and they said they walked into my office, and I was sitting there in a shirt and tie and everything, and they felt quite intimidated by me, and took me seriously, which I thought was fascinating . . .
> (lecturer, early career, male, old university)

Authority was also an issue for heads of department and professors: it was common for them to explain that they had begun to wear much smarter clothes when they were promoted. Once dress codes have shifted in the direction of casual dress, constructing an authoritative image is more complex; the suit can no longer exclusively be relied upon to do this (Rucker et al, 1999: 60):

> I remember when I became [head of department] I made an effort to buy smart blazers and trousers, and a pair of shoes that weren't trainers. And I had a series of little outfits that I'd trot out for exam boards or an important meeting . . .
> (principal lecturer, experienced, female, new university)

> From the time when I first became head of department, I have been rather more conscious of the fact that I've become what some people call a 'suit'. At times I don't like that. At other times, I feel I'm making too much of a statement if I don't put on a shirt and tie and jacket. Sometimes I'd like to be more relaxed about the way I dress, particularly in vacations. Sometimes I am—I mean, if the weather gets really nice, that's when I feel sort of able to shed the image. It's partly that you're never quite sure, as a head of department or dean, or whatever, who might come to see you, and what expectations they might have—and it's odd, because the university as a whole doesn't have a dress code, you can dress pretty much how you like . . .
> (professor, experienced, male, old university)

Dress was used by some respondents to create an identity as 'authoritative teacher'. These respondents said that, although they might wear some form of casual dress on other occasions, if they were teaching, they chose to dress smartly:

> If I'm teaching, I dress better than if I'm not teaching. I think if you teach a big group, and you're coming to a class professionally dressed, you make a better impression. I don't know if this is true, but it's sufficiently ingrained in my mind that I believe it to be true. I think students listen to you more, and they respect you more, if you're professionally dressed . . .
> (lecturer, early career, male, old university)

> . . . For myself, I always try and look smart when I'm teaching. I *never*, for instance (and I'm sure I'm not alone in this), teach in jeans. I always wear something reasonably smart, whether it's a dress, skirt or trousers, I never wear complete scruff to teach . . .
> (lecturer, mid-career, female, new university)

These comments provide further evidence of the way in which dress is used in the 'performance' of teaching, to assist in the creation of a professional identity as 'authoritative expert'.

Women and Dress

Given the identification of academia with rationality and masculinity, it is not surprising that women were particularly aware of the need to establish credibility. In her study of women professors' clothing choices, Green argues that female academics routinely 'watch themselves' via personal surveillance of their appearance, as part of the process of establishing themselves as serious academics. She points to the tensions which women experience when faced with the need to present themselves as professional and authoritative, while also signalling what are perceived to be acceptable levels of femininity (Green, 2001: 98–99).

> Basically, I wear a uniform. I wear clothes that I don't wear at the weekend. I think that I need to look smarter than I would choose to be at home. That, to me, is probably to do with being a woman, and working in a high-powered institution. I think that I have to portray an image of myself as professional . . .
> (lecturer, early career, female, old university)

Women were also aware of the need to avoid appearing as sexual beings. Entwistle argues that women have developed particular strategies for managing the gaze of others, particularly men, in public spaces at work; their strategies both reflect the gendered nature of the workplace and represent an adaptation to this in terms of their experience of it (Entwistle, 2001: 50). Exuding sexiness is not powerful, so women need to take especial care in managing their appearance in this regard (Johnson and Lennon, 1999: 5):

> . . . I wouldn't wear sort of tight trousers to work, because I just don't like the impression that would give. I think I need a little bit of respect . . . I think I would feel very uncomfortable, because I'm not with my peers, I'm with a load of students—and you want people to respect you for what you're doing, you don't want people to be looking at how tight your trousers are.
> (lecturer, early career, female, new university)

> I try to wear something that doesn't attract attention, not too outrageous, quite conservative, and then neat and clean . . . I suppose I go for neutral colours. I wouldn't wear anything too flouncy. I try to choose clothes that are 'work-like' in some way. Because I don't want, both with colleagues, and I suppose especially vis-à-vis the students, I don't want attention attracted to what I'm wearing. I want attention attracted to what I'm saying, and how I'm doing my job . . . you know, I enjoy clothes in my spare time, and I enjoy wearing things that might attract a bit of attention, and are not conservative. But I wouldn't enjoy that during my work, because I feel that's an inappropriate place, and I also think that I want to be taken seriously.
> (lecturer, early career, female, old university)

The data from this study and from others provides evidence that being a female legal academic is problematic in many ways; the attitudes towards dress revealed by these respondents provide yet another example of the way in which these women have to 'manage' their professional identities in order to gain acceptance within the culture of academic law.

Men in Suits?

As far as contemporary legal academics are concerned, 'corporatisation' does not seem to have greatly affected the cultural norms relating to dress; there is substantial evidence from my survey that the culture remains resolutely casual.

However, it would be surprising if recent changes in higher education had had no effect at all on the way in which legal academics dress, and it is inevitable that some people will embrace change more enthusiastically than others. Some respondents felt that the effect of ideas springing from new public management, and the 'corporatisation' of universities was to undermine the 'casual culture' of the academy; they detected an increasing tendency towards smarter dress:

> I think there's an increasing sort of thing that you will be dressed more smartly. I suppose to a certain extent I go along with it—most people seem to be going that way, sort of, but if I got to the stage where I didn't have a particular shirt or something, I'd just wear a t-shirt and jeans . . .
> (senior lecturer, experienced, male, old university)

> I think you can't turn up to faculty meetings or senate in a 'woolly pully', though I probably would have done in the past. So I think it has something to do with the projection of the image. And it probably goes hand-in-hand with the fact that we have become more bureaucratised, that we have become more like businesses—and there's more of an expectation that you will dress in a businesslike way.
> (professor, mid-career, male, old university)

Corporatisation too, is deeply gendered, and that is reflected in relation to dress, as it is in other ways, as one of the respondents pointed out:

> . . . I think there's less expectation of what you're supposed to wear in our job than in other jobs, though I think to an extent that's changing. There's a kind of managerial ethos developing, whereby suits are on the increase. There's a sort of Boy's Own gang, who dress alike, and comment on each other's style, and what they're wearing, which is giving a message. It's all done in a jokey way, but I think it's basically saying, 'If you want to mix with the other big boys, then there are certain expectations with regard to dress' . . .
> (senior lecturer, experienced, female, old university)

Green's research into women professors reveals the ways in which that 'corporatisation' was impinging upon the dress choices of her respondents. They made their clothing choices with an eye to the necessity of deference to the formal dress codes of 'management', but also revealed a strong desire to signal originality and difference via womanly bodies which challenge the male 'suits'. At the same time they want to avoid being taken for secretaries or junior administrators. But the key message they relayed through dress, comments Green, '. . . is one which reinforces the power and status attached to their professional role, and must not be deflected by "girly" or submissive clothes' (Green, 2001: 104).

Dress Codes?

In order to find out whether the respondents perceived that they were subject to any kind of 'dress regulation', within this apparently 'go-as-you-please' culture, I asked whether the respondents thought that there was a dress code (formal or informal) in their department. All the respondents were clear that no formal dress codes existed; several people mentioned how inappropriate such a code would be in the context of a university. While the majority of respondents also thought that there was no informal dress code either, about a fifth of respondents, in both old and new universities thought that informal codes did exist. In most cases, these informal rules related to the wearing of smart clothes by senior staff:

> I suppose there is an informal dress code, in the sense that, by and large, the more senior staff tend to dress more formally. Whether that is because of their position, or because of their age, I don't know. Although it is noticeable that one or two people who, during the time that I have been here, have been raised to dizzy heights seem to have upped their dress. They were far more casual and are now far more inclined to wear a suit than they once were . . .
> (lecturer, early career, male, new university)

> There's an informal one, in the sense that, as a matter of fact, all of the professors wear suits . . .
> (lecturer, early career, male, old university)

> My suspicion *is*, yes, a certain sort of dress *is* expected of one. I mean, I can think of things that one wouldn't wear, and I would have thought that colleagues wouldn't wear—I mean, I couldn't imagine many people here coming in very, very short shorts in the summer, something like that. But I haven't really thought about it—my gut reaction is that we all probably think we have to dress in a certain way—not necessarily suits and jackets, but there would be certain things that would be inappropriate. I can certainly think of things that I would think are inappropriate to come to work in—revealing clothes, tarty sort of things—not necessarily Doc Martens etc—but revealing clothes.
> (principal lecturer, mid-career, female, new university)

> I am sure there is [an informal dress code]. I think if you dressed in certain ways you might become a laughing-stock. I don't know how—in a way that was seen as inappropriate . . .
> (lecturer, mid-career, male, new university)

'Appropriate' dress for legal academia seems as if it is clothing which conveys an aura of somewhat conservative respectability:

> Well—people wear the same sort of clothes. If someone turned up in bright orange, it would be commented on. We have 'open day outfits'—jackets, etc. In the vacation, people turn up in jeans. But mostly, we're quite regimented. Nothing's ever said—but there are sort of accepted things to wear.
> (lecturer, mid-career, female, new university)

> Oh yes, there's an informal code—for blokes, I mean. I can't comment on women's dress, which I've never really understood. But there is, definitely. I mean, it's enforced—by comments—ostensibly light, amusing comments, kind of friendly, *but* the subtext is always query, is this quite acceptable. I'm not even sure that the people making those comments are actually aware of what they're doing, I mean that is actually my deconstruction of what's happening. But it is very noticeable. You know, I

could guarantee it, I could elicit those comments for you. I could come in in certain ties and so on, and I could set you up to observe it, and I could guarantee it—I'd put money on it. It's not nasty, or anything, it's just *so* predictable.
(senior lecturer, mid-career, male, old university)

... I know that nobody would walk in with a skirt that was too short, or anything like that. They just wouldn't do it. [So there's a sort of informal dress code?] Yes, there is. I mean, you couldn't turn up to the exam board in shorts, put it that way ... there are certain things you wouldn't do.
(lecturer, early career, female, new university)

In addition to those respondents identifying informal restrictions on dress, a further group (who did not think there was any sort of dress code) made comments about the informal regulation of dress which were also revealing. These comments amounted to a feeling that dress regulation for legal academics consists of clothing that is 'neutral', not showy or 'way out' in any way:

... I think of all academics, legal academics are probably the most conformist of the lot, so there's probably an element of that [in what I choose to wear to come to work].
(lecturer, early career, male, old university)

People basically wear what they like—not too outrageous ...
(senior lecturer, experienced, male, old university)

... People don't dress a long way down, so to speak, nor do they dress a long way up, for the most part. There's quite a range of attire—if you just arrived unannounced on an ordinary day in term, I think you'd see a fair variety of clothing on display, none of it of any great distinction, I have to add.
(lecturer, experienced, male, old university)

I think there's a kind of—you can wear what you like, but if you didn't dress up on the occasions when it was expected, then it would be commented on ...
(lecturer, experienced, female, old university)

I think there's a huge variety of personal styles, and it's a personal matter. I think most people try to dress quite neutrally. Even if you're naturally a more casual person, I still think they give some thought to what they wear ...
(lecturer, early career, female, old university)

Digressing from the generally casual atmosphere by dressing smartly (other than for reasons of seniority) would be to break the informal code as much as by wearing clothes that draw a lot of attention to themselves:

No, I don't think there is a dress code—except I think if anybody did dress in a suit on a regular basis we'd think that they were a little bit odd. But I don't think anybody would say anything.
(lecturer, early career, female, new university)

I get my leg pulled, especially when term ends, and I walk in and I've got my jeans on. Someone will say 'Why don't you dress like that more often?' ...
(lecturer, early career, male, old university)

Although it is true to say that the 'dress-culture' of legal academia as a whole was casual in nature, it was interesting that twice as many men as women

196 Identity Matters

described their dress style as definitely 'casual'. Membership of this category of 'anti-fashion' appears to coincide most closely with the stereotype of the academic as absent-minded professor, in cord trousers, shirt, and jacket with leather patches on the elbows. 'Grey—and badly-dressed', as one respondent put it. This is, of course, a masculine stereotype, and it reinforces the identification of academia with rationality ('clothes are unimportant, it's the ideas that matter'), itself associated with masculinity. It is perhaps unsurprising that less women felt comfortable with identifying themselves with a stereotype which arguably has strong masculine connotations.

The casual dress code which generally permeates the law school serves to sharply differentiate legal academia from legal practice. It is yet another reminder of the professional identity of legal academics *as academics* and reinforces the culture of academic law as one which is part of the academy. It reflects the fluidity of the public/private divide which is also a feature of the culture of academic law. However, the most noticeable feature of this analysis of dress in the legal academy is that it is deeply gendered. Collier, in his examination of the 'nutty professors', 'men in suits' and 'new entrepreneurs', reminds us that not only are these images of masculinity, they are images of heterosexual masculinity (Collier, 1998). For both Collier (1998) and Skidmore (1999) dress 'codes' such as those I have uncovered here represent another aspect of the privileging of the homosocial culture and practices which permeate the law school.

CONCLUSION

This chapter, as its title suggests, is primarily concerned with matters of professional identity. However, it is clear that the construction of a professional identity as 'legal academic' is profoundly affected by the culture within which that construction takes place. Law school culture privileges the white, the heterosexual and the male; those possessing alternative identities have, to use Goffman's term, to 'manage' their performances as legal academics differently. The debate about the ways in which gender plays out in the law school is well-established; the results of this study reveal that it is a debate which has taken firm roots in the culture—it is not just women who are aware of the privileges afforded to particular types of men. Analysis of dress as a 'situated bodily practice' not only adds to our knowledge of the culture of academic law, but throws further light on our understanding of gender in the law school.

There remain some aspects of identity, notably sexuality and race, which it has not been possible to explore in sufficient detail to fully appreciate their effects on the professional identities of academic lawyers; there is still much research to be done.

9

Conclusion

INTRODUCTION

THE PURPOSE OF THIS book has been twofold: to throw light upon the discipline of law, and to add to our knowledge of the academic profession, by exploring, in both cases, the lived experience of academic lawyers. I have engaged in 'conversations with a purpose' (Burgess, 1984) with a large number of legal academics working in widely differing types of institution and have examined, with their help, a range of aspects of the culture of academic law, and the construction of the professional identity of 'academic lawyer.' In using these two concepts to analyse the data I gathered, I have tried to show the utility and applicability of theoretical position I set out at the beginning of the book, emphasising the interplay between the culture of the discipline as a whole, and the individual academic identities forged within it. My understanding of culture, informed primarily by cultural anthropology and organisation studies, has led me to examine the explicit and tacit assumptions held by academic lawyers; I have been interested in beliefs, values, and customs (Billington et al, 1991: 4). Equally, I have looked at academic lawyers' understanding of 'who they are' (Jenkins, 1996: 4–5), and the ways in which that understanding relates to the culture in which the 'lived experience' takes place. Now I am in a position to bring together the insights which I have been able to draw from the project as a whole.

LAW AS A DISCIPLINE

The data I have gathered tells us that law is a discipline in transition, moving away from traditional doctrinal analysis towards a more contextual, interdisciplinary approach. When they talked to me, the legal academics I interviewed were evenly divided between those describing themselves as 'black-letter' (ie ‚adopting a doctrinal approach) and those describing themselves as 'socio-legal /critical legal.' However, given the propensity of those adopting a socio-legal approach to stress the necessity for an understanding of cases and statutes before more theoretical analysis can be undertaken, and the equally strong comments made by the great majority of 'black-letter' lawyers about the importance of introducing contextual issues into their analysis, one could accurately characterise the dominant mode of academic law as 'concerned both with doctrine *and* with placing those doctrinal materials in their social context.' The precise balance of these factors will lie with individuals; academic lawyers' view of their approach to their discipline is likely to vary, depending upon where they stand on the 'doctrinal—socio-legal—critical legal' spectrum. However, the majority of them were clear that the socio-legal approach to law will certainly become more important in the future. There is clear evidence from my study that the discipline of law as a whole has long left behind the pure doctrinal analysis with which it started when it was first taught in English universities at the end of the nineteenth century.

In embarking on the journey away from its purely doctrinal roots, academic law is cutting its closest ties with the legal profession, and bringing itself much nearer to the heart of the academy. It is not solely the increased participation in socio-legal work, and insights drawn from other disciplines which is bringing this about. Feminist research also appears to have had a not insubstantial effect on the discipline, with just under half the respondents (both men and women) saying that they used such materials in their teaching. The influence of feminism provides another indication of the 'academic' nature of law in the university, and is a further illustration of the way in which the discipline is now affected by the intellectual currents flowing through the academy as a whole.

In some respects, there is still a noticeable lack of intellectual self-confidence about academic lawyers. Overall, the respondents retained the view which Becher's original study uncovered (Becher, 1989: 30), that in order to be an academic lawyer, you do not really have to be intellectual. Here, too, however, the discipline is changing. Although being intellectual was not regarded as a *necessary* quality, the majority of my respondents thought to produce the *best* work in academic law, you would need to be an intellectual. Thus, in law as in other disciplines, it is that which is most 'academic' which is most highly regarded.

Despite its growing socio-legal nature, law is not yet strongly interdisciplinary. Only a few respondents said that they had contacts with experts in other subjects. Academic lawyers who use research from other disciplines in their research or teaching tend to do so without perceiving a need to get particularly involved in any other discipline. Some respondents had strong concerns about the consequences of such attitudes on the discipline, fearing that without training, particularly in the social sciences, the development of socio-legal research may suffer, a concern shared by the Socio-Legal Studies Association (Cowan et al, 2003).

Not only was there minimal contact with academics from other disciplines; neither was it the case that there was much contact with the legal profession. 'Outsiders' may confuse academic lawyers with practising lawyers, but the academics themselves were clear that the two inhabit different worlds. Most of the respondents who did make such contacts regarded the relationship between the academy and practitioners as uneasy; their view was that the majority of practitioners regard academic lawyers with considerable suspicion.

Nevertheless, academic law may not be quite as self-contained as these indications might suggest. The growing propensity of academic lawyers to include materials other than the strictly 'legal' in their teaching and research suggests that law may be becoming what Becher and Trowler would term a 'loose' disciplinary community, ie, rather like geography, where 'the cognitive border zones with other subject fields are liable to be ragged and ill-defined' (Becher and Trowler, 2001: 59).

Despite what others think of them (and despite what some legal academics say about themselves) my study suggests that the changes in academic law as a whole indicate that no longer will members of other disciplines accurately be able to say, as one of Becher's original respondents did, that academic lawyers are 'an appendage to the university world' (Becher, 1989: 30). The evidence coming from my data is that law is a discipline in flux—but the direction in which it is moving is clear: it is moving away from its exclusive concern with doctrine and in doing so it is moving closer to the heart of the academy.

THE CHANGING CULTURE OF ACADEMIC LAW

The culture of academic law, in the sense of the explicit and tacit assumptions that academic lawyers hold, and their 'ways of doing things,' is also changing fast, since knowledge and culture continuously interact with one another (Tierney, 1991: 205). It is in keeping with the disciplinary developments which I have discussed above that law is a culture which thinks of itself, to an increasing extent, as 'academic,' with distinctive values and norms, separate from those of the legal profession. Academic lawyers become university lecturers because they want to be part of academia; many of them have contemplated (or actually tried) working as a practising lawyer first, and they are clear that this is not what they want to do. The academic lawyers I interviewed were overwhelmingly (though quietly and privately) proud to be legal academics, and certainly did not see their career choice as 'second best' to the pursuit of a career at the Bar or as a solicitor. In this regard, they displayed a considerable amount of self-confidence. Their objectives are very different from those of the legal profession; their personal view of success is largely related to personal reputation as a researcher, and to a lesser extent, to helping students to learn. They do not perceive themselves as preparing young people for entry to the legal profession; their main pedagogical concern is to 'teach the students to think.' The skills which they value in each other are those which make for academic success— analysis, critical thinking, being articulate and able to communicate ideas readily, both orally and on paper. When one looks for the qualities which are likely to lead to promotion, in terms of obtaining a chair, research output, in law as elsewhere in the academy, is what is valued and rewarded. The culture of academic law is firmly embedded in the university.

The Changing Culture—Effects of the RAE

In law as elsewhere, 'the way we do things,' has been significantly affected by the RAE. The changes in the discipline which I identified above are being accelerated by the RAE, aided by the criteria used by the law panel in the 2001 Exercise; student textbooks and works for practitioners (once the primary research output of academic lawyers) were only accepted as research provided they contained 'significant scholarly material' (RAE 1999, para 3.28.11). The majority of respondents who were research-active regarded the RAE as altering their research practices, in terms of the type of work they engaged in and where they published it. Publication in practitioner journals was largely abandoned in favour of refereed academic journals; there was also an increased emphasis on the publication of monographs. This is a significant move away from the 'textbook tradition' which has for so long been a major feature of the culture of academic law (Sugarman, 1986).

Respondents did not, on the whole, regard the RAE positively. They have considerable doubts about the credibility of the exercise, in terms of the criteria and methodology used, and worry that the existence of the RAE has encouraged the publication of too much poor quality research. They also dislike the 'transfer-market' effect, and the damage to collegiality due to the unhappiness brought about for those who are not included. The RAE was also seen as yet another vehicle for 'managerialism' and as another way of eroding the autonomy which these respondents, like other academics, regard as a core feature of their professional identities. Although the RAE affects the culture as a whole, it is far from gender-neutral. Early-career academics and women appeared to be more affected by it than mid-career and experienced men, with women in particular emphasising how they felt subjected to a constant pressure to publish.

It is certainly the case that the RAE has had the negative effects outlined by the respondents, and analysed by a number of commentators (Henkel, 2000; Talib, 2001; Vick et al, 1998; Campbell et al, 1999) to which I will return later in this concluding section. However, there appears to be little doubt that its effects on the discipline of law have been to increase the rate of its move away from the legal profession (and, by implication, from doctrinalism) towards the centre of the academy.

DIFFERENT PERSPECTIVES ON THE CULTURE OF LAW: OLD AND NEW UNIVERSITIES

While legal academics working in old and new universities shared many attitudes and experiences, differences between the two sectors also became apparent, which were reflected in some varying cultural perspectives. This is not surprising, given the historical differences between the two types of institutions (Ainley, 1994; Fulton, 1996).

The research orientation of old universities was greater than that in new universities—but not overwhelmingly so, apart from the one institution I visited which had no interest in research. Differences in research orientation were reflected in the qualities which legal academics working in the two types of institution identified as being necessary to be a 'good' academic lawyer. While respondents working in both types of institution stressed the need for analytical skills and communication skills, those working in old universities identified two extra types of skill which they regarded as crucial: time management skills and the need for persistence and perseverance (which was largely related to research). The RAE was also regarded differently; it would appear that the RAE has been more effective in new universities than in old in acting as a vehicle for managerialism, with significantly more respondents working in new universities reporting that their research had been affected by the RAE.

Respondents indicated that institutional attitudes to teaching varied considerably between old and new universities, with new universities placing considerably more emphasis upon teaching than old universities. Exploration of cultural expectations relating to administration revealed another difference between old and new universities. In new universities in particular, there was a marked tendency for administrative burdens to be shouldered disproportionately by women, many of whom appeared to be fulfilling the role of 'handmaiden' or 'dutiful daughter' set out by Thornton (Thornton, 1996).

The effects of recent changes in higher education policy also appear to have impacted differently upon legal academics working in old and new universities. In old universities, respondents discussing the effects of these changes tended to point to the increased pressure to research and publish, whereas those working in new universities placed most emphasis upon the increasing numbers of students and the types of demands made by an increasingly diverse student body, together with the increasingly bureaucratic nature of academic life and the increased presence of audit and other monitoring mechanisms.

Although in this section I have enumerated the differences between legal academics working in old and new universities, overall, legal academics working in the two types of institution shared a great deal of experience, both in terms of culture and identity. As others have noted, institution is important, but so is the discipline (Henkel, 2000).

KEY ASPECTS OF PROFESSIONAL IDENTITY

Teaching

Teaching was important to the legal academics I interviewed. They gained real satisfaction from helping students to learn, especially when they sensed excitement or enthusiasm on the part of their students. Being a 'good' teacher was an important part of their professional identity, regardless of the fact that half of them believed that teaching was not valued by their institution. For these legal academics, teaching, particularly lecturing, involved a self-conscious 'performance,' involving humour and rhetoric, in order to retain the interest and attention of their student 'audience.' Respondents enthusiastically analysed the strategies they use to achieve these objectives, providing a rich array of evidence that they are indeed managing their performance in the ways suggested by Goffman (Goffman, 1990). The most highly-valued effect, however, was that of naturalism—any suggestion that law lecturing consists merely of reading out a script was rejected outright.

Research

The majority of respondents were involved in research, and were enthusiastic about it, particularly the opportunity it provides for the satisfaction of intellectual curiosity. For a significant number, research was the key aspect of their professional identity, and the one which gave them more personal satisfaction than any other aspect of their job. Respondents noted that one of the effects of the RAE has been to engender a considerable increase in the value placed on research within the culture of academic law. The strong orientation towards research displayed by the majority of respondents, together with the evidence of changes in the culture brought about by the RAE, provides further evidence that legal academics are consolidating their place within the academy.

Administration

Administration seems to bring out the worst in legal academics—another trait which they share with the other inhabitants of the academy. In all the departments I visited, respondents readily identified a group of 'good citizens' (who were both male and female) who could be relied upon to carry out administrative tasks effectively and without fuss, though such unselfish behaviour is rarely rewarded. The general view adopted by my respondents was that administration is a necessary evil, whose burdens are unevenly distributed among academic staff, because some people are very good at getting out of it. A range of strategies were used to avoid administration; appearing to be incompetent at it was a common one, as was being 'difficult' when asked to take on an administrative task, in the expectation that it would instead be passed on to a less aggressive colleague. Sharing these attitudes with the rest of the academy is one of the less attractive features of the culture of academic law.

OTHER IDENTITY MATTERS

The 'identity matters' of gender, class, race and sexuality include some of the least explored areas of legal academia, Yet this study provides evidence that they have significant effects, not only upon the professional identities of legal academics, but also on key aspects of the culture of academic law, such as teaching and research.

In terms of class, while the overall view of respondents was that their class background had little effect upon their professional identities, half of them immediately qualified this by saying that in fact it had affected their research interests, or their desire to be involved in education. Additionally, a significant minority of respondents did not feel at ease in the middle-class milieu of the legal academy. While rejecting the notion that class had any particular effects upon the culture, the reality appears to be that it is a significant factor for many academics working in law schools, which could easily be ignored if one too readily accepted the initial reactions of the respondents I interviewed. Being a legal academic was unequivocally regarded as being a middle class occupation, but since 80 per cent of the respondents came from a family where neither parent had been to university, they appear to have brought with them considerably less cultural capital than might be implied by some commentators (Collier, 2002: 28; Wells, 2001: 136). Arguably, in the future, it will become even more important to understand the effects of class in the legal academy; Ryan and Sackrey argue that the general effects of 'managerialism' have special consequences for the class-mobile person in the academy Ryan and Sackrey, 1984: 18).

Race and sexuality remain almost wholly unexplored aspects of the culture of academic law (and, indeed, of academia as a whole). The work which has been done (eg, Goodrich and Mills, 2001; Heward et al, 1997; Collier 1998, 2002) suggests that these would be fruitful areas for future research. The position of women in the legal academy, on the other hand, is widely acknowledged as problematic by the majority of academic lawyers, both men and women. Women feel uncomfortable with many aspects of the legal academy. The 'ruthless ambition' which is perceived to be a necessary quality of those who get to the top may be common to the university as a whole, but the ability to cultivate informal contacts, and the important role they play in advancement, appear to be facets of the culture of academic law in particular; all of these things mitigate against women achieving their rightful place in the legal academy. When their attention is specifically directed towards the issues, there is a high level of awareness of the differential treatment of women legal academics among both men and women working in the legal academy, and a particularly high level of awareness of the small number of women occupying chairs in law departments. Only a small number of my respondents (mostly men) appeared to be unaware of gender issues. Respondents canvassed a wide rage of explanations for the situation which exists, reflecting, in various ways, upon the power of hegemonic masculinity which researchers analyse in terms of 'the gendered organisation' (Hearn, 2001). This study has provided additional insights, gathered from both men and women, about the ways in which gender plays out in the law school, but there is still much to be done, especially, as I argued in chapter 8, in the light of the fact that awareness of gender issues, though widespread among legal academics, may be somewhat superficial in nature.

Dressing the Part

Of all the questions I asked in my interviews, it was those on dress which the respondents found most surprising. The data gained in response to these questions has, however, proved to be some of the richest. Given the importance of the notions of 'culture' and 'identity' to my analysis, dress was an important area to explore, because as a 'situated bodily practice' (Entwistle, 2001) it inhabits precisely the juncture between those two fundamental concepts in which I was interested. Dress is a key part of the management (in Goffman's sense) of the 'performance' of being a legal academic (Goffman, 1990). The casual dress-codes which are an apparently almost universal feature of the culture of legal academia are deceptive. Heads of department and other senior members of the department also used dress to manage their 'performance' and enhance their 'gravitas.' Women do not join in the 'relaxed' mode of dressing to the same extent as men; instead, they use dress to gain credibility within the law school and to establish themselves as authoritative legal experts, as do early career academics of both sexes. They were also much more aware of the need to avoid appearing as sexual beings than men were; this appeared to relate to women's desire to manage their appearance so as to avoid any danger that they would not be taken seriously. The 'corporatisation' of universities, with its associations with masculinity/managerialism, increases the pressures on all legal academics (but particularly on women) to become 'suits,' although, as yet, the dress culture of legal academia remains generally casual.

Although respondents firmly rejected the notion that dress codes formed part of the culture of academic law, they were able to identify a considerable amount of informal regulation of appearance, which reveals the culture of academic law as one of 'conservative respectability'; presentation of self as flamboyant, while probably tolerated, would attract adverse comment.

'CULTURE', 'IDENTITIES' AND THE DISCIPLINE OF LAW

Overall, the picture which emerges from my study is one about which it is possible to be cautiously optimistic. The discipline of law is embedding itself firmly within the academy; as it does so, it is gaining in intellectual strength. The new knowledge which will emerge as there is increasing engagement with a variety of different approaches to research in law is likely to offer exciting new insights into legal phenomena and their place in the world. Legal academics, although not yet convinced that it is necessary to be an intellectual to be a good academic lawyer, nevertheless regarded such people as likely to produce the best work in their discipline; this provides further evidence for my thesis that law is moving closer to the heart of the academy, since defining oneself as an intellectual appears to be a broad common value held by members of the academy (Clark, 1987: 129). In the future, law is likely to find itself increasingly affected by the great intellectual currents which swirl around the university, and, almost more importantly, the developments in the discipline which this study has uncovered make it more likely that the somewhat self-contained world of the academic lawyer will produce ideas which are of more than passing interest to other members of the academy. The evidence provided by this study of changes in the discipline of law suggests that it is increasingly becoming part of the intellectual mainstream; this is a development which should give academic lawyers grounds for optimism (Twining, 1997).

The legal academics I interviewed displayed considerable attachment to core academic values. The factor they most often identified as being the thing they liked most about being a legal academic was the freedom to organise one's own working life. The extent to which autonomy is a key part of their professional identities is something which academic lawyers share with other members of the academy (Henkel, 2000). However, the professional identities of legal academics, like their colleagues elsewhere in the academy, are under considerable pressures from the changes in higher education which have seen not only the move from an elite to a mass system of higher education, but also increasing efforts to introduce managerialism and corporatisation to the academy. It is these sorts of pressures which have led some commentators to suggest that legal academics are currently subject to a process of 'proletarianisation' which is taking place across the higher education sector (Collier, 2002: 30). The paradox which emerges here is a common feature of academic culture; on the one hand, academics are immensely proud to be doing their job, and would not wish to do any other; on the other, they express a sense of personal strain (Fulton, 1996: 419).

Much discussion of policy change in higher education has arguably paid insufficient attention to what sociologists call 'agency,' ie, the behaviour of the groups and individuals who are the subjects of these structural changes (Trowler, 1998: 110). The data I have gathered about legal academics suggests they have strong attachments to core parts of their academic identity, which are focused on their discipline—on researching and teaching law as part of an independent community of scholars which is still concerned with 'speaking truth to power.' These strong attachments make it much more likely that they will be able to resist, or undermine, policy changes which threaten those core values (Fulton, 1996: 435). Some readers may regard this as an overly positive view, but it is one which is not merely based on personal optimism. It is a view shared by others. Even Halsey, despite highlighting *The Decline of Donnish Dominion* (1992), notes that if the surveys conducted over the period 1964–1989 reveal an ever-increasing bitterness among academics, they also affirmed the survival of a strong belief in academic values (Halsey, 1992: 270). Henkel's position is even clearer; she concluded, on the basis of her large-scale study of academic identities and policy change in higher education, that in the face of numerous challenges academics engaged in a range of more or less conscious strategies to conserve their collective and individual academic identities (Henkel, 2000: 261).

At the end of his in-depth qualitative study of 'NewU,' Trowler argues that one of the contributions of studies of the 'underlife' of higher education is to enable us, through greater understanding of the sector, to put in perspective the policy changes and structural forces which have to date received the bulk of attention from researchers in higher education:

> The ideologies, beliefs, assumptions, values, principles, tastes and the taken-for-granted recurrent behaviours stemming from them which comprise culture are not easily disposable. In fact, they are remarkably durable, and this durability stems from their social rather than individual character.
> (Trowler, 1998: 152)

I would argue that in this study of legal academics, I have found considerable evidence of the enduring nature of certain core aspects of the culture of academic law, which suggest that the professional identities of legal academics may be more resistant to pressure than some commentators have acknowledged. Their prime objective as teachers was to teach students to think; despite benchmarks, audit and other forms of quality assessment they did not talk in terms of 'transferable skills' or increasing the employability of their students. When asked about their personal view of success, their aim was to establish themselves as an expert in their field, who would be respected by other academics; other than in highly specialised fields, they did not look outside academia for peer approval. The qualities they identified as being desirable in a legal academic, such as powers of analysis and communication, were those which have traditionally been valued in the academy. Academic lawyers are subject to the changes taking place in higher education just as much as members of other 'academic tribes.' They teach more students, they are subject to almost constant surveillance, and not surprisingly, they feel under pressure, especially the women. However, overall, the culture of academic law and the professional identities constructed within it display a great deal of resilience, both retaining a fundamentally academic orientation.

Bibliography

Abel-Smith, B & Stevens, R (1967) *Lawyers and the Courts: a sociological study of the English Legal System 1750–1965* Heinemann, London.
Acker, J (1990) 'Hierarchies, Jobs, Bodies: a theory of gendered organisations' 4 *Gender and Society* 139–58.
—— (1992) 'Gendering Organisational Theory' in A Mills & P Tancred (eds), *Gendering Organisational Analysis* Sage, London.
Acker, S (1994) *Gendered Education* Open University Press, Buckingham.
Acker, S & Feuerverger, G (1996) 'Doing Good and Feeling Bad: the work of women university teachers' (26.3) *Cambridge Journal of Education* 401–22.
ACLEC (1996) *First Report on Legal Education and Training* Lord Chancellor's Advisory Committee on Legal Education and Conduct (ACLEC), London.
Adams, D (1998) 'Examining the Fabric of Academic Life: an analysis of three decades of research on the perceptions of Australian academics about their roles' 36 *Higher Education* 421–35.
Adams, JN & Brownsword, R (1999) *Understanding Law* (2nd edn), (Sweet & Maxwell, London).
Addison, W & Cownie, F (1992) 'Overseas Law Students: language support and responsible recruitment' (19.4) *Journal of Law and Society* 467–82.
Adkins, L (2002) 'Reflexivity and the Politics of Qualitative Research' in T May (ed), *Qualitative Research in Action* (Sage, London).
Adler, PA & Adler, P (1987) *Membership Roles in Field Research* (Sage, London).
Ainley, P (1994) *Degrees of Difference: higher education in the 1990s* (Lawrence and Wishart, London).
Aisenberg, M & Harrington, M (1988) *Women of Academe: outsiders in the sacred grove* (University of Massachusetts Press, Amherst).
Allen, M (1993) 'Teaching Quality Exercise' Winter 1993 *SPTL Reporter* 25.
Altbach, P & Lewis, L (1996) 'The Academic Profession in International Perspective' in P Altbach (ed), *The International academic Profession: portraits of fourteen countries* (The Carnegie Foundation for the Advancement of Teaching, Princeton, NJ).
Alvesson, M (1993) *Cultural Perspectives on Organisations* (Cambridge University Press, Cambridge).
Alvesson, M (2002) *Understanding Organizational Culture* (Sage, London).
Alvesson, M & Billing, Y (1997) *Understanding Gender and Organisation* (Sage, London).
Alvesson, M & Skoldberg K (2000) *Reflexive Methodology* (Sage, London).
Anderson, P & Williams J (2001) (eds), *Identity and Difference in Higher Education: 'outsiders within'* (Ashgate, Aldershot).
Anderson, P (2001) 'Betwixt and Between: classifying identities in higher education' in P Anderson & J Williams (eds), *Identity and Difference in Higher Education: 'outsiders within'* (Ashgate, Aldershot).
Andre, R & Frost, PJ (1997) *Researchers Hooked on Teaching: Noted Scholars Discuss the Synergies of Teaching and Research* (Sage, Thousand Oaks, California).

Bibliography

Archer, L, Pratt, S & Phillips, D (2001) 'Working-Class Men's Constructions of Masculinity and Negotiations of (Non) Participation in Higher Education' (13.4) *Gender and Education* 431–49.

Atiyah, P (1970) *Accidents, Compensation and the Law* (Weidenfeld & Nicolson, London).

Atkins, S & Hoggett, B (1984) *Women and the Law* (Blackwell, Oxford).

Austin, A (1998) *The Empire Strikes Back: outsiders and the struggle over legal education* (New York University Press, New York and London).

AUT (2001) *Lesbian, Gay and Bisexual Participation in UK Universities* (Association of University Teachers, London).

Bannerji, H et al (1991) *Unsettling Relations: the university as a site of feminist struggle* (Women's Press, Toronto).

Bar Council (2002) List of Institutions Recognised as Providing Qualifying Law Degrees. www.legaleducation.org.uk

Barley, N. (1986) *The Innocent Anthropologist: notes from a mud hut* (Penguin Books, London).

Barnett, H & Yach, D (1985) 'The Teaching of Jurisprudence and Legal Theory in British Universities' *Legal Studies* 151–243.

Barnett, R (1990) *The Idea of Higher Education* (Society for Research into Higher Education & Open University Press, Buckingham).

Bauman, Z (1999) *Culture as Praxis* (Sage, London).

Becher, T (1989) *Academic Tribes and Territories: intellectual enquiry and the culture of disciplines* (SRHE & Open University Press, Milton Keynes).

—— (1991) 'Perspectives on Academic Life: an apologia for meso-qualitative research' 16(3) *Higher Education in Europe* 119–36.

Becher, T & Kogan M (1992) *Processes and Structure in Higher Education* (Routledge, London).

Becher, T & Trowler, P (2001) (2nd edn) *Academic Tribes and Territories: intellectual enquiry and the culture of disciplines* (SRHE & Open University Press, Buckingham).

Bell, J (1999) 'Benchmarking: a pedagogically valuable process?' *Web Journal of Current Legal Issues* (http://webjcli.ncl.ac.uk/1999/issue2/bell2.html)

Bell, J & Engle, G (1995) (3rd edn) *Statutory Interpretation; by the late Sir Rupert Cross* (Butterworths, London).

Bell, D & Valentine, G (1995) 'The Sexed Self: strategies of performance, sites of resistance' in S Pile & N Thrift (eds), *Mapping the Subject: geographies of cultural transformation* (Routledge, London).

Billington, R, Strawbridge, S, Greensides, L & Fitzsimmons A (1991) *Culture and Society: a sociology of culture* (Macmillan, Basingstoke).

Birks, P (1992) *Examining the Law Syllabus: The Core* (Oxford University Press, Oxford).

—— (1993) *Examining the Law Syllabus: Beyond The Core* (Oxford University Press, Oxford).

—— (1994) *Reviewing Legal Education* (Oxford University Press, Oxford).

—— (ed), (1996) *Pressing Problems in the Law Volume 2: What Are Law Schools For?* (Oxford University Press, Oxford).

—— (1996a) 'Editor's Preface' in P Birks (ed), *Pressing Problems in the Law Volume 2: What Are Law Schools For?* (Oxford University Press, Oxford).

Blaxter, L Hughes, C & Tight, M (1998) *The Academic Career Handbook* (Open University Press, Buckingham).

Bosworth, J (1987) *The Birmingham Law Faculty: the first sixty years* (University of Birmingham, Faculty of Law).
Bourdieu, P (1977) *Outline of a Theory of Practice* (Cambridge University Press, Cambridge).
—— (1984) *Homo Academicus* (Editions de Minuit, Paris).
Boyer, E, Altbach, P & Whitelaw, MJ (1994) *The Academic Profession: an international perspective* (Carnegie Foundation for the Advancement of Teaching, Princeton, NJ).
Bradney, A (1990) 'Paying the Piper' (24) *The Law Teacher* 137–49.
—— (1992) 'Ivory Towers and Satanic Mills: choices for university law schools' *Studies in Higher Education* 5–20.
—— (1996) 'The Quality of Teaching Quality Assessment in English Law Schools' *The Law Teacher* 150–67.
—— (1997) 'The Rise and Rise of Legal Education' 4 *Web Journal of Current Legal Issues* http://www.webjcli.ncl.ac.uk/1997/issue4/bradney4.html
—— (1998) 'Law as a Parasitic Discipline' *Journal of Law and Society* 71–84.
—— (1999) 'Benchmarking: A pedagogically valuable process? An alternative view' *Web Journal of Current Legal Issues* http://webjcli.ncl.ac.uk/1999/issue2/bradney2.html
—— (2001) 'The Quality Assurance Agency and the Politics of Audit' *Journal of Law and Society* 430–42.
—— (2002a) 'Give Us the Money' *The Reporter* (The Newsletter of the Society of Legal Scholars) Spring 2002, 1.
—— (2002b) 'Welcome' *The Reporter* (The Newsletter of the Society of Legal Scholars) Winter 2002, 1.
—— (2002c) 'Accountability, the University Law School and the Death of Socrates' *Web Journal of Current Legal Issues* www.ncl.ac.uk/~nlawwww/
—— (2003) 'On Academic Freedom' *The Reporter* (The Newsletter of the Society of Legal Scholars) Spring 2003, 1.
—— (2003a) *Conversations, Choices and Chances: the liberal law school in the twenty first century* (Hart Publishing, Oxford).
Bradney, A & Cownie, F (1996) 'Working on the Chain Gang?' 2.2 *Contemporary Issues in Law* 15–30.
—— —— (1998) *Transformative Visions of Legal Education* (Blackwell, Oxford).
Bradney, A & Cownie, F (1999) *Teaching Legal System* (NCLE, Warwick).
Bradney, A & Cownie, F (2000) 'British University Law Schools' in D Hayton (ed), *Law's Future(s)* (Hart Publishing, Oxford).
Brayne, H (1996) 'Law Students as Practitioners: developing an undergraduate clinical education programme at Northumbria University' in J Webb & C Maugham (eds), *Teaching Lawyers' Skills* (Butterworths, London).
Brayne, H, Duncan, N & Grimes, R (1998) *Active Learning in Your Law School* (Blackstone Press, London).
Brew, A (1999) 'Research and Teaching: changing relationships in a changing context' (24.3) *Studies in Higher Education* 291–302.
Bridge, JW (1975) 'The Academic Lawyer: mere working mason or architect?' 91 *Law Quarterly Review* 488–501.
Bright, S & Sunkin, M (1991) *Commercial Sponsorship of Legal Education* (Institute of Advanced Legal Studies, London).
Brooks, A (1997) *Academic Women* (SRHE & Open University Press, Buckingham).

Brooks, A & Mackinnon, A (2001) (eds), *Gender and the Restructured University* (SRHE & Open University Press, Buckingham).

Brown, G & Atkins, M (1988) *Effective Teaching in Higher Education* (Routledge, London).

Brownsword, R (1994) 'Teaching Quality Assessment in Law Schools: a cause for concern?' *Journal of Law and Society* 529–44.

—— (1996) 'Where Are All the Law Schools Going?' 30 *The Law Teacher* 1–27.

—— (1999) 'Law Schools for Lawyers, Citizens and People' in F Cownie (ed), *The Law School: Global Issues, Local Questions* (Ashgate, Aldershot).

Buchanan, D, Boddy, D & McCalman, J (1988) 'Getting in, getting on, getting out and getting back' 53–67 in A Brymer (ed), *Doing Research in Organisations* (Routledge, London).

Burgess, R (1982) 'Styles of Data Analysis: approaches and implications' in R Burgess (ed), *Field Research: A Sourcebook and Field Manual* (Allen & Unwin, London).

—— (1983) *Experiencing Comprehensive Education: A Study of Bishop McGregor School* (Methuen, London).

—— (1984) *In The Field* (Routledge, London).

Burrell, G & Hearn, J (1989) 'The Sexuality of Organization' in J Hearn, D Sheppard, P Tancred-Sherriff & G Burrell (eds), *The Sexuality of Organization* (Sage, London).

Burton, F, Martin Clement, N, Standley, K, Williams, C (1999) *Teaching Family Law* NCLE, Warwick.

Butler, J (1999) *Gender Trouble: feminism and the subversion of identity* (Routledge, London).

Cain, M & Hunt, A (1978) (eds), *Marx and Engels on Law* (Academic Press, London).

Campbell, CM & Wiles, P (1976) 'The Study of Law in Society in Britain' 10 *Law and Society Review* 547–78.

Campbell, K, Vick, DW, Murray, AD & Little, GF (1999) 'Journal Publishing, Journal Reputation and the United Kingdom's Research Assessment Exercise' *Journal of Law and Society* 470–501.

Cane, P (1997) *The Anatomy of Tort Law* (Hart Publishing, Oxford).

Caplan, P (1993) *Lifting a Ton of Feathers: a woman's guide to surviving in the academic world* (University of Toronto Press, Toronto).

Card, R (2002) 'The Legal Scholar' *The Reporter* (Newsletter of the Society of Legal Scholars) 5–12.

Census (1992) *Definitions Great Britain* (HMSO, London).

Cheffins, BR (1999) 'Using Theory to Study Law: a company law perspective' 58 *Cambridge Law Journal* 197–221.

Chrisler, J (1998) 'Teacher Versus Scholar: role conflict for women?' pp. 107–34 in LH Collins, JC Chrisler, K Quina (eds), *Career Strategies for Women in Academe* (Sage, London).

Clark, BR (1983) *The Higher Education System: Academic Organization in Cross-National Perspective* (University of California Press, Berkeley, Los Angeles, London).

—— (1987) *The Academic Life. Small Worlds, Different Worlds* (Carnegie Foundation, Princeton).

—— (1995) 'Complexity and Differentiation: the deepening problem of university integration' in D Dill & B Sporn (eds), *Emerging Patterns of Social Demand and University Reform* (IAU & Elsevier Science Ltd, Oxford).

Clinch, P (1999) *Teaching Legal Research* (NCLE, Warwick).

Coffey, A (1999) *The Ethnographic Self: Fieldwork and the representation of Identity* (Sage, London).
Collier, R (1991) 'Masculinism, Law and Law Teaching' 19 *International Journal of the Sociology of Law* 427–51.
Collier, R (1998) 'Nutty Professors', 'Men in Suits' and 'New Entrpreneurs': corporeality, subjectivity and change in the law school and legal practice' 7 *Social and Legal Studies* 27–53.
Collier, R (1998a) '(Un)sexy Bodies: the making of professional masculinities' in C McGlynn (ed), *Legal Feminisms: Theory and Practice* (Ashgate, Aldershot).
Collier, R (2002) 'The Changing University and the (Legal) Academic Career—rethinking the relationship between women, men and the "private life" of the law school' 22 *Legal Studies* 1–32.
Collier, R (2003) 'Useful Knowledge and the "new economy": an uncertain future for (critical) socio-legal studies?' 39 *Socio-Legal Newsletter* 3.
Collinson, D & Hearn, J (1996) 'Men' at 'Work' : multiple masculinities / multiple workplaces' in M Mac an Ghaill (ed), *Understanding Masculinities* (Open University Press, Buckingham).
Conaghan, J (2002) 'Reassessing the Feminist Theoretical Project in Law' (27.3) *Journal of Law and Society* 351–85.
Cotterell, R (1987) 'Power, Property and the Law of Trusts: a partial agenda for critical legal scholarship' in P Fitzpatrick, & A Hunt, (eds), (1987) *Critical Legal Studies* (Basil Blackwell, Oxford).
—— —— (1995) *Law's Community: Legal Theory in Sociological Perspective* (Clarendon Press, Oxford).
Cotterell, RBM & Woodliffe JC (1974) 'The Teaching of Jurisprudence in British Universities' *Journal of the Society of Public Teachers of Law* 89.
Court, S (1996) 'The Use of Time by Academic and Related Staff' (50.4) *Higher Education Quarterly* 237–60.
Cowan, D, Wheeler, S & Hillyard, P (2003) 'What is the State of Socio-Legal Training in UK Law Schools? SLSA Questionnaire Results' (39) *Socio-Legal Newsletter* 1.
Cownie, F (1998) 'Women Legal Academics—A New Research Agenda?' 25 *Journal of Law and Society* 102–15.
—— (1999) 'Searching for Theory in Legal Education' in F Cownie (ed), *The Law School: Global Issues, Local Questions* (Ashgate, Aldershot).
—— (1999a) (ed), *The Law School: Global Issues, Local Questions* (Ashgate, Aldershot).
—— (2000) 'The Importance of Theory in Law Teaching' 7(3) *International Journal of the Legal Profession* 225–38.
—— (2000a) 'From Doctrinalism to Pluralism: a brief history of English legal education' 271–88 in P Torremans (ed), *Legal Convergence in the Enlarged Europe of the New Millenium* (Kluwer, The Hague).
—— (2000b) 'Women in the Law School—Shoals of Fish, Starfish or Fish Out of Water?' in P Thomas (ed), *Discriminating Lawyers* (Cavendish Publishing, London).
Cownie, F & Addison, W (1996) 'International Students and Language Support: a new survey' (21.2) *Studies in Higher Education* 221–31.
Craik, J (1993) *The Face of Fashion: cultural studies in fashion* (Routledge, London).
Crompton, R (1998) (2nd edn) *Class and Stratification: an introduction to current debates* (Polity Press, Cambridge).

Crompton, R & Jones, G (1988) 'Researching White Collar Organisations: why sociologists should not stop doing case studies' in A Brymer (ed), *Doing Research in Organisations* (Routledge, London).

Cross, R & Harris, J (1991) (4th edn) *Precedent in English Law* (Clarendon Press, Oxford).

Csordas, T (1990) 'Embodiment as a Paradigm for Anthropology' (18) *Ethos* 5–47.

Csordas, T (1994) 'Introduction: the body as representation and being-in-the-world' in T Csordas (ed), *Embodiment and Experience: the existential ground of culture and self* (Cambridge University Press, Cambridge).

CVCP (1985) *Report of the Steering Committee for Efficiency Studies in Universities* (CVCP, London).

Davies, S, Lubelska, C & Quinn, J (1994) (eds), *Changing the Subject: women in higher education* (Taylor & Francis, London).

Dean, JP, Eichorn, RL & Dean, LR (1967) 'Observation and Interviewing' in JT Dolby (ed), *An Introduction to Social Research* (Meredith Corporation, Des Moines, Iowa).

Delamont, S (1992) *Fieldwork in Educational Settings* (Falmer, Lewes).

—— (1996) 'Just Like The Novels? Researching the Occupational Culture(s) of Higher Education' in R Cuthbert (ed), *Working in Higher Education* (SRHE & Open University Press, Buckingham).

Delamont, S & Atkinson, P (1995) *Fighting Familiarity: essays on education and ethnography* (Hampton Press, Crosskill, NJ).

Denzin, N K (2000) 'The Art and Politics of Interpretation' in NK Denzin & Y K Lincoln (eds), *Collecting and Interpreting Qualitative Materials* (Sage, CA).

Dicey, AV (1883) 'Can English Law be Taught at the Universities?' Inaugural Lecture, 21 April 1883, (MacMillan & Co, London).

Douglass, W (1992) 'Anthropological Methodology in the European Context' in J de Pina-Cabral & J Campbell (eds), *Europe Observed* (Macmillan, London).

Duxbury, N (2001) *Jurists and Judges* (Hart Publishing, Oxford).

Eagleton, T (2000) *The Idea of Culture*.

Edgell, S (1993) *Class* (Routledge, London).

Enders, J & Teichler, U (1997) 'A Victim of Their Own Success? Employment and working conditions of academic staff in comparative Perspective' 34 *Higher Education* 347–72.

Entwistle, J (2001) 'The Dressed Body' in J Entwistle & E Wilson (eds), *Body Dressing* (Berg, Oxford).

ESRC (1994) *Review of Socio-Legal Studies: Final Report* (ESRC, Swindon).

Evans, C (1988) *Language People: the experience of teaching and learning modern languages in British universities* (SRHE & Open University Press, Milton Keynes).

—— (1993) *English People: the experience of teaching and learning English in British universities* (SRHE & Open University Press, Buckingham).

Everett, J E & Entrikin, LV (1994) 'Changing Attitudes of Australian Academics' 27 *Higher Education* 203–77.

Falk Moore, S (1978) *Law as Process* (Routledge & Kegan Paul, London).

Fehl, N (1962) *The Idea of the University in East and West* (Chung Chi College, Hong Kong).

Finch, J & Mason, J (1990) 'Decision-Taking in the Fieldwork Process: theoretical Sampling and Collaborative Working' in R Burgess (ed), *Studies in Qualitative Methodology vol. 2 1990: Reflections on Field Experience* (JAI Press, London).

Fitzpatrick, P & Hunt, A (1987) (eds), *Critical Legal Studies* (Basil Blackwell, Oxford).
Frost, P (1997) 'Learning to Teach: lessons from a life in business and academia' in R Andre & P Frost (eds), *Researchers Hooked on Teaching: noted scholars discuss the synergies of teaching and research* (Sage, Thousand Oaks, CA).
Fulton, O (1996) 'The Academic Profession in England on the Eve of Structural Reform' 391–437 in P Altbach (ed), *The International Academic Profession: portraits of fourteen countries* (The Carnegie Foundation for the Advancement of Teaching, Princeton, NJ).
Geertz, C (1975) *The Interpretation of Cultures* (Hutchinson & Co., London).
—— (1976) 'Toward an Ethnography of the Disciplines' (Princeton Institute for Advanced Study, Mimeo).
—— (1983) *Local Knowledge: further essays in interpretative anthropology* (Basic Books Inc, New York).
Gelsthorpe, L (1992) 'Response to Martin Hammersley's Paper on Feminist Methodology' 20(2) *Sociology* 213–18.
Gerson, K & Horowitz, R (2002) 'Observation and Interviewing: options and choices in qualitative research' in T May (ed), *Qualitative Research in Action* (Sage, London).
Gibson, S (1990) 'Define and Empower: women students consider feminist learning' 1 *Law and Critique* 47–60.
Giddens, A (1988) (2nd edn) *The Class Structure of the Advanced Societies* (Hutchinson, London).
—— (1991) *Modernity and Self-Identity* (Polity Press, Cambridge).
—— (1984) *The Constitution of Society* (Polity Press, Cambridge).
Gilligan, C (1982) *In A Different Voice: Psychological theory and Women's Development* (Harvard University Press, Cambridge, Massachusetts).
Goffman, E (1990) *The Presentation of Self in Everyday Life* (Penguin Books, London).
Gold, R (1958) 'Roles in Sociological Field Observation' (36.3) *Social Forces* 217–23.
Goode, J (2000) 'Is the position of academic women changing?' in M Tight (ed), *Academic Work and Life: what it is to be an academic, and how this is changing* (JAI Elsevier, New York).
Goodhart, A (1931) *Essays in Jurisprudence and Common Law* (Cambridge University Press, Cambridge).
Goodrich, C (1991) *Anarchy and Elegance: confessions of a journalist at Yale Law School*, (Little, Brown, Boston).
Goodrich, P (1986) *Reading the Law* (Basil Blackwell, Oxford).
—— (1992) 'Critical Legal Studies in England: Prospective Histories' (12.2) *Oxford Journal of Legal Studies* 195–236.
—— (1999) 'The Critic's Love of the Law: intimate observations of an insular jurisdiction' (10) *Law and Critique* 343–60.
—— (1996) 'Of Blackstone's Tower: Metaphors of Distance and Histories of the English Law School' in P Birks (ed), *Pressing Problems in the Law Volume Two: What Are Law Schools For?* (Oxford University Press, Oxford).
Goodrich, P & Mills, LG (2001) 'The Law of White Spaces: Race, Culture and Legal Education' 51 *Journal of Legal Education* 15–38.
Gower, LCB (1950) 'English Legal Training: a critical survey' 13 *Modern Law Review* 137–205.
Green, E (2001) 'Suiting Ourselves: women professors using clothes to signal authority, belonging and personal style' in A Guy, E Green, & M Banim, (eds), *Through the Wardrobe: women's relationships with their clothes* (Berg, Oxford).

Grigg-Spall, I & Ireland, P (1992) (eds), *The Critical Lawyers' Handbook* (Pluto Press, London).

Grimes, R (1996) 'The Theory and Practice of Clinical Legal Education' in J Webb & C Maugham (eds), *Teaching Lawyers' Skills* (Butterworths, London).

Grimes, R, Klaff, J & Smith, C (1996) 'Legal Skills and Clinical Legal Education—a Survey of Law School Practice' 30 *The Law Teacher* 44.

Grodecki, JK (1967) 'Legal Education, Dilemmas and Opportunities: an inaugural lecture delivered in the University of Leicester 18 October 1966' (Leicester University Press, Leicester).

Gunter, H (2001) 'Gender, Identity and Working Lives' (13.4) *Gender and Education* 451–55.

Guy, A, Green, E & Banim, M (2001) (eds), *Through the Wardrobe: women's relationships with their clothes* (Berg, Oxford).

Hagan, J & Kay, F (1995) *Gender in Practice* (Oxford University Press, Oxford).

Hakin, C (2000) *Work-Lifestyle Choices in the Twentieth Century: preference theory* (Oxford University Press, Oxford).

Hall, S (1996) 'Introduction: Who Needs Identity?' in S Hall & P Du Gay (eds), *Questions of Cultural Identity* (Sage, London).

Halpern, D (1994) *Entry Into the Legal Professions: The Law Student Cohort Study Years 1 and 2*, (The Law Socirty, London).

Halsey, AH (1992) *Decline of Donnish Dominion: the British academic professions in the twentieth century* (Clarendon Press, Oxford).

Hammersley, M & Atkinson, P (1995) *Ethnography: Principles in Practice* (2nd edn), (Routledge, London).

Hannerz, U (1992) *Cultural Complexity: studies in the social organisation of meaning* (Columbia University Press, NY).

Harley, S (2002) 'The Impact of Research Selectivity on Academic Work and Identity in UK Universities' (27.2) *Higher Education* 187–205.

Harris, P & Bellerby, S with Leighton, P & Hodgson, J (1993) *A Survey of Law Teaching, 1993* (Association of Law Teachers).

Harris, P & Jones, M (1997) 'A Survey of Law Schools in the United Kingdom, 1996' 31(1) *The Law Teacher* 38–126.

Harrison, J (1991) 'Confess'n the Blues: some thoughts on class bias in law school hiring' (42.1) *Journal of Legal Education* 119–25.

Hearn, J (2001) 'Academia, Management and Men: making the connections, exploring the implications' in A Brooks & A Mackinnon (eds), *Gender and the Restructured University* (SRHE & Open University Press, Buckingham).

Hearn, J & Parkin, W (1987) *Sex at Work* (Wheatsheaf, Brighton).

Henkel, M (2000) *Academic Identities and Policy Change in Higher Education* (Jessica Kingsley Publishers, London).

Henry, M (1994) 'Ivory Towers and Ebony Women: the experiences of black women in higher education' in S Davies, C Lubelska & J Quinn (eds), *Changing the Subject: women in higher education* (Taylor & Francis, London).

Hepple, B (1992) 'The Integration of Contract and Tort' in P Birks (ed), *Examining the Law Syllabus: The Core* (Oxford University Press, Oxford).

—— (1996) 'The Renewal of the Liberal Law Degree' *Cambridge Law Journal* 470–87.

Herman, D & Stychin, C (1995) (eds), *Legal Inversions: lesbians, gay men and the politics of law* (Temple University Press, Philadelphia).

HESA (2002) *Resources of Higher Education Institutions 2000/01* (Higher Education Statistics Agency, Cheltenham).
Heward, C, Taylor, P, & Vickers, R (1997) 'Gender, Race and Career Success in the Academic Profession' (21.2) *Journal of Further and Higher Education* 205–18.
Hicks, A (1995) 'Legal Practice is an Academic Matter' (Spring) *SPTL Reporter* 6.
Holdsworth, WS (1925) 'The Vocation of a Public Teacher of Law' [1925] *Journal of the Society of Public Teachers of Law* 1–11.
Holland, L & Spencer, L (1992) *Without Prejudice? Sex Equality at the Bar and in the Judiciary* (TMS Management Consultants, Bournemouth).
Housee, S (2001) 'Insiders and/or Outsiders: black female voices from the academy' in P Anderson & J Williams (eds), *Identity and Difference in Higher Education: 'Outsiders Within'* (Ashgate, Aldershot).
Howie, G & Tauchert, A (2002) *Gender, Teaching and Research in Higher Education: challenges for the 21st century* (Ashgate, Aldershot).
Huber, M et al (1997) *Scholarship Assessed: Evaluation of the Professoriate* (Carnegie Foundation for the Advancement of Teaching, Princeton, NJ).
Hudson, L (1966) *Contrary Imaginations* (Penguin Books, Harmondsworth).
Hunt, A (1986) 'The Case for Critical Legal Education' 20 *The Law Teacher* 10–20.
—— (1987) 'The Critique of Law: what is 'critical' about critical legal studies?' 5–19 in P Fitzpatrick & A Hunt (1987) (eds), *Critical Legal Studies* (Basil Blackwell, Oxford).
Jenkins, R (1992) *Pierre Bourdieu* (Routledge, London).
—— (1996) *Social Identity* (Routledge, London).
Johnson, K & Lennon, S (1999) (eds), *Appearance and Social Power* (Berg, Oxford).
Johnston, R (1996) 'Managing How Academics Manage' in R Cuthbert (ed), *Working in Higher Education* (SRHE & Open University Press, Buckingham).
Joint Statement (1999) 'A Joint Statement Issued by The Law Society and the General Council of the Bar on the Completion of the Initial or Academic Stage of Training by Obtaining an Undergraduate Degree'. www.legaleducation.org.uk
Jones, G (1996) 'Traditional' Legal Scholarship: a personal view' in P Birks (ed), *Pressing Problems in the Law Volume 2: What Are Law Schools For?* (Oxford University Press, Oxford).
Kahn-Freund, O (1966) 'Reflections on Legal Education' 29 *Modern Law Review* 121–36.
Keenan, W (2001) 'Introduction: *Sartor Resartus* restored: dress studies in Carlylean perspective' in W Keenan (ed), *Dressed to Impress: looking the part* (Berg, Oxford).
Kennedy, D (1982) Legal Education and the Reproduction of Hierarchy 32 *J Legal Educ* 591–615.
Kennedy, D (1992) 'Legal Education as Traning for Hierarchy' pp. 51–61 in I. Grigg-Spall & P Ireland, *The Critical Lawyers' Handbook* (Pluto Press, London)
Kennedy, D (1997) *Academic Duty* (Harvard University Press, Cambridge, Mass).
Knorr-Cetina, K & Cicourel, AV (1981) (eds), *Advances in Social Theory and Methodology: Toward an Integration of Micro- and Macro- Sociologies* (Routledge & Kegan Paul, London).
Kogan, M & Hanney, S (2000) *Reforming Higher Education* (Jessica Kingsley Publishers, London).
Kogan, M & Henkel, M (1992) 'Constraints on the Individual Researcher' in TG Whiston & RL Geiger *Research and Higher Education: the United Kingdom and the United States* (SRHE & Open University Press, Buckingham).

Kolb, DA (1981) 'Learning Styles and Disciplinary Differences' in A Chickering (ed), *The Modern American College* (University of Chicago Press, Chicago).

Kramer, M (1996) 'Review of Patterns of American Jurisprudence by Neil Duxbury' (55) *Cambridge Law Journal* 150–2.

Laurie, H & Gershuny, J 'Couples, Work and Money' in R Berthoud & J Gershuny (eds), *Seven Years in the Lives of British Families* (Policy Press, Bristol).

Lawson, FH (1968) *The Oxford Law School 1850–1965* (Clarendon Press, Oxford).

Lawton, F (1980) 'Legal Education and the Needs of the Legal Profession' 4 *The Law Teacher* 163–7.

Le Brun, M & Johnstone, R (1994) *The Quiet Revolution: improving student learning in law* (Law Book Company, Sydney).

Leighton, P (1996) 'Law Teachers in 1996: traditions, challenges and paradoxes' (Professorial Lecture, School of Law, Manchester Metropolitan University).

Leighton, P (1998) 'New Wine in Old Bottles or New Wine in New Bottles?' in A Bradney & F Cownie (eds), *Transformative Visions of Legal Education* Special Issue of the Journal of Law and Society (vol 25.1).

Leighton, P, Mortimer, T & Whatley, N (1995) *Today's Law Teachers: Lawyers or Academics?* (Cavendish, London).

Letherby, G & Shiels, J (2001) 'Isn't He Good But Can We Take Her Seriously?: gendered expectations in higher education' in P Anderson & J Williams (eds), *Identity and Difference in Higher Education: outsiders within* (Ashgate, Aldershot).

Llewellfryn Davies, DJ (1956) 'Problems of Legal Education' [N.S. 3] *JSPTL* 198–206.

Lloyd, G (1984) *The Man of Reason: 'male' and 'female' in Western philosophy* (Routledge, London).

Lynch, B, Moodie, P, & Salter, D (1992) 'The Teaching of Foundation Legal Instruction' *The Law Teacher* 216–43.

Malleson, K & Banda, F (2000) *Factors Affecting the Decision to Apply for Silk and Judicial Office* (Lord Chancellor's Department Research Series 2/00, LCD, London).

Manning, P (1992) *Erving Goffman and Modern Sociology* (Polity Press, Cambridge).

Martin, E (1999) *Changing Academic Work: developing the learning university* (SRHE & Open University Press, Buckingham).

Mason, J (1996) *Qualitative Researching* (Sage, London).

McAuslan, P (1989) 'The Coming Crisis in Legal Education' 16 *Journal of Law and Society* 310–18.

McDowell, L (1995) 'Body Work: heterosexual gender performances in City workplaces' in D Bell & G Valentine (eds), *Mapping Desire: geographies of sexualities* (Routledge, London).

—— (1997) *Capital Culture: gender at work in the City* (Blackwell, Oxford).

McGlynn, C (1998) *The Woman Lawyer: Making the Difference* (Butterworths, London).

—— (1999) 'Womem Representation and the Legal Academy' (19.1) *Legal Studies* 68–92.

McIntyre, S (1995) 'Gender Bias within the Law School: "The Memo" and its impact' in The Chilly Collective (eds), *Breaking Anonymity: the chilly climate for women faculty* (Wilfred Laurier University Press, Waterloo, Ontario).

McNay, L (1999) 'Gender, Habitus and the Field: Pierre Bourdieu and the limits of reflexivity' 16(1) *Theory, Culture and Society* 95–117.

Minogue, M et al (2000) (eds), *Beyond the New Public Management: changing ideas and practice in governance* (Edward Elgar Publishing, Cheltenham).

Mirza, H (1995) 'Black women in Higher Education: defining a space / finding a place' in L Morley, & V Walsh (eds), *Feminist Academics: creative agents for change* (Taylor & Francis, London).

Montgomery, A (1997) 'In Law and Outlaw? The Tale of a Journey' in L Stanley (ed), *Knowing Feminisms* (Sage, London).

Moran, L (1996) *The Homosexual(ity) of Law* (Routledge, London).

Morley, L (1995) 'Measuring the Muse: feminism, creativity and career development in higher education' in L Morley, & V Walsh, (eds), *Feminist Academics: creative agents for change* (Taylor & Francis, London).

—— (2002) 'A Comedy of Manners: quality and power in higher education' in P Trowler (ed), *Higher Education Policy and Institutional Change: intentions and outcomes in turbulent environments* (SRHE & Open University Press, Buckingham).

Morley, L & Walsh, V (1995) (eds), *Feminist Academics: creative agents for change* (Taylor & Francis, London).

—— —— (1996) (eds), *Breaking Boundaries: women in higher education* (Taylor & Francis, London).

Morison, J & Leith, P (1992) *The Barrister's World and the Nature of Law* (Open University Press, Buckingham).

Morris, A & O'Donnell, T (1999) (eds), *Feminist Perspectives on Employment Law* (Cavendish Publishing, London).

Muetzelfeldt, M (1989) 'Fieldwork at Home' in J Perry (ed), *Doing Fieldwork* (Deakin University Press, Geelong, Victoria).

Murlis, H & Hartle, F (1996) 'Does It Pay to Work in Universities?' in R Cuthbert (ed), *Working in Higher Education* (SRHE & Open University Press, Buckingham).

Naffine, N (1990) *Law and the Sexes: explorations in feminist jurisprudence* (Unwin Hyman, Sydney).

—— (1993) 'Assimilating Feminist Jurisprudence' (11.1) *Law in Context* 78–94.

Newman, JH (1960) *The Idea of a University* (Holt, Rineholt & Winston, London).

Nicolson, D & Bibbings, L (2000) (eds), *Feminist Perspectives on Criminal Law* Cavendish Publishing, London.

Nicolson, D & Webb, J (1999) *Professional Legal Ethics* (Oxford, Oxford University Press).

Nixon, J (1996) 'Professional Identity and the Restructuring of Higher Education' (21.1) *Higher Education* 5–16.

O'Dair, DRF, (1997) 'Ethics by the Pervasive Method—the Case of Contract' 17 *Legal Studies* 305–22.

—— (1998) 'Recent Developments in the Teaching of Legal Ethics—A UK Perspective' in K Economides (ed), *Ethical Challenges to Legal Education and Conduct* (Oxford, Hart Publishing).

O'Donovan, K (1985) *Sexual Divisions in Law* (Weidenfeld & Nicolson, London).

Pakulski, J & Waters, M (1996) *The Death of Class* (Sage, London).

Park, S (1996) 'Research, Teaching and Service: why shouldn't women's work count?' (67.1) *Journal of Higher Education* 46–84.

Parker, P (2000) *Organizational Culture and Identity: Unity and Division at Work* (Sage, London).

Partington, M (2002) 'SLRUF Highlights Way Forward' (37) *Socio-Legal Newsletter* 5.

Pettit, P H (1983) 'The Society of Public Teachers of Law—the first seventy five years' 3 *Legal Studies* 231–47.

Pollitt, C (1993) (2nd edn) *Managerialism and the Public Services: cuts or cultural change in the 1990s?* (Blackwell, Oxford).

Prichard, C (2000) *Making Managers in Universities and Colleges* (SRHE and Open University Press, Buckingham).

RAE (1999) *Assessment Panels' Criteria and Working Methods, RAE Circular 5/99* http://www.rae.ac.uk/Pubs/

Ramazanoglu, C (1987) 'Sex and Violence in Academic Life, or You Can Keep a Good Woman Down' in J Hanmer & M Maynard (eds), *Women, Violence and Social Control* (Macmillan, London).

Ramsden, B (1996) 'Academic Staff: information and data' in R Cuthbert (ed), *Working in Higher Education* (SRHE & Open University Press, Buckingham).

Riemer, J (1977) 'Varieties of Opportunistic Research' (5.4) *Urban Life* 467–77.

Robbins, S & Okonska, M (1999) *Bibliography on Women in Legal Education* www.aals.org/wle99/biblio.html

Roberts, G (2003) *Review of Research Assessment* (HEFCE, Gloucester).

Roberts, K, Cook, F, Clark, S & Semenoff, E (1977) *The Fragmentary Class Structure* (Heinemann, London).

Robson, R (1998) *Sappho Goes to Law School: fragments in Lesbian Legal Theory* (Columbia University Press, New York).

Rose, M (2000) 'Future Tense? Are growing occupations more stressed out and depressive?' Working Paper 3 ESRC Work Centrality and Careers Project, University of Bath, www.bath.ac.uk/~hssmjr.

Roseneil, S (1993) 'Greenham Revisited' in D Hobbs & T May (eds), *Interpreting the Field* (Clarendon Press, Oxford).

Rowland, S (1996) 'Relationship between Teaching and Research' (1.1) *Teaching in Higher Education* 7–20.

Rucker, M, Anderson, E & Kanglas, A (1999) 'Clothing, Power and the Workplace' in K Johnson, & S Lennon (eds), *Appearance and Social Power* (Berg, Oxford).

Ryan, D (1998) 'The Thatcher Government's Attack on Higher Education in Historical Perspective' (227) *New Left Review* 3–32.

Ryan, J & Sackrey, C (1984) *Strangers in Paradise: academics from the working class* (South End Press, Boston, Mass).

Salter, B & Tapper, T (1994) *The State and Higher Education* (Woburn Press, Ilford).

Sanders, A (1997) 'Criminal Justice: the development of criminal justice research in Britain' in PA Thomas (ed), *Socio-Legal Studies* (Dartmouth, Aldershot).

Savage, N & Watt, G (1996) 'A "House of Intellect" for the Profession' in P Birks (ed), *Pressing Problems in the Law Volume 2: What Are Law Schools For?* (Oxford University Press, Oxford).

Scott, P (1984) *The Crisis of the University* (Croom Helm, Beckenham).

—— (1995) *The Meanings of Mass Higher Education* (Open University Press, Buckingham).

Scott-Hunt, S & Lim, H (2001) (eds), *Feminist Perspectives on Equity and Trusts* (Cavendish Publishing, London).

Shattock, M (2001) 'The Academic Profession in Britain: a study in the failure to adapt to change' (41) *Higher Education* 27–47.

Sheldon, S & Thomson, M (1998) (eds), *Feminist Perspectives on Health Care Law* (Cavendish Publishing, London).

Sherr, A (1998) 'Legal Education, Legal Competence and Little Bo Peep' (32) *The Law Teacher* 37–63.
Sherr, A & Sugarman, D (2000) *Theory in Legal Education* Special Issue (7.3) *International Journal of the Legal Profession*.
Skeggs, B (1992) 'Techniques for Telling the Reflexive Self' in T May (ed), *Qualitative Research in Action* (Sage, London).
Skidmore, P (1999) 'Dress to Impress: employer regulation of lesbian and gay appearance' (8.4) *Social and Legal Studies* 509–29.
Skidmore, P (2001) 'A Legal Perspective on the Sexuality of Organisations: a lesbian and gay case-study' (paper delivered at the annual conference of the Law and Society Association, Budapest).
SLSA (2001) 'Statement of Ethical Practice' pp xix–xxviii in *SLSA Directory 2001*.
Smart, C (1989) *Feminism and the Power of Law* (Routledge, London).
Snaith, I (1990) 'Company Law on Degree Courses: survey report' *The Company Lawyer* 177.
Snow, CP (1959) *The Two Cultures and the Scientific Revolution. The Rede Lecture 1959* (Cambridge University Press, New York).
Sommerlad, H & Sanderson, P (1998) *Gender, Choice and Commitment: women solicitors in England and Wales and the struggle for equal status* (Dartmouth, Aldershot).
Spencer, A & Podmore, D (1987) 'Women Lawyers—Marginal Members of a Male-Dominated Profession' in A Spencer and D Podmore (eds), *In A Man's World: essays on women in male-dominated professions* (Tavistock, London).
Squirrell, G (1989) 'Teachers and Issues of Sexual Orientation' (1.1) *Gender and Education* 17–34.
Stallybrass, WT (1948) 'Law in the Universities' [N.S. 1] *JSPTL* 157–69.
Stanley, J (1995) 'Pain(t) for Healing: the academic conference and the classed/embodied self' in L Morley & V Walsh (eds), *Feminist Academics: creative agents for change* (Taylor & Francis, London).
Stanley, L & Wise, S (1983) *Breaking Out: feminist consciousness and feminist research* (Routledge, London).
—— —— (1993) *Breaking Out Again: feminist ontology and epistemology* (Routledge, London).
Stychin, C & Herman, D (2000) *Sexuality in the Legal Arena* (Athlone Press, London).
Sudman, S et al (1983) *Asking Questions* (Jossey Bass, San Francisco).
Sugarman, D (1983) 'The Legal Boundaries of Liberty: Dicey, Liberalism and Legal Science' 46 *Modern Law Review* 102–11.
—— (1986) 'Legal Theory and the Common Law Mind: The Making of the Textbook Tradition' in WL Twining (ed), *Legal Theory and the Common Law Mind* (Blackwell, Oxford).
Swadling, W (1992) 'Teaching Property Law: an Integrated Approach' in P Birks (ed), *Examining the Law Syllabus: The Core* (Oxford University Press, Oxford).
Talburt, S (2000) *Subject to Identity: knowledge, sexuality, and academic practices in higher education* (State University of New York Press, Albany, NY).
Talib, A (2001) 'The Continuing Behavioural Modification of Academics since the 1992 Research Assessment Exercise' (33.3) *Higher Education Review* 30–46.
Taylor, P (1999) *Making Sense of Academic Life* (SRHE & Open University Press, Buckingham).

220 Bibliography

Tett, L (2000) 'I'm Working Class and Proud of It': gendered experiences of non-traditional participants in higher education' (12.2) *Gender and Education* 183–94.

Thomas, K (1990) *Gender and Subject in Higher Education* (SRHE & Open University Press, Buckingham).

Thomas, PA (1997) 'Socio-Legal Studies: The Case of Disappearing Fleas and Bustards' in PA Thomas (ed), *Socio-Legal Studies* (Dartmouth, Aldershot).

Thomson, A (1987) 'Critical Legal Education in Britain' in P Fitzpatrick, & A Hunt, (eds), *Critical Legal Studies* (Basil Blackwell, Oxford).

Thornton, M (1996) *Dissonance and Distrust: women in the legal profession* (Oxford University Press, South Melbourne, Australia).

—— (1998) 'Technocentrism in the Law School; why the gender and colour of law remain the same' 36 *Osgoode Hall Law Journal* 369–98.

—— (2000) 'Among the Ruins: Law in the Neo-Liberal Academy'. Paper presented as keynote address at 'The Challenge of Change: rethinking law as a discipline' Workshop on Legal Knowledge and Legal Education in the Twenty-First Century, University of British Columbia, Vancouver, Canada.

Thorsen, E (1996) 'Stress in Academe: what bothers professors?' 31 *Higher Education* 471.

Tierney, WG (1988) 'Organizational Culture in Higher Education: Defining the Essentials' 59 *Journal of Higher Education* 2–12.

Tierney, WG (1991) 'Academic Work and Institutional Culture: constructing knowledge' (14.2) *The Review of Higher Education* 199–216.

Tierney, WG & Rhoads, RA (1993) *Enhancing Promotion, Tenure and Beyond*. ASHE / ERIC Higher Education Report No 6, The George Washington University and ASHE, Washington, DC.

Tight, M (2002) 'Editorial' 27(4) *Studies in Higher Education* 365–8.

Trow, M (1975) 'The Public and Private Lives of Higher Education' 104 *Daedalus* 113–27.

Trowler, P (1998) *Academics Responding to Change: new higher education frameworks and academic culture* SRHE & Open University Press, Buckingham.

Trowler, P & Knight, P (1999) 'Organisational socialization and induction in universities: reconceptionalising theory and practice' 37 *Higher Education* 177–95.

Tushnet, M (1991) 'Critical Legal Studies: a political history' 100 *Yale Law Journal* 1515–44.

Twining, WL (1967) 'Pericles and the Plumber: prolegomena to a working theory for lawyer education' 83 *Law Quarterly Review* 396–426.

—— (1974) 'Some Jobs for Jurisprudence' 1 *British Journal of Law and Society* 149–74.

—— (1980) Goodbye to Lewis Eliot: the academic lawyer as scholar' 15 *Journal of the Society of Public Teachers of Law* 2–19.

—— (1982) 'The Benson Report and Legal Education: A Personal View' in A. Thomas (ed), *Law in the Balance*.

—— (1988) 'Legal Skills and Legal Education' 22 *The Law Teacher* 4–13.

—— (1989) '1836 and All That: Laws in the University of London 1836–86' in R. Rideout & J. Jowell (eds), *Current Legal Problems: 1989* (Stevens & Sons, London).

—— (1994) *Blackstone's Tower: the English Law School* (Sweet & Maxwell, London).

—— (1995) 'What Are Law Schools For?' 46 *Northern Ireland Legal Quarterly* 291–303.

—— (1996) 'Rethinking Law Schools: a response to Schlegel' 21 *Law and Social Inquiry* 1007–16.

—— (1997) *Law in Context: Enlarging A Discipline* (Clarendon Press, Oxford).
—— (1997a) 'Reflections on 'Law in Context' in WL Twining, *Law in Context: Enlarging A Discipline* (Clarendon Press, Oxford).
—— (1997a) 'Introduction: Wandering Jurist' in W Twining *Law in Context: Enlarging A Discipline* (Clarendon Press, Oxford).
—— (1998) 'Thinking About Law Schools: Rutland Revisited' 25 *Journal of Law and Society* 1–13.
Valimaa, J (1998) 'Culture and Identity in Higher Education Research' 36 *Higher Education* 119–38.
Vick, D W, Murray, AD, Little, GF & Campbell, K (1998) 'The Perceptions of Academic Lawyers Concerning the Effects of the United Kingdom Research Assessment Exercise' *Journal of Law and Society* 536–61.
Warnock, M (1989) *Universities: knowing our minds. What the Government should do about higher education* (Chatto & Windus, London).
Webb, J (1996) 'Why Theory Matters' in J Webb & C Maugham (eds), *Teaching Lawyers' Skills* (Butterworths, London).
Webb, J & Maugham, C (1996) (eds), *Teaching Lawyers' Skills* (Butterworths, London).
Weidner, D (1997) 'The Crises of Legal Education: a wake-up call for faculty' 47 *Journal of Legal Education* 92
Wells, C (2000) 'Exceptional Women or Honorary Men?' in M. Freeman (ed), *Current Legal Problems* Vol 53, (Oxford University Press, Oxford).
—— (2001) 'Working Out Women in Law Schools' 21 *Legal Studies* 116–36.
—— (2001a) 'Ladies in Waiting: the Women Law Professors' Story' 3 *Sydney Law Review* 167–84.
—— 2002) 'Women Law Professors—Negotiating and Transcending Gender Identities at Work' 10 *Feminist Legal Studies* 1–38.
Wheeler, S & Shaw, J (1994) *Contract Law: Cases, Materials and Commentary* (Clarendon Press, Oxford).
Williams, G (1990) Review of 'Academic Tribes and Territories: intellectual enquiry and the culture of disciplines' *Studies in Higher Education* 351–3.
Williams, J (2000) *Unbending Gender: why family and work conflict and what to do about it* (Oxford University Press Inc, New York).
Williams, R (1983) *Keywords* (London, Fontana).
Wilson, G (1987) 'English Legal Scholarship' 50 *Modern Law Review* 818–54.
Wilson, J (1966) 'A First Survey of Legal Education in the United Kingdom' *Journal of the Society of Public Teachers of Law* 5–144.
—— (1993) 'A Third Survey of University Legal Education in the United Kingdom' *Legal Studies* 143–82.
Wilson, J & Marsh, S (1975) 'A Second Survey of Legal Education in the United Kingdom' *Journal of the Society of Public Teachers of Law* 241–330.
—— —— (1978) 'A Second Survey: Supplement No. 1' (Institute of Advanced Legal Studies, London).
—— —— (1981) 'A Second Survey: Supplement No. 2' (Institute of Advanced Legal Studies, London).
Witherspoon, S (2002) 'Research Capacity: A Crisis in Waiting?' (37) *Socio-Legal Newsletter* 1.
Woolf, H (2000) 'The Education the Justice System Requires Today' 34 *The Law Teacher* 263–70.

Wortley, BA (1965) 'Some Reflections on Legal Research After Thirty Years' (8) (*New Series*) *Journal of the Society of Public Teachers of Law*, 249–60.

Young-Eisendrath, P & Wiedemann, F (1987) *Female Authority* (The Guilford Press, London).

Index

Accountability, 163–4
  experience of being a legal academic, 109–10
Acker, 138, 147, 168, 171, 184
Adams, 50, 69, 102, 104, 105
Addison, 15
Adkins, 21
Adler, 24
Administration, 143–50
  identity, 202
  women and, 146–8, 170
Ainley, 200
Aisenberg, 89, 90, 155
Allen, 164
Altbach, 163
Alvesson, 4, 5, 10, 26, 73
Ambition, 88–90
Analysis, skills in, 81–2
Anderson, 181, 184
Andre, 7
Anson, 40
Anthias, 167
Anti-intellectualism, 69–72
Approaches to law, 49–54
  anti-intellectualism, 69–72
  black-letter law, 49–50, 54–6, 58, 59–60, 63–5, 197
  competing paradigms, 59–60
  critical legal studies, 51–3
  doctrinal law, 49–50, 54–6, 58, 59–60, 63–5, 197
  feminism and law, 53–4
  future difficulties, 65–7
  future of legal discipline, 63–5
  socio-legal studies, 50–1, 56–7, 59–60, 68–9, 198
Archer, 167
Atiyah, 77
Atkins, 53, 83
Atkinson, 23, 97
Audit,
  experience of being a legal academic, 109–10
Austin, 39, 59
Autonomy,
  experience of being a legal academic, 104–5

Banda, 80
Bannerji, 89
Barley, 23

Barnett, 30, 70, 83, 121
Bauman, 5
Becher, 2, 3, 8, 9, 10, 18, 20, 27, 49, 69, 78, 87, 92, 108, 124, 148, 153, 154, 155, 181, 182, 184, 198, 199
Beertz, 5
Bell, 34, 68, 183, 184
Bentham, 39
Billing, 6
Billington, 6, 7, 167, 197
Birks, 29, 30, 33
Black-letter law, 49–50, 54–6, 58, 59–60, 63–5, 197
Blackstone, 39, 42
Blaxter, 153
Bourdieu, 3, 12, 13, 25, 97, 167, 175, 186
Bradney, 22, 27, 29, 30, 34, 35, 39, 40, 51, 54, 65, 102, 103, 110, 118, 135, 150, 155, 164
Brayne, 15, 19, 22, 28, 29
Brew, 106
Bridge, 38, 69
Bright, 34
Brooks, 7, 19, 89, 168
  becher, 7
Brown, 83
Brownsword, 31, 34, 50, 69, 110, 135, 164
Buchanan, 15
Bureaucracy, 107, 163–4
Burgess, 17, 21, 23, 24, 197
Burrell, 184
Burton, 29
Butler, 11, 126

Cain, 52
Campbell, 27, 34, 36, 58, 68, 141, 200
Cane, 36
Caplan, 147
Card, 28
Career, legal academic, 73–95
  ambition, 88–90
  culture of academic law, 73
  gender, 88, 90–1
  getting on in profession, 86–92
    administrative route, 91–2
    ambition, 88–90
    gender, 88, 90–1
    informal contacts, 87–8
    masculinity, 89–90
    research output, 86–7
  informal contacts, 87–8

Career, legal academic (*cont.*):
  philosophy of education, 75–7
  qualities and skills of good academic lawyer, 81–6
    analysis, 81–2
    communication skills, 82–3
    organisation skills, 84–5
    persistence, 85–6
  reading law, 73–5
  reasons for choosing, 79–81
  research, 86–7
  second best, whether, 79–81
  vocational or academic, 75–8
Chrisler, 147
Cicourel, 4, 13, 143
Clark, 1, 2, 3, 13, 17, 25, 167, 205
Class,
  identity, 175–81
Clinch, 29
Clothes. *See* Dress
Cofey, 23
Collier, 19, 39, 44, 45, 89, 90, 91, 102, 108, 113, 116, 118, 138, 165, 168, 171, 172, 174, 175, 176, 185, 186, 196, 203, 205
Collinson, 184
Communication skills, 82–3
Conaghan, 37, 53
Cotterell, 30, 51, 68
Court, 85
Cowan, 66, 198
Cownie, 15, 19, 22, 28, 30, 31, 40, 47, 51, 54, 102, 130, 155, 168, 174, 175
Craik, 186, 187
Critical legal studies, 36, 37, 51–3, 54
Critical race theory, 43, 53
Crompton, 15, 176
Cross, 68
Csordas, 187, 189
Culture,
  academic law, studying, 9–12, 199–200
  different perspectives, 200–1
  higher education, approach to researching, 7–9
  identity and, 4, 143, 204–6
  meaning, 5
  studying legal academics, 4, 5–10

Davies, 28, 168
Dean, 24
Delamont, 6, 14, 97
Denzin, 17
Dicey, 31–2
Discipline, law as a, 197–9
  See also Approaches to law
Doctrinal law, 49–50, 54–6, 58, 59–60, 63–5, 197

Douglass, 23
Dress, 204
  codes, 193–6
  culture, 188–9
  men in suits, 192–3
  smart clothes, 189–91
  theorising, 186–7
  women and, 191–2
Duncan, 29
Duxbury, 39, 69, 95

Eagle, 68
Eagleton, 5
Edgell, 176
Enders, 98
Entrikin, 102
Entwistle, 187, 192, 204
Ethnicity, 9, 43–4
  identity, 181–3, 203–4
Evans, 9–10, 17, 20, 75, 81, 86, 128
Everett, 102
Experience of being a legal academic, 97–119
  accountability, 109–10
  audit, 109–10
  autonomy, 104–5
  bureaucracy, 107
  dislikes, 107–11
  home working, 111–13
  job satisfaction, 101–3
  negatives, 107–11
  positive factors, 97–107
  pressure, 110–11
  pride, 97–101
  variety, 105–7
  work-life balance, 97, 113–18

Falk-Moore, 4
Feminism, 21, 37, 45–7
  impact, 60–3
  law and, 53–4
  masculinity and, 44
Feuerverger, 147
Finch, 17
Fitzpatrick, 29, 36, 51
Frost, 7
Fulton, 129, 160, 200, 205

Geertz, 2, 6, 20, 49, 97
Gelsthorpe, 21
Gender, 9, 19–20
  career, legal academic, 88, 90–1
  identity, 168–75, 203–4
Gershuny, 169
Gerson, 17
Giddens, 11, 12, 167, 177
Gilligan, 172
Glaser, 17

Goffman, 11–12, 13, 124, 125, 126, 187, 196, 202, 204
Gold, 23
Goldthorpe, 176
Goode, 86
Goodhart, 68
Goodrich, 36, 43, 44, 50, 52, 53, 54, 129, 182, 183, 203
Gower, 38, 69
Green, 189, 191, 192, 193
Grigg-Spall, 29
Grimes, 15, 19, 22, 28, 29, 30
Gunter, 184
Guy, 186

Hagan, 80, 157
Hakim, 169
Hall, 11, 126
Halpern, 60, 162, 177
Halsey, 7, 18, 87, 102, 106, 111, 124, 165, 176, 177, 206
Hammersley, 23
Hanney, 108, 159, 161
Harrington, 89, 90, 155
Harris, 42, 68, 159, 161, 182
Harrison, 176
Hartle, 134
Hearn, 89, 184, 204
Henkel, 4, 14, 17, 81, 92, 95, 102, 104, 118, 121, 141, 148, 159, 163, 200, 201, 206
Henry, 181
Hepple, 29, 33, 38
Herman, 184
Heward, 88, 182, 203
Hicks, 136
Hodsworth, 28
Hoggett, 53
Holland, 80, 157
Horowitz, 17
Housee, 181, 183
Howie, 89
Huber, 3, 133
Hudson, 74
Hunt, 29, 51, 52

Identity, 167–96
  administration, 202
  class, 175–81
  culture and, 4, 143, 204–6
  device for analysing culture of academic law, 13–14
  dress 186–96. *See also* Dress
  ethnicity, 181–3, 203–4
  gender, 168–75, 203–4
  meaning, 10–12
  multiple, 11
  professional, 11–13
  project of the self, 167

race, 181–3, 203–4
research, 202
sexual orientation, 183–6
teaching, 201–2
Insider research, 22–5
Ireland, 29

Jarrett report, 159
Jenkins, 11, 12, 13, 25, 97, 121, 167, 175, 197
Johnson, 192
Johnstone, 83, 145
Jones, 15, 58, 159, 161, 182

Kahn Freund, 32, 33
Kay, 80, 157
Keenan, 187
Kennedy, 36, 69, 150
Kluckholm, 5
Knight, 18
Knoee-Cetina, 143
Knorr-Cetina, 4, 13
Kogan, 18, 92, 108, 121, 124, 148, 159, 161
Kolb-Biglan classification, 78
Kramer, 43

Lacey, 68
Laurie, 169
Law schools,
  contemporary, increased pressure in, 160–1
  history, 40–1
Lawson, 40
Le Brun, 83, 121
Legal education,
  approaches to law, 35–7
  critical legal studies, 36–7
  empirical studies, 41–2
  historical perspective, 39–41
  journals, 28
  live experience of academics, 27–47
  pedagogy, 28–30
  policy, 30–5
Legal profession, 156–8
Leighton, 38, 42, 81–2, 92, 93, 116, 182
Leith, 129
Lennon, 192
Letherby, 175
Lewis, 163
Lim, 37
Lived experience, 27–47
  See also Experience of being a legal academic
  legal education, 27–47
  meaning, 1
  private life of academia, 42–7
  studying, 1
Lloyd, 171
Lynch, 30

226   Index

McAuslan, 34, 38
McDowell, 168, 185, 188
McGlynn, 19, 20, 37, 45, 46, 57–9, 63, 88, 91, 168, 170, 174
McIntyre, 168
Mackinnon, 19
McNay, 13, 97
Malleson, 80
Manning, 12
Marsh, 41
Martin, 78, 83, 159, 161, 162, 163
Masculinity, 44–5, 89–90, 171–3
Mason, 17
Maugham, 29
Mills, 43, 44, 182, 183, 203
Mirza, 181
Moley, 138
Montgomery, 183
Moran, 184
Morison, 129
Morley, 19, 89, 141, 163
Morris, 37
Muetzlfeldt, 16
Murlis, 134

Naffine, 52, 171
Networking, 153–5
New public management, 108
Newman, 70
Nicolson, 69

O'Dair, 28
O'Donnell, 37
O'Donovan, 53, 171
Okonska, 168
Organisation skills, 84–5

Pakulski, 176
Park, 145, 147
Parkin, 184
Partington, 66
Performance, teaching, 124–9
Pettit, 40
Podmore, 80, 157
Pollitt, 107, 108
Pride,
   experience of being a legal academic, 97–101
Professional identity 11, 12–13. *See also* Identity
Professional organisations, 156
Psychoanalysis, 53

Qualifying law degrees, 17
Qureshi, 183

Race,
   identity, 181–3, 203–4

RAE, 135–41, 163–4, 200, 201, 202
Ramsden, 181
Reading law, 73–5
Reimer, 23
Research, 133–41
   career, legal academic, 86–7
   identity, 202
   RAE, 135–41, 200, 201, 202
Rhoads, 13
Robbins, 168
Roberts, 177
Robson, 186
Rose, 98
Roseneil, 23, 24
Rowland, 106
Rucker, 190, 191
Rush, 36
Ryan, 111, 180, 203
Ryle, 6

Sackmann, 6, 7, 53
Sackrey, 180, 203
Salter, 159
Sanderson, 80, 157
Savage, 33, 58
Scott, 17, 21
Scott-Hunt, 37
Sexual orientation,
   identity, 183–6
Shattock, 17
Shaw, 36
Sheldon, 37
Sherr, 29, 38
Shiels, 175
Skeggs, 21
Skidmore, 184, 196
Skills of academic lawyer, 81–6
   analysis, 81–2
   communication skills, 82–3
   organisation skills, 84–5
   persistence, 85–6
Skoldberg, 26
Smalle-Baker, 40
Smart, 171
Smith, 40
Snaith, 30
Snow, 7
Socio-legal studies, 50–1, 56–7, 59–60, 68–9, 198
Sommerland, 80, 157
Spencer, 79–81, 157, 1457
Squirrel, 186
Stallybrass, 28
Stanley, 21, 153
Stevens, 40
Strauss, 17
Student pressures, 161–3
Studying legal academics,

academic discipline of law, effect on, 3
culture, 4, 5–10
  academic law, using to study, 9–10
  higher education, use to study, 7–9
disciplinary culture, 2, 3–4
higher education, cultural approach to
    researching, 7–9
identity, 10–12
lived experience. *See* Lived experience
method, 14–26
  access, 15
  conversations with a purpose,
    20–2
  insider research, 22–5
  interviewing, 15–16
  location, 25–6
  location of the self, 20–2
  sampling, 17–20
objectives, 1–4
professional identity, 11, 12–13
reasons for, 1–4
semi-autonomous legal field, 4
social factors, 3
Stychin, 184
Sugarman, 29, 31, 40, 50, 158, 200
Sunkin, 34
Swadling, 29

Talburt, 183–4
Talib, 135, 200
Tapper, 159
Tauchert, 89
Taylor, 73, 159
Teaching, 121–33
  identity, 201–2
  institutional attitude, 130–3
  performance, 124–9
  professional identity, 129–30
Teichler, 98
Tett, 167
Theory,
  law and, 68–9
Thomas, 35, 51, 89
Thomson, 36, 37
Thornton, 35, 50, 89, 91, 102, 133, 147, 148,
    168, 170, 171, 201

Thorsen, 19, 102
Thorton, 45
Tierney, 199
Tight, 7
Toma, 49
Trow, 2–3
Trowler, 7, 8, 9, 10, 18, 27, 49, 78, 87, 88, 102,
    145, 153, 154, 155, 181, 182, 184, 199,
    205
Tushnet, 59
Twining, 32, 33, 35, 36, 40, 41, 42, 43, 51, 55,
    70, 103, 158, 205

Usher, 21

Valentine, 183, 185
Valimaa, 3, 7, 10, 13, 143, 151, 153
Vick, 34, 136, 141, 200

Walsh, 19, 89
Warnock, 78
Waters, 176
Watt, 33, 58
Webb, 28, 69, 130
Weber, 5
Weidner, 103
Wells, 19, 46, 90, 91, 133, 149, 168, 170, 171,
    174, 175, 176, 203
Wheeler, 36
White Paper *The Future of Higher Education*,
    106
Wiedemann, 138
Wiles, 27, 36, 58, 68
Williams, 5, 8, 169, 184
Wilson, 34, 41–2
Winstanley, 69
Wise, 21
Witherspoon, 66
Woodliffe, 30
Woods, 20
Woolf, 39
Work-life balance, 97, 113–18
Wright, 176

Yach, 30
Young-Eisendrath, 138